Cambridge Studies in the History and Theory of Politics

EDITORS

MAURICE COWLING   G. R. ELTON
F. KEDOURIE J. G. A. POCOCK
J. R. POLE   WALTER ULLMANN

REGICIDE AND REVOLUTION

REGICIDE AND REVOLUTION

SPEECHES AT THE TRIAL OF LOUIS XVI

EDITED WITH AN INTRODUCTION BY
MICHAEL WALZER
Professor of Government, Harvard University

TRANSLATED BY
MARIAN ROTHSTEIN

CAMBRIDGE UNIVERSITY PRESS

Published by the Syndics of the Cambridge University Press
Bentley House, 200 Euston Road, London NW1 2DB
American Branch: 32 East 57th Street, New York, N.Y. 10022

ISBN: 0 521 20370 8

First published 1974

Photoset in Malta by St Paul's Press Ltd
Printed in the United States of America

PREFACE

In their speeches at the trial of Louis XVI, writes Thomas Carlyle, the deputies of the revolutionary Convention 'welter amid law of nations, social contract, juristics, syllogistics; to us barren as the east wind'. He goes on to ask a question that may occur to other readers of the opinions and orations translated here: 'What can be more unprofitable than the sight of 749 ingenious men struggling with their whole force and industry, for a long course of weeks, to do at bottom this: To stretch out the old formula and law phraseology, so that it may cover the new, contradictory, entirely *un*coverable thing?' The uncoverable thing is the killing of the king; indeed, it is the revolution itself, of which regicide is only a symbolic representation – and what old formula could cover that? 'This stretching out of formulas till they crack, is especially in times of swift change, one of the sorrowfulest tasks poor humanity has.' But why did that task elicit the whole force and industry of 749 revolutionaries? Why was it a *task* at all? Surely the answer is that the revolution was not something men found, as if it had been left, outrageous and naked, by the side of the road. It was something they made, and while they were making it, they needed the old formulas so as to know, or better, so as to argue about what they were doing. In the winter of the first year of the French Republic, the shape of the revolution had not yet been determined. It was being disputed. Law of nations, social contract, juristics, syllogistics – this was the language in which the dispute was carried on. There was and there could be no other.

Like the Huguenot pamphlets of the French civil wars and the debates of the New Model army in the English Revolution, the speeches of the *conventionnels* belong to the history of political theory. They were delivered at one of those moments in time when men of action literally cannot act without becoming theorists. I do not mean that their decisions are necessarily fixed by this or that interpretation of the social contract: no doubt, there were political reasons, of both a high and low sort, for bringing and for not bringing Louis to trial. But the event had a meaning beyond its political reasons, for the king was a mythic figure, the embodiment of the old regime, and all Frenchmen might expect to learn something of their own future from his treatment. In disputing the prerogatives of kings and the forms of revolutionary justice, the deputies were forced to explain themselves and their intentions more fully, perhaps, than on any other occasion. That they were forced to do so with all the immediacy of speech (for there was no time for treatises) means that their explanations are not as careful or as structured as they might otherwise have been. But they are probably all the more revealing for that.

I have selected eleven speeches from the several hundred that were delivered, printed as pamphlets, or placed in the Convention's record between 7 November 1792, when the Legislative Committee reported on the king's trial, and 15 January 1793, when the roll-calls began. These are, I think, the most important theoretical statements, and they turn out, mostly, to be those of the greatest revolutionary leaders. But not all the great men of the Convention are represented. Danton never spoke at the trial; he managed to be out of Paris during most of the debate, returning only to vote. The speech of his close friend and associate Camille Desmoulins was too confused to reproduce here. In effect, there was no *dantoniste* position on the king's trial. Brissot's major address was concerned almost entirely with the possible effects of Louis' execution on foreign affairs; it is not to our purpose. Barère is usually said to have played a crucial part in determining the outcome of the second roll-call (on the appeal to the people), but his speech is not theoretically interesting. For the rest, lesser men followed the cues of the leaders. Except for Saint-Just, no new spokesmen emerged in the course of the trial. I have not included the king's defense, worked out by that old friend of the *philosophes*, Malesherbes, and delivered by the young lawyer de Sèze. Its main points were anticipated by Morisson in the course of the debate itself and had already been dealt with in a number of important speeches before de Sèze spoke.

My own introduction is not concerned with the previous history of the French Revolution – the constitutional experiment, the defeat of the moderates, the overthrow of the monarch, and so on. I have tried instead to say something about kingship itself and to distinguish this act of regicide (and its earlier English counterpart) from the long history of murder and assassination which is at the same time the history of kingly rule. I have tried also to do something more ambitious, perhaps more presumptuous: to judge the king's judges and their judgment. For the trial is not an event in front of which a man can or should remain silent and detached, and it has parallels in our own time which even more obviously require moral understanding. So I have resurrected an old question: what should be done with Louis the Last? — and attempted an answer, not out of concern for the historical reputations of Jacobins or Girondins, but because justice and the terror that comes when justice fails are abiding issues, especially so for those of my contemporaries who retain some vestiges of revolutionary hope.

The introduction was written in the course of a year that I spent at the Center for Advanced Study in the Behavioral Sciences in Stanford, California. I am grateful to the staff of the Center for the constant assistance its members provided and to my colleagues of that year for their friendship and conversation.

TRANSLATOR'S PREFACE

The better to convey the period flavor of the original speeches, I have tried to simulate later eighteenth-century English oratory, and have, as much as possible, avoided words or expressions not in use between 1750 and 1810. The French text can be found in the *Archives Parlementaires*, première série, vols. 53–6 (Paris, 1898–9). The text of the Constitution and the Declaration of Rights is taken from an English translation printed in the *Annual Register* (London, 1791) pp. 151–77. The citations from Montesquieu and Rousseau are taken from standard English texts. Finally, Thomas Paine did not require the services of a translator; his speeches are reprinted from *The Writings of Thomas Paine*, ed. M. D. Conway, vol. 3 (New York, 1895).

CONTENTS

For
FRANK E. MANUEL
AND
SAMUEL H. BEER

I

TWO KINDS OF REGICIDE

In writing about regicide, it is important not to 'tell sad stories of the death of kings'. There are stories enough to tell, brutal tales of deposition, imprisonment, and murder, moving legends of the last days of this or that ruler. It is no doubt a central feature of kingship that kings are so prone to be killed. But the sad stories are of no help in the study I propose here, of European monarchy and its fall, or rather, of how monarchy was destroyed in the person of two of its leading representatives, Charles I of England and Louis XVI of France. By themselves, moreover, they only make the survival of royal authority until those two executions seem strange indeed: why did the death-before-their-time of so many kings have so little effect upon the magic and even upon the everyday effectiveness of kingship?

Monarchy depends upon an ideology of personal rule. While it acquires over time a great variety of justifications, including utilitarian justifications, it remains fudamentally dependent upon a set of beliefs about the person of the king. Subjects must feel some awe in the royal presence; they must sustain some faith in the king's sanctity, power, and wisdom; they must believe in his inviolability. The murderers of kings presumably do not share these feelings and beliefs, though we may doubt that they escape them entirely. For much of European history, entire disbelief was a species of atheism, rarely encountered; and most royal assassins, though not those who thought themselves divinely inspired, must have died fully expecting to suffer in hell forever. In any case, their skepticism, if it existed, was never communicated to the mass of the king's subjects. Popular faith in the royal person, indeed, in the medieval and early modern periods, the faith of practically everyone, seems to have been readily transferable from dead to living monarchs. Nor did it matter a great deal that the death of the old king was brutally unnatural, though it sometimes made trouble that the claim of the new king was illegitimate. The personal suffering and degradation of a particular monarch, once thought almighty and godlike, was never to my knowledge made into an argument against monarchy. One reason for this is obvious: in Christendom, God himself was thought to have suffered and died. He had not, however, been succeeded by a rival claimant, and so there must be other, more political reasons for the success of irregular and unnatural successions.

Until the English Revolution, kings were killed by would-be kings or by lonely assassins in the pay of would-be kings. Again, exception must be made for religious zealots like the muderers of Henry III and Henry IV of France, whom no-one needed to pay, but they too struck down the old ruler in the hope of a new one more firmly formed in the image of their own faith. It never occurred to them, as Albert Camus says in his essay *The Rebel*, that the throne might remain empty.[1] Nor was it ever in the interests of the new rulers, for obvious reasons, that monarchy itself should be called into question. They intrigued and killed precisely in order to become kings, and in this way offered their own deeply felt testimony to the power of kingship. Once installed, they sought always to preserve for themselves the personal authority of the man at whose death they had connived; so they connived again at the perpetuation of the myths of monarchy and sometimes at their invention. Thus, the behavior of Henry IV of England, after deposing and (apparently) planning the murder of Richard II: he had himself annointed with a mysterious oil, given, it was said, by the Virgin Mary to Thomas Becket many years before.[2] The oil continued to be used until the coronation of James I, who refused it; his claims to divine right required other sorts of symbols. A recent biographer of Richard has argued that 'medieval divine right' died with that unhappy king, 'smothered or starved in Pontefract Castle'.[3] I doubt very much that this is true. Divine right is not subject to smothering or starvation and certainly not to smothering or starvation in the hidden recesses of Pontefract Castle. Nor is there any evidence that Englishmen during the reign of Henry V (for example) felt radically differently about the royal person than Englishmen had felt two reigns earlier. A line of succession was broken in 1399, but that is something quite different from – and much more frequent than – the death of divine right.

Richard's deposition was cited during the trial of Charles, but it was not a good precedent. Henry had worked hard to make sure that it would not be. Above all, he had resisted anything that resembled a parliamentary trial. Richard had not been deposed, according to his successor, he had

---

[1] *The Rebel: An Essay on Man in Revolt*, trans. Anthony Bower (New York, 1956), p. 112. Camus' essay contains one of the most recent and most important discussions of the trial of Louis XVI.
[2] Marc Bloch, *Les rois thaumaturges* (Paris, 1961), pp. 241–2; see also Percy Schramm, *A History of the English Coronation*, trans. L. G. W. Legg (Oxford, 1937), p. 137.
[3] Anthony Steel, *Richard II* (Cambridge, 1962), p. 288.

willingly, even 'cheerfully' abdicated. Parliament had merely recognized the abdication.[1] Then Richard had died, somehow, in the North, far from Henry's hand. According to most accounts, the new king never admitted that Richard had been murdered, but Shakespeare, following a different tradition, has Henry acknowledge the murder and then repudiate the murderer: 'With Cain, go wander through the shade of night.' The new king admits no responsibility for the death of the old. It is even more important that Parliament was not in any sense complicitous. And though a group of prominent Londoners had called for Richard's execution when he was first brought to the Tower, he was not killed at their call. In the matter of regicide, the nation was not involved.

So kings for centuries were killed in corners, the murders hushed up, the murderers unthanked, neglected, condemned. That is the substance of the sad stories. And monarchy survived. Even in the eighteenth century, the slaughter went on. Indeed, there is no piece of dynastic history more bizarre and bloody than that of the Romanoffs in the Age of Enlightenment: it included the murder of a crown prince by his father and of a reigning czar by his wife. Yet living monarchs in the rest of Europe watched, congratulated the survivors, and apparently felt the spectacle no threat to their own pretensions.[2] More philosophic onlookers managed to discover in the triumph of Catherine a victory for enlightened despotism – the short-lived legatee of divine right kingship. Even they could not imagine an empty throne. In Russia, at the end of it all, Paul II, half-mad, expecting his assassin every day, nevertheless proclaimed his absolute authority, reasserted divine right, and established a succession that lasted for more than a century. The murders of Alexis, Ivan VI, Peter III, and finally of Paul himself, did not weaken the hand of nineteenth century czars. They were not driven to modify their claims, their subjects were not encouraged to challenge their rulers or deny those claims. Faith in the person of the czar survived, embodied as late as the Revolution of 1905 in the pathetic monk Gapon and the thousands of workers who marched behind him.

But there is another kind of regicide that changes monarchy forever.

---

[1] G. Lapsley, 'The Parliamentary Title of Henry IV', *English Historical Review*, 49: 423–49, 577–606 (1934). Steel follows this account of Richard's fall. If it is accurate, then William Prynne was right in 1648 when he denied that Richard's deposition provided any basis for the trial of Charles: *Speech in the House of Commons . . . the Fourth of December 1648* (London, 1649), p. 78.

[2] Thus Louis XV, writing to his ambassador after the accession of Catherine: 'The dissimulation of the empress and her courage at the moment of execution of her project [that is, the murder of her husband] indicate a princess capable of conceiving and executing great deeds.' Quoted in Albert Sorel, *Europe Under the Old Regime*, trans. F. H. Herrick (New York, 1964), p. 41.

It is best revealed, perhaps, in a remark Oliver Cromwell is supposed to have made to Algernon Sidney on the eve of the condemnation of Charles I: 'I tell you, we will cut off his head with the crown on it.'[1] What is apparent here is the fixed commitment — it is a revolutionary commitment — not only to kill Charles but to kill him in his public character and in public. Sidney was reluctant to do any such thing, and no doubt many other members even of the purged Parliament were reluctant also. Yet the charge brought before the tribunal they constituted is clear enough: 'A charge of High Treason ... exhibited ... for and on behalf of the People of England against Charles Stuart King of England.' In France there were important disagreements as to the precise status of the king at the time of his trial. Formally he was no longer King of France but *le ci-devant roi*, plain Louis Capet, and many of the revolutionaries hoped that he would be tried like any other citizen. The public stage could not, however, be denied the public person: all France and all Europe knew that a king was on trial. Though Louis' citizenship was, as I will argue later on, an important theoretical discovery, his trial testified nevertheless to the practical way in which monarchy resisted legal and political egalitarianism. The king defeated and brought low remained somehow a royal figure; the king imprisoned was still, as Charles insisted, 'no ordinary prisoner.'[2] To try him and then to execute him in public was to challenge monarchy itself.

Cromwell's 'we' is as important as his insistence that the crown and not only the king be brought to the scaffold. It was not the royal we, though that was a form of address Oliver would one day adopt. The king was condemned by a group of men who represented his successors — however that succession is conceived: the People of England, the Commons, the army. And the members of that group were public men, who signed their names, boldly or fearfully, and accepted responsibility for the solemn execution that their signatures authorized. The executioner wore a mask; not so the judges. Whatever legal subterfuges the trial of the king required and whatever excuses individual regicides later offered, their participation could not be denied. We do not know what happened at Pontefract Castle; the proceedings at Westminster and Whitehall were published to the world. Here, then, were *ci-devant* subjects, who judged and killed their king and (some of them) boasted of the act.

'This subjugation, which forces the sovereign to take the law from his

---

[1] J. G. Muddiman, *Trial of Charles the First* (Edinburgh, n.d.), p. 70.
[2] Muddiman, p. 93.

people, is the last calamity that can fall upon a man of our rank.' So wrote Louis XIV not of the first but of the second Charles.[1] He was referring to the king's dependence, after the Restoration, upon parliamentary appropriations. But it might better be said that the 'last calamity' of kings is not to take the law in the form of legislation, but to take it, that is, to receive it, in the form of justice. Public regicide is a denial not of the king's legislative power or his executive prerogative, but of his personal inviolability – and therefore of all the mysteries of kingship without which the practical powers of monarchy cannot survive for long. The importance of mystery to the integrity of monarchic rule and the importance of its denial to the establishment of democratic regimes form a large part of my subject in this essay. Once the king has been judged by his peers, I will argue, monarchy is never the same; it can survive a thousand assassinations but not one execution. The invasion of the *arcana imperii* by commoners and assemblymen is, after that, a relatively easy matter. Kings may return for a time, but, as Jean Jaurès says in his monumental history of the French Revolution, 'they are never more than phantoms'.[2] Majesty cannot be restored. Though they called themselves godlike, there was no resurrection for kings; divine right itself was killed at Whitehall and the *Place de la Révolution*.

Public regicide is an absolutely decisive way of breaking with the myths of the old regime, and it is for this very reason, the founding act of the new. It might be compared with other such acts, for the history of political foundation, as Machiavelli teaches us, is a history of murder and violence. Beginnings are bloody, because there are always rival claimants to power, while 'to found a republic, one must be alone'.[3] That harsh sentence helps explain the fratricidal struggles of the revolutionary period and the dictatorship which most often follows upon them. The trial and execution of the king, however, are founding acts of another kind. To found a republic, the regicides say, one must kill the man who claims to rule alone. The difference is important. Machiavelli is dealing with foundation *ex nihilo*: before Romulus there was no Rome. But English and French revolutionaries each confront an old regime and a royal house long established. 'What has Louis in common with the French people?' asked the Jacobin St Just.[4] The answer is obvious: he and his family, they and

---

[1] Quoted in John B. Wolf, 'The Formation of a King', in J. C. Rule, ed., *Louis XIV and the Craft of Kingship* (Columbus, Ohio, 1969), p. 124.

[2] *La Convention* (Paris, n.d.), II, p. 962.

[3] Machiavelli, *The Discourses*, I, 9.

[4] *Archives Parlementaires de 1787 à 1860* (Paris, 1899), 53: 391 (first series).

their ancestors, share a thousand years of history. The revolution necessarily involves a judgment on those years, and that judgment is given
when Louis is brought to trial and publicly killed. The Jacobins would have
settled for the execution alone; they opposed the trial for reasons I will
examine below. But the majority of the revolutionaries in both England
and France thought the trial necessary so that the killing of the king would
appear not merely to be justifiable but to be (what they thought it was) an
act of justice and an explicit denial of the king's claim to rule. Only the trial
could make it clear that Louis was being killed in accordance with new
political principles, and only then would his execution mark the triumph
not of a new set of men but of new kind of government.

These straightforwardly political purposes account for many of the
doubts that have been expressed over the years about the trial of Louis
and also about that of Charles, its historical model.[1] The use of judicial
or semi-judicial processes to destroy a political enemy was not new, of
course, to either England or France. Kings, like the men who eventually
defeated them, had often found it wise or prudent to turn to their judges
rather than to their assassins and to charge their victims with treason rather
than simply to have them murdered. The treason laws had even been used
against the advisors and friends of the king himself by opposition groups
unwilling or unable to touch the royal person. Nor had there been qualms
on either side about inventing treasons after the fact to catch ambitious or
powerful men who had probably not done anything illegal. But revolutionary justice is not *ex post facto* in this usual sense, for now it is not only
the laws that are new but also the regime. The men who fall before the
justice of the revolution are condemned in alien courts and assemblies and
they are condemned by their triumphant opponents. That makes for a very
peculiar kind of justice indeed, which may not warrant the name, even
though it cannot dispense with the appearance.

In the French case, regicide is often described as the beginning of the
terror, the first act in the bloody assizes of the modern age.[2] It is true
that the terrorists, like the regicides, exploited the forms of law for
political purposes. Yet I shall try in the last section of this essay to draw
a line between the two and to give reasons for doing so. First, however,
it will be necessary to say something about the old regime, for if every
trial is a kind of settlement with the past, this is true in a special sense
of the trials of Charles and Louis. The revolutionaries could not attend

---

[1] Otto Kirchheimer, *Political Justice: The Use of Legal Procedure for Political Ends* (Princeton, 1961),
pp. 304ff. – an especially helpful discussion of the problems raised by these and similar trials.
[2] Camus, *The Rebel*, is the classic example of this view.

6

only to the king's actions; in the turmoil of the revolutionary struggle the precise status of those actions, as of the king's person, was radically unclear. They had to attend to his kingship as well. It was monarchy itself that established the context within which the king acted and the background against which, finally, he was judged.

The crucial issue before the Convention in its first months was the relation of the monarchy and the revolution, and this was the topic of the extraordinary debate among the delegates in November and December 1792, when the trial was being prepared. St Just's dramatic question was meant to deny that there was any relation at all (except that of war): he intended to raise the most serious doubts about the very possibility and also about the moral necessity of doing justice to a king. And although he was a resolute foe of monarchy, and not only of Louis XVI, his program had something in common with that of earlier regicides. They were unwilling to challenge the legitimacy of kingship; he was unwilling to grant that kingship had ever been legitimate. On either view, the measured confrontation of a public trial (or any other process suggesting the possibility of limited obedience and constitutional resistance) was radically inappropriate. The only way to deal with a king (earlier regicides would have said, the only way to deal with *this* king) was to kill him out of hand. The opponents of the Mountain had another view not only of revolutionary justice, but also of what it meant to be a king under the old regime — a view which represented (as I shall argue) a more thoroughgoing renunciation of monarchic mystery. They thought the king a citizen, one among many, a man with peers, who had committed a specific crime. The historicity of either of these positions is less important than the fact that both were focused on the past. In this sense, at least, regicide was like punishment rather than like terrorism: it was backward looking in the most profound way.

7

2

THE OLD REGIME

THE IDEOLOGY OF KINGSHIP

There is no single way of describing a king. The ideology of kingship in the West draws upon many distinct traditions of thought – classical, oriental, Germanic, feudal, and Christian – and the long process of amalgamation and distortion has a succession of outcomes, which parallel, though they do not narrowly reflect, changes in the political structure of the monarchic regime. I shall focus largely on the last of these, royalism before the revolution, the ideology of absolute monarchy. But I shall venture to argue also that this last amalgamation was the most important and the most characteristic form of royalist doctrine. This is not to deny that it remained possible, even at the end, to tear the strands apart and weave a new pattern: many of the revolutionaries were trying to do just that. Nor do I want to suggest that every previous king wanted to write like James I or rule (though this is more likely) like Louis XIV. No doubt, their practical aspirations were limited by their immediate possibilities, as well as by the particular idealism of their time and place. There was never a perfected kingship, established once and for all by God, immune from political conflict. There was never a perfected tyranny, embodiment of kingly arrogance and aribitrary power, awaiting the climactic attack of the people.

Centralized monarchy as the regicides confronted it, the king sovereign in more than name: these are late and relatively short-lived achievements. They are the work of latter-day kings or of their ministers and they formed, as Tocqueville insisted, the immediate inheritance of the revolution.[1] Age-old monarchy had been something different, and because of what it had been, revolutionary arguments against royal absolutism were rarely new. Except for brief moments, it was the usual lot of European kings to endure extensive limits on their authority, imposed by a universal church or a locally entrenched aristocracy and justified in the most elaborate fashion. But these limits, practical or moral, have no essential form – no more than

---

[1]Alexis de Tocqueville, *The Old Regime and the French Revolution*, trans. Stuart Gilbert (New York, 1955), pp. 32ff.

royal power itself. They vary with time. So historians can trace the rise and fall of dynasties, the decline and resurgence of monarchic authority. They can record that this or that ruler could not act without these allies; lost out to those opponents; granted these rights, withdrew those; faltered before or heroically overcame the sheer disorganization of his realm, and so on. The possibilities are at least as various for the life as for the death of kings.

Despite all this, there are deep similarities in the pretensions of kings, in the claims they have made and struggled to enforce over the centuries. If there is no essential kingship, there are nevertheless characteristic patterns of royal aggrandizement. Even more important for my purposes here, there are profound continuities in the myths – what the revolutionaries in England and France called the 'superstitions' – that both underlay and served this aggrandizement. Though these were consciously sponsored by kings and their publicists, they cannot be regarded simply as propaganda. The attained to the status of popular beliefs, were probably believed by kings and their publicists, and lived on until and even after monarchy was decisively overthrown. They helped to determine the character of the overthrow. No doubt the forms of power, argument, and mythic elaboration varied a great deal. Through it all, there can be detected a kind of regal optimism that is almost always the same. It is as if every king until the revolution preened himself before the same magic mirror and saw the same gratifying images: himself God's deputy, head and soul of the body politic, sole knower of the mysteries of state, father of his subjects, husband of the realm, healer, peacemaker, sovereign lord. The characteristic sin of kings is pride. Perhaps this is part of what St Just meant when he said, 'No man can reign innocently.'[1] Even the burdens of kingship can be, indeed must be, a source of pride:

> ... What infinite heart's ease
> Must kings neglect that private men enjoy!

The famous lines of Shakespeare's Henry V are a boast, not a lament as is commonly thought, for it is a boast to envy one's own subjects the enjoyment of the protection provided by oneself. (It is the poet's, not the king's irony that the subjects so envied are soldiers awaiting battle, some of whom will die the next day in the king's war.) Henry has no desire that private men join him in neglecting their hearts' ease. The attempt would be treason. Nor does he believe any such sharing possible, for

[1] *Archives Parlementaires*, 53: 391.

9

'gross brain little wots/ What watch the King keeps . . .'. This is the pride of monarchs, the inescapable moral corollary of the claim to rule alone.

To see kingship in this way, as a set of abiding pretensions variously asserted and acted out, is no doubt dangerous. It pays too much attention to royalist argument and ceremonial and too little attention to the theoretical and practical limits on royal authority. These last will be considered later on, for they figured significantly in the arguments of the revolutionaries. In the century and a half before each of the revolutions, however, kings were triumphant, and they did not hesitate to draw upon the ancient arsenal of kingly pretension. They acted as kings had long claimed it was right for them to act. And the content, the force, and the wide acceptance of these claims go a long way toward explaining why such different institutional arrangements as those of England and France yielded in similiar ways to monarchic self-assertion and then to popular rebellion. The similarity requires explanation, since so much has been made of the differences. Thus, the distinguished historian Walter Ullmann marks off two radically opposed patterns of monarchic rule, peculiar, he argues, to the French and the English. He names them theocratic and feudal kingship, and after a long and impressive description of the two, concludes that 'The former led to revolution, the latter to evolution'.[1] If this is a reference to the actual histories of France and England, and not to some idea of historical development, it is plainly wrong. Both patterns 'led to' revolution. Two European kings were defeated, imprisoned, charged with treason against their own people, condemned, and brought to the block. It is true that the English have a monarch still, while the French do not, and these outcomes and other more significant differences in the two regimes probably have a great deal to do with the histories Ullmann has studied. But it is also true that these histories are marked by strikingly similar eruptions, and so historians must search for common causes.

Among these, the 'superstitions' of kingship must rank high, even if they are regarded as nothing more than the intellectual weapons of social and political forces. For men must fight with the instruments and ideas they have to hand; they cannot choose their weapons, as if political conflict were a duel. The early modern Europeans who found a strong central government in their interests did not choose to be royalists. In their world, there was no alternative to royalism (and 'superstition'). Nor has there often been an alternative, for until very recent times, kingship, indeed,

[1] *Principles of Government and Politics in the Middle Ages* (London, 1961), p. 211.

sacred kingship was pervasive in human history – a fact which suggests a certain independence from sociological determination. Royalism is the ruling idea of a ruling class consisting ultimately of only one man, and to account for the range of nations and classes within which it has been believed is not a task to be undertaken lightheartedly.[1] I shall not undertake it here, but only insist upon the central importance of this strange and yet commonplace creed which taught one man to rule and everyone else to obey. By 1640 and 1789, its tenets were widely doubted, perhaps, and yet the two revolutions cannot be understood without continual reference to the terms it had fixed. Charles and Louis were killed in large part because of what kingship was: not simply because they were unlucky enough to be kings at the moment revolution broke out, but rather because, confronted with revolution, they were stubbornly loyal to royalist ideology. The more moderate revolutionaries – Cromwell himself in England, Mirabeau, Barnave, Roland among the French – literally pleaded with them to surrender (some of) their royal pretensions. Ordinary men though they were, they would not yield on what seemed to them points of right. Poor Louis XVI can hardly have believed that he ruled in God's place, yet when he vowed 'to drink the cup until the last dregs', he knew he was acting the way kings were supposed to act. It was a triumph of ideology over mere personality.

But the complex and elaborate belief system that I have called 'royalism' included more than one man's claim to rule. It suggested and justified the kind of political order that could only be ruled by one man. The ideology of kingship was also the ideology of the old regime. If members of the aristocratic opposition often doubted this, they paid a price for their skepticism: they developed, willy nilly, the crucial ideas of the revolution. What has often been called bourgeois political thought was first of all the work of aristocrats and of writers in their pay. The notion that a man's home was his castle, protected even against royal invasion, was first put forward by men whose castles were their homes. The rights of the people were systematically confused, by many noblemen, with their own

Nice.

---

[1] The relative power of particular kings obviously has to be explained at least partly by reference to the balance of social forces. In his *Origin of the Family, Private Property and the State*, Engels puts forward such an explanation for both Bonapartism and absolute monarchy: rulers like Elizabeth I, Louis XIV, and Napoleon, he argues, exploited the near-equality of social classes, playing one against the other in order to maintain their own positions (Moscow, 1952, p. 281). One would have to look to other factors, however, to explain the stability and persistance of monarchic, as distinct from Bonapartist, institutions. Kingship was not easily overthrown, even when the balance of social forces radically shifted. On the prevasiveness of royalism, see A. M. Hocart, *Kingship* (Oxford, 1927).

privileges, and owe much of their original elaboration to that confusion. The noblemen thought of themselves as the natural leaders of the people against the overbearing power of the king. In fact, they could not dispense with the king, however they might challenge him, any more than the Pope and the bishops could dispense with the king, despite their long struggle against royal sovereignty. And kings, though they won out against the Pope and the barons, could not preside for long over a society of equals. 'For where there is equality of estates' wrote James Harrington, '. . . there can be no monarchy'.[1] The great men of the old regime required one another, for their privileges were of essentially the same sort. James I was right when he said, no bishop, no king; and Louis XVI might equally well have told his aristocratic opponents of 1787 and '88, no king, no notables.

'The state is in the person of the prince', Bishop Bossuet taught the *dauphin* of France.[2] If this was not, could not be literally true, it was true that the old regime was often conceived and understood with reference exclusively to the king's person. The idea of the state was included in the idea of the prince. Social and political historians have told us a great deal about the nature of the old regime, but they have rarely speculated as to why it required or was susceptible to such a strange intellectual embodiment. The answer surely lies in the patterns of inequality that prevailed under the old regime and required bishops and aristocrats every day to make claims on other men of the same sort that the king made on all men. Royal authority was symbolically portioned out even when it was not shared in practice; most often, of course, it was shared in practice. Throughout society, inequality was radically personal in a nature, and it was at least partly explained by reference to the personal attributes of the king.[3] He had been touched by God, singled out as divine deputy; hence he was godlike and living proof that heaven itself intended men to be unequal in rank and privilege. The king was quite simply a different sort of person, and lesser men were different too in ways that had to be respected by still lesser men, who shared only a common humanity. This social hierarchy was most readily and familiarly represented in organic terms, as a body which God had created and the king now headed, all of whose parts

[1]*The Political Writings of James Harrington*, ed. Charles Blitzer (New York, 1955), p. 97: this is probably the only sociological limit on monarchic rule – and even it is called into question by anthropological studies of African kingship.

[2]Jacques Benigne Bossuet, *Politique tirée des propres paroles de l'Ecriture sainte*, ed. Jacques Le Brun (Geneva, 1967), p. 185.

[3]Schramm describes how the principle of hierarchy was ceremonially acted out at the coronation of the king: 'On that day the feudal pyramid . . . appeared in visible shape.' *English Coronation*, p. 69.

were as naturally differentiated as were the royal head and the plebeian feet. The state in theory was the king's body politic, and it will be necessary to look closely at this body, first of all because its extended form was the form of the old regime, secondly because it made the old regime killable, as it were, in the person of the king. The monarchy could only be destroyed, however, if it was the king as embodiment and not only the king as a natural body that was put to death. Hence the distinction already made, between public regicide and the assassination or secret murder of kings, a distinction which directly parallels the mystery of the king's two bodies. This important theme of royalist ideology has been so brilliantly treated by Ernst Kantorowicz that I need only allude to his discussion here and stress (as he does not) its central importance in the explanation of regicide.[1] Royal publicists claimed that the king's body politic was immortal; the king with his crown could not die, even if an assassin struck down the man who wore the crown. But the public trial and execution of the king could and did destroy the king's body politic along with the man himself. It was precisely because he was 'twice-born', as body and embodiment, that the king had to die and to die in public. It was royalist ideology that inextricably bound together revolutionary change and the killing of kings.

Kantorowicz's own view of the two revolutions is rather different from this. He emphasizes the way in which Parliament, during the early 1640s, was able to exploit the mystery of the king's two bodies: it claimed to be fighting the king (body) in the name of the King (embodiment), Charles Stuart in the name of the Crown of England. But he is wrong, I think, when he suggests that the revolutionaries actually 'succeeded ... in executing solely the king's body natural without affecting seriously or doing irreparable harm to the king's body politic – in contradistinction with the events in France in 1793.'[2] In fact, irreparable harm was done if not to monarchy itself, then precisely to the king's body politic. After the revolution, kings no longer claimed to embody the realm or attempted to draw practical conclusions from their royal headship; or, if they did, they were quickly reminded of their new condition. Nor did any major political theorist describe English monarchy after 1649 in such flattering terms as Bossuet provided for the French. Like Ullmann (and many other historians), Kantorowicz underestimates the radicalism of the English, though not of the French, revolution. This is especially curious in his case, for it was the English who brought a reigning king to the bar, while the French

---

[1] *The King's Two Bodies: A Study in Medieval Political Theology* (Princeton, 1957).
[2] Kantorowicz, p. 23.

Convention officially summoned *citizen* Louis Capet. It is only fair to say, however, that in both cases the king's two bodies proved inseparable.

The emperor Caligula is said to have wished that the Roman people had but one neck, that he might cut it through with one blow. The sentence suggests how much easier it is or should be to fight against kings than to subjugate peoples. Yet the revolutionaries, whose enemies in fact had but one neck, found it extraordinarily difficult to strike the blow that would destroy them. And though only one head dropped into the basket at Whitehall in 1649, the moan that went through the crowd expressed a general loss. It was painful to kill the king, not only for the king, because the regime he embodied was both divine and natural in a way no other regime could ever be. This special and inimitable character of the royal embodiment can be explained in two ways. It might be said simply that kingship cannot be defended except by calling it divine and natural. No utilitarian argument will do the job for long, and so royal publicists had no choice but to work out the two mysteries of the king as divine deputy and head of the body politic. Insofar as they were believed, men found the mysteries comforting and mourned their loss. True enough, perhaps, but that does not explain why they were so widely believed. It might better be said that kingship lent itself to these sorts of mystic representation; the mysteries were not only morally satisfying but also convincing. They were convincing because the king ruled alone, like God, and because he had a body like other men in which the body politic was made visible and actual. J. N. Figgis has offered a partial defense of the theory of the divine right of kings by saying that it kept alive the organic conception of the state.[1] One might say also that it kept alive an anthropomorphic theology. It could hardly help but serve both these (dubious) purposes, so long as God was deputized and the regime represented by a single, biologically distinct, humanly shaped organism. Moreover, the state was in fact governed by the rhythmic forces of growth and decay when it was ruled by a king, and God was actually incarnate as he never would be again once sovereignty had been vested in impersonal and abstract powers.

THE KING'S DIVINE RIGHT

Monarchy is no doubt compatible with a great variety of religious systems. But Christian monarchy is best understood as a reflection of Christian monotheism: the king is not only made, like other men, in God's image; he is specially marked out to represent the will of God on earth. This is

[1] John Neville Figgis, *The Divine Right of Kings* (Cambridge, 1914), pp. 25off.

by no means implausible, for though one can imagine a God who has no politics at all, it is hard to imagine a politically active and interested God who works his will through Parliaments. Assemblies of priests have at times claimed divine inspiration, as if God could rule through them as he presumably ruled Israel through priests and judges before the time of Saul. Israel, writes Bossuet, 'was a kind of republic, which had God for king.'[1] During the late Middle Ages, Conciliarist writers defended the prerogatives of priestly assemblies and perhaps had such a republic in mind. But Christian theocracy culminated in the Papal Monarchy, in the rule of a priest, not of priests, indeed, in the most centralized and absolute of medieval governments. In his *curia*, the Pope resembled God in his heavenly court, where government is also centralized and absolute: 'God', as Bossuet said, 'is the true king.' And 'kings are justly called Gods', declared James I of England, 'for that they exercise a manner or resemblence of divine power upon earth. For if you will consider the attributes of God, you shall see how they agree in the person of a King.'[2] The argument is unanswerable, so long as one is committed to talk in terms of resemblances. However one pictures God, he does not look like a council or a crowd.

Yet divine omnipotence, which royal power only resembles and cannot equal, poses a problem for this way of thinking. Every regime that exists surely exists in accordance with God's will; there is no power that is not of God, whether it is exercised by kings, oligarchs, or popular tribunes. Bossuet at least recognizes that this is true and then is driven to the strange locution that monarchy is 'the most conformable (*le plus conforme*) to the will of God'.[3] The phrase suggests some special knowledge of that will, of which there is no sign in his *Politique*. But how, in any case, can conformity to the will of God be a matter of more or less? Is it possible that God only creates monarchies when political conditions on earth allow him to do so? The same problem comes up with regard to the argument from nature that I will consider later on. Some writers say flatly that republican or mixed regimes are unnatural, even monstrous, but Bossuet calls monarchy only 'the most natural' regime, arguing from the frequency of its appearance in history — as if the daisy were said to be more natural than some rare species of orchid. Behind these improbable assertions there stands a vision rather than an argument, a vision of the state as a reflection

---

[1] *Politique tirée*, p. 52.
[2] *Politique tirée*, p. 44; *The Political Works of James I*, intro. by C. H. McIlwain (Cambridge, Mass., 1918), p. 307.
[3] *Politique tirée*, p. 63.

of God's universe, a microcosm which can indeed take different forms but which reaches perfection only when it is presided over by an image of divinity. God's presence is not guaranteed by the mere existence of a ruling will – hence the political neutrality of the idea of sovereignty – but only by an actual or symbolic embodiment of his person in human flesh, that is, only by a king.

The king's 'resemblence' to God is one of the oldest and most common themes of Christian political thought, the basis of all historically specific assertions of divine right. The most famous of these is that of King James, which differs from earlier versions not in its listing of the parallel attributes of God and king, but in its insistence upon the descent of the divine resemblence through the blood royal and in its assimilation of the legal doctrin of absolute sovereignty. In his edition of James' *Political Works*, C. H. McIlwain rightly fixes on all that was new in the king's position (or new to common lawyers and parliamentarians) and argues that the attempt to act out divine and hereditary sovereignty as James conceived it made the revolution 'almost inevitable'.[1] That it made some sort of resistance to the king highly probable is probably true. It should also be said that the underlying doctrine of Christian kingship made the appearance of theories like those of James equally probable. Kantorowicz has demonstrated the long pedigree of some of his most provocative assertions and also, more importantly, of the metaphors and symbols within which his innovations fit so neatly. It required only a king (or a would-be king) with intellectual as well as divine pretensions to seize the opportunity offered by the old ideas. (In fact, it required less than that, for in France similar doctrines were put forward by jurists, ministers, and court preachers.)

When James made his claims, he also made divine right more vulnerable than it had ever been before, not because he screwed it to its highest pitch, but because some of his subjects did not believe it anymore at any pitch. 'A king is a thing', John Selden said (but did not write), 'men have made for their own sakes, for quietness' sake. Just as in a family one man is appointed to buy the meat.'[2] This is a far greater innovation than any argument put forward by King James, and its radical denial of any sort of divine resemblance has more to do with the 'inevitability' of the revolution than does the king's claim to divine sovereignty. Many years before, Richard II, apparently believed and acted upon views something like those of the first Stuart, though he unhappily wrote no books. But

[1]'Introduction', p. xl.
[2]John Selden, *Table Talk*, ed. Frederick Pollock (London, 1927), p. 61.

if some of his subjects were ready to risk offending the divine image in his person, they at least lied about what they were doing and so simultaneously paid tribute to that very image. They did not think Richard a 'thing', nor would they have said that Bolingbroke was newly chosen to buy the meat. And so they made no revolution. Revolutions come when the old regime is attacked in its fundamentals, not in the most recent exaggerations or absurdities of its leaders and spokesmen.

What was fundamental to divine right was the notion that the king was somehow godlike. That gave him a reason for pretending to political omnipotence (and no reason for not pretending), but it required him to assert only his difference from other men and not any particular doctrine of state power. The king is superior 'in essence', court writers told the French on behalf of Henry IV. 'A subject and a sovereign are clean different things', Charles I bravely announced on the scaffold, though he knew his head would drop like any other man's.[1] He was not pointing – as even Selden might have done – to a functional distinction. He meant to describe a personal difference. We can best get at the nature of that difference by turning immediately to the consecration ceremony that was once thought to establish it. The anointing of the king by a bishop of the Church was probably the most important ritual of Christian monarchy. It has its origins as a Christian rite in the time of Charlemagne, and with it comes also, as Fritz Kern has pointed out, the all-important phrase announcing that the anointed king rules 'by the grace of God'.[2] Not that God's grace moved the bishop to perform the ceremony. The king himself did that. What God did was actually to perform the miracle that the anointing symbolized. 'The grace of God hath this day changed thee into another man, and by the holy rite of unction hath made thee partaker in its divinity' – so the archbishop of Mainz spoke to the new German king.[3] The rite was thought in those early times to be a sacrament, and the new ruler, as a result of the mysterious transformation that it effected or proclaimed, emerged as a priest-king, an adopted son of God and of the Church, different from ordinary Christians because of his priesthood, different from other priests because of his kingship.

The Gregorian revolution in the Church succeeded in abolishing the king's priesthood and in denying the sacramental character of royal

[1] Roland Mousnier, *L'Assassinat d'Henri IV* (Paris, 1964), p. 228; Muddiman, *Trial*, p. 262.
[2] *Kingship and Law in the Middle Ages*, trans. S. B. Chrimes (New York, 1970), pp. 42–3. On the importance of consecration, see also Bloch, *Rois thaumaturges*, ch. 3, and Schramm, *English Coronation*, pp. 6–8. After the English reformation, the ceremony was devalued: Schramm, p. 139.
[3] Kern, *Kingship*, p. 37.

unction. Gregory and his successors insisted that the king was a layman, inferior to the lowest cleric on the spiritual hierarchy. It would have been a greater victory had they succeeded as well in making the spiritual hierarchy more effective in the world. As it was, the Church lost control over the mystery of kingship; the fact that the king was now less than priestly did not make him in his own or in his subjects' eyes less than god-like.[1] The divinity that 'hedges' a king became for the Church Militant as well as for later revolutionaries a superstition – though this was a superstition from which local church officials could rarely dissociate themselves. Carolingian kings had argued that they received from their annointing a 'a quality that could not be taken away without the verdict of the Church'. Hence churchmen had their say in the deposition of kings: Louis I (the Pious) was solemnly degraded by a synod of bishops before he was deposed and sent off to a monastary in 833. But when the Church's verdict was to take away that magical quality, not from this or that king, but from kings in general, the argument shifted. Richard II believed more simply that 'his hallowing was indelible'.[2] No synod could take it away (and perhaps it was because he could not be degraded that he had to be murdered).

> Not all the water in the rough rude sea
> Can wash the balm off from an annointed king.

If this was right, if there was no possibility of an ecclesiastical impeachment, then any attack on the king was an attack also on the divinity in which he partook. Opposition to kings was rebellion against God, who had not merely appointed them but who had also invested them with something of his own divinity. Hence the religious abhorrence in which rebels were held, at least by kings and their supporters, and the tendency of defeated kings (from Richard to Charles and Louis) to identify themselves with the God who died and to make of their defeat a Passion. There is probably something in the hatred we still feel for traitors that derives from that religious identification, though it is much easier to call the king's enemy a Judas than to apply that name to an enemy of the impersonal and secular state. The Pope, it should be said again, denied the identification altogether and sanctioned rebellion, when he thought it in the Church's interest, simply by freeing subjects from their oath of allegiance. He did

---

[1] For a time, however, a lesser oil was used in the consecration of the king than in the annointing of a priest: Schramm, *English Coronation*, pp. 127–28.

[2] So he told Chief Justice Thirning in 1399, who presumably did not agree: Steel, *Richard II*, p. 284.

not feel it necessary to wash off the balm, since he did not recognize its sacramental quality. It is interesting to note that it was not until 1682 that the French king succeeded in definitively repudiating the Pope's right to release his subjects from obedience.[1] Long before that, however, political theology had triumphed over theology itself and given the king a divine status that the Pope could not hope to challenge. He could inspire occasional assassins, but not revolutionaries.

The most extraordinary, though not the most important, power derived from the indelible hallowing of the king – and ritually acted out by French and English rulers from the early Middle Ages until the revolutionary years – was the power to heal men and women suffering from scrofula, the King's Evil. This ability, unique to kings, was sometimes quietly, sometimes vociferously denied by the Gregorian Popes and their publicists. It might nevertheless be said to represent the (self imposed) limit of royalist ideology, for it involved no priestly power: the king claimed to heal bodies, not to cure souls. The Roman objection was to the fact that he did not also claim to be especially skillful (even by the grace of God) in the practice of medicine. His work was entirely miraculous. In performing it, he literally acted the part of God, without claiming to be God, but also without the mediation of a clerical servant. '*Le roi te touche, Dieu te guerit.*' Marc Bloch is surely right to let this miracle stand for all the mysteries of kingship. Though it does not suggest an application of divine mercy to political life itself – the king does not similarly heal the ills of the body politic – the ritual touching of thousands of assembled subjects is obviously a matter of political significance. The Long Parliament recognized this when in 1647 it took up again, all unknowing, the work of Hildebrandine monks and appointed a committee to prepare 'a Declaration . . . to the People, concerning the superstition of being touched for the healing of the King's Evil'.[2]

Despite its efforts, touching for scrofula was restored along with Charles II, and that king and his brother touched their subjects at an unprecedented rate, as if seeking through the old ritual to regain all the other features of their divine resemblence. William of Orange and then the Hanoverians gave up the attempt; they were not restored, but simply post-revolutionary kings, without pretensions to sacred kingship. In France too, before the revolution, faith was waning, even the faith of the royal miracle-workers themselves. Bloch notes a revealing shift to the conditional in the formula

[1]McIlwain, 'Introduction', p. lxix(n.).
[2]Bloch, *Rois thaumaturges*, p. 374.

spoken by the king: '*Le roi te touche, Dieu te guerisse.*'[1] Nevertheless, Louis XVI touched 2400 devout and hopeful men and women on the day after his consecration in 1775, and apparently continued the practice until he became, briefly, a constitutional monarch. His election by the French people was no renewal of his mysterious powers. He is the last of the thaumaturgic kings.

If kings defied Rome by remaining godlike and working miracles long after the Papacy claimed a monopoly on religious mystery, they also defended the Church and even the faith, in part because they thought themselves godlike. They seized the opportunities, but also accepted the responsibilities, entailed by their divine resemblence. So they would have said, at any rate, and in the case of the last two kings, the assertion has some truth. Both Charles and Louis were obviously more interested in being Christian kings than in being *rois medicins*, though the two identities were, as we have seen, ideologically connected. The decline of Roman power and the rise of something like national states had enabled the kings of England and France to reclaim their religious offices as the natural corollary of the sacral character they had never lost. In the sixteenth and seventeenth centuries, they made their country's churches effectively their own, royal *eigenkirchen*, and justified their new power by reference to their age-old representation of God (and touched the scrofulous to prove the title). The priest-king returned, though without canonical justification or sacramental power. Thus the English king came to call himself not only Defender of the Faith – a title first granted by the Pope who did not foresee that the faith might be defended against himself – but also Head of the Church, whose body, it must be remembered, was still regarded as the Body of Christ. He did not thereby call himself a god; these were Christian kings. But he did claim, once again, to act in God's place and with something of his character.

This was a claim that Charles I took very seriously. More than any other royal pretension, it stood in the way of a political accommodation with Parliament. The king vacillated and lied, even signed a treaty with the Scots that committed him to ecclesiastical reforms he clearly found repugnant, but he probably did ultimately place a higher price on his religious than on his physical body.[2] The case was similar in France,

[1] Bloch, p. 403; the decline of faith is more harshly revealed by Voltaire's comment that Louis XIV could not heal one of his mistresses, though she had been '*tres bien touchée*' (p. 398).

[2] See the *Eikon Basilike*, which I shall take, following its most recent editor, to be based on a substantial 'core of material' composed by the king himself: 'Introduction', by Philip A. Knachel to the Folger Library edition (Ithaca, New York, 1966). For Charles' view of himself as defender of the Church, see esp. pp. 81, 101ff.

though Louis was even less resolute. The French king, according to royal publicists of the late seventeenth and early eighteenth centuries, was '*chef et première personne écclesiastique*'. He was given the (honorary) title 'Christ' by Bossuet, called 'sacred' both because of his unction and his duty as 'representative of the divine majesty'.[1] It is hard to be sure what Louis himself believed and impossible to doubt his private modesty, yet, like his English predecessor, he tried to live up to the responsibilities thus imposed on him by God and the ideology of kingship. Hence his abhorrence of the Civil Constitution of the Clergy, the greatest affront of the Revolution, not perhaps to his regal power but to his personal dignity. Both English and French revolutionaries sought to attack the Church while still bargaining with the king. The king's sense of himself made that extraordinarily difficult: the Church was, like the state, 'in the person of the prince'. To touch the Church was to lay hands on the king's extended body, and he could not withdraw from the religious establishment he headed without leaving some substantial part of his kingship behind. One should add, that this was true only in a manner of speaking, but that is the manner in which kings actually spoke.

Once again, the crucial point here is not the degree of ecclesiastical power claimed by any particular king. That varied a great deal, depending on the relative balance of forces within the Church and the state. What is important is the claim of virtually every king, or every Christian king, to partake in divine authority, to be an image and deputy of God.[2] Then the Church and state that he embodied partook in turn of the inequality he represented, and bishops and secular lords too ruled as lieutenants of a Captain who sometimes had, in their case, a proper as well as an ineffable name. The old regime was peopled by 'little gods', each with his retinue of servants and subjects.

THE KING'S BODY POLITIC

Because the God who made kings made everything else, one might expect the natural world to be organized, like the social world, on monarchic principles. The appeal to natural monarchy was, in fact, a central feature of royalist ideology. It depended, above all, on the description of political

---

[1]*Politique tirée*, pp. 65–7.

[2]Geoffrey Elton has argued that 'religion formed the ceremonial dress rather than the passionate essence of post-medieval kings by right divine'. Perhaps; but one would have to stress how important it is that kings not be naked. See Elton's 'Introduction' to the Harper Torchbook edition of Figgis' *Divine Right of Kings* (New York, 1965), p. xxi.

society as a body, a living organism, to whose various parts the names of different social classes were more or less plausibly attached. The image is very old, and it was apparently first elaborated in detail with reference to the Church and on behalf of Christ and his Roman vicar. The Church was a mystic body, that is, really the body of Christ, though the embodiment remained mysterious and Christ himself invisible. Kantorowicz has emphasized the degree to which medieval political thinking imitated and even reproduced the theology of the mystic body, drawing again and again the parallel of the king and Christ and developing finally a mysticism of state which absolutist writers like James I freely exploited. 'And just as men are joined together spiritually in the spiritual body, the head of which is Christ . . . so are men joined together morally and politically in the *respublica*, which is a body the head of which is the Prince.'[1] The parallel is crucial to the argument; a great deal of the appeal of body imagery clearly derives from its theological resonance.

But that is not, I think, the whole story, for the body politic has a pre-Christian history and a post-Christian appeal. There is something peculiarly comforting about the notion of the state as a product of nature and not of mere human inventiveness. If the precise character of the political union remains, on this view, mysterious and the body politic invisible, the point of reference is nevertheless familiar. We are intimate with our own bodies as we are not with God's, and the straightforward description of the state as a natural organism carries conviction, or may do so, even in the absence of theological reinforcement. To say that the body politic must have a single head is not simply to express a poetic fancy; it is to make an argument rooted in our knowledge of our own bodies and our desire for a world that is precisely not mysterious but homely and easily imagined. There may well be no argument for monarchy that is more elegant and economical than this one. Similarly, when King James says, 'I am the husband, and all the whole island is my lawful wife', he is building on medieval arguments whose source is the mystical marriage of Christ and the Church.[2] But he is also referring his listeners to their own experience of family life in a patriarchal society. That experience itself has theological endorsement, characteristically expressed in *Ephesians* 5 in

---

[1] The passage is from the fourteenth century Italian jurist Lucas de Pena, quoted in Kantorowicz 'Mysteries of State: An Absolutist Concept and its Late Medieval Origins', *Harvard Theological Review*, 48: 78–9 (1955).

[2] *Political Works*, p. 272.

body imagery: 'The man is the head of his wife, and the wife the body of the man.' Along with its theological supports, patriarchalism rests on what was thought to be a naturalistic base, that is, on the superior rational capacity of the male and the sheer 'bodyness' of the female – homely truths indeed!

Though royal headship was a mystery and a subject fit for the greatest schoolmen, it nevertheless required no great intellectual versatility to draw out the central implications of body imagery for political life. This was done again and again by popular preachers and pamphleteers. The image bore repetition and lent itself to a considerable range of stress and elaboration. But there remained always the basic and indisputable truth that the body had but one head, organically connected to the rest, not elected by the other members, whose loss was death for all of them. This same head, moreover, was the only thinking part of the body; though it needed, as it were, to consult with the five senses, its own ideas and projects were necessarily those of the whole, and the whole was uniquely its concern and not that of any other member. A wounded leg might ache, an empty stomach growl, but only the head could seek out the necessary dressing or the necessary food. Translated into political terms, all this meant in effect that the king was the only public person. All other men and women were private, limited in their functions, dependent, members of the body politic only because of the unifying role of the king. The king's plans determined the actions of the state: state policy, one might say, was in the mind of the prince. A wise prince would consult with his subjects and especially with those through whom he planned to act, but they had no political existence independent of his own.

Nor had they any claim to know his innermost thoughts. These were mysteries of state, which only the head of state had the capacity to understand. Other men might have their trades and handicrafts, but the trade of ruling belonged exclusively to the king, and here the others must bow to his wisdom, keeping 'in their own bounds', as James I told his Parliament, and never daring to 'dispute what a king can do'.[1] It is important to stress that the allusion in the phrase 'mysteries of state' is not to any particular body of knowledge that the king had mastered. There were many things, indeed, that a king needed to know, and so he called lawyers and generals to his side and hired tutors for his sons. But the art

---

[1]*Political Works*, pp. 333–4.

and mystery of kingship itself no man could teach him. It was a divine gift, perhaps, like the gift of healing, or a natural capacity inherent to the royal person.[1] In any case, it could not be shared, except perhaps with other kings; among his subjects the king had no political equals; he lived, like the head, perched high above the body, with a sense of distance and power and a degree of understanding that were his alone. For this reason, the king could not survive for long as an enlightened despot, however hard he might try to defend his prerogative by doing what other men thought right, convincing himself of the virtues of this or that fashionable philosophy. The king could not rule by the common light, and he could not survive the scrutiny of equally enlightened subjects. The whole history of monarchy and the weight of royalist ideology told against the attempt. Without mystery, the king was lost. His claim to rule rested upon another claim: to an inner light, however derived, that was as dark to the king's subjects as Protestant illumination was to the unregenerate mass.

If the king could not share his knowledge, he could no more share his power. A body with two heads would be a monster. This was a common argument in the pamphlet literature (on behalf of both monarchy and patriarchy), even though it might appear to suggest the existence of more monsters in nature than natural causes could easily account for. I have already referred to the alternative: to call monarchy 'more natural' than other historical regimes and to drive the point home (since it is not obvious) by multiplying examples and analogies. The crucial analogies are also the easiest ones: 'all the laws of nature point toward monarchy', wrote Jean Bodin, 'whether we regard the microcosm of the body, all of whose members are subject to a single head ... or whether we regard the macrocosm of the world, subject to one almighty God'.[2] The difficulties of this sort of argument are of less interest here than its main thrust, which is to describe presumptuous subjects as rebels not only against God but also against nature, madmen at war with their own bodies, intent on self-injury. A body politic might wage war against an 'outward power', argued a royalist pamphleteer during the English Revolution, 'but not (as now) by one part of it set against the head ... for that tends to the dissolution

[1] Explanations of the king's gift varied, though it was most commonly traced to God: thus, Bishop Grosseteste told Henry III that it was his consecration that gave him 'insight into the ordering of things temporal and spiritual'. Schram, *English Coronation*, p. 129. The French humanist Guillaume Budé, writing during the reign of Francis I, said more simply that 'the heart of the king received its impetus from God'. W. F. Church, *Constitutional Thought in Sixteenth Century France* (Cambridge, Mass., 1941), p. 47.

[2] *The Six Books of a Commonwealth*, trans. M. J. Tooley (Oxford, n.d.), p. 199.

of the whole'.[1] The state was a functional unity; every member had his task — not assigned to him by some bureaucratic chief, but naturally his own — upon the fulfillment of which the life of the whole depended. And it was not the task of the hands to batter the head or even to meddle in its business; that was unnatural and anarchic behavior, a threat to the survival of the entire body. Regicide can be imagined, not implausibly, as an experiment designed to falsify this view of political life.

Royalist writers took great delight in pointing out that so long as the king was physically attached to the state (that is, alive and in command), he was certain to be morally attached to it. He could be no more powerful and prosperous, no more 'lusty' (in Hobbes' phrase) than his subjects were, for they were the members of his own body.[2] The argument is even stronger in the case of hereditary monarchy, where the king's own flesh and blood will inherit not merely his physical possessions but his body politic. Indeed, these two inheritances are not easy to distinguish, for it was often said that the king had a property right in his kingship and in his realm.[3] When John Locke argued that all men 'own' their own bodies, he was generalizing on a royalist theme. And just as, for Locke, this personal ownership did not give rise to an absolute right of self-disposal or self-destruction, so with the king's body. The realm was an entailed estate or a grant from God, the ultimate owner, and the king was morally bound to preserve it and pass it on intact to his legitimate heir. It was also in his interest to do so. Self-love made him love the state, the same self-love that set other men, who had only their own physical bodies to care for, at odds with it. And paternal affection bound the king to the future of the state: 'the love that he has for his kingdom', wrote Bossuet, 'is confounded with his love for his family'.[4]

The necessary benevolence of kings might be suggested in another way. If the king were husband to his realm (in which the qualities of wife, body, and property were, like the king's love, confounded), then he might also be called the father of his subjects. The precise character of his generative capacity need not be investigated too closely. In any case, the image clearly

[1] Henry Ferne, quoted in Herbert Palmer, *Scripture and Reason Pleaded for Defensive Arms* (London, 1643), p. 14. For a similar argument used against the Huguenots, see Church, *Constitutional Thought*, p. 125.

[2] The frontispiece of the first edition of Hobbes' *Leviathan* shows a huge king whose body is literally made up of the tiny bodies of all his subjects.

[3] Herbert Rowen, 'L'état, c'est à moi:' 'Louis XIV and the State', *French Historical Studies*, 2: 83–98 (1961).

[4] *Politique tirée*, p. 57.

has origins independent of the congery of ideas associated with the body politic. It is one of the oldest ways of thinking about political rulers, and it has outlasted kings, though not without losing at their downfall a great deal of its evocative power. Men are not accustomed to elect their fathers, and it is difficult to believe wholeheartedly in the paternal wisdom and benevolence of one's own agents. For all effects and purposes, revolution marks the end of political fatherhood.[1] No great commitment to psychoanalytic theory is required to describe it as the successful struggle of the 'brethren' against the father, and after it is over, the brethren are alone, without a political father, just as they are without a natural head. *No man is born to rule his fellows* – this is the central axiom of modern politics and a direct contradiction to royalist ideology, which holds not merely that some men are so born, but that *this* man is, a figure as particular as one's own father, this man, to whom the rest of us are like children.

The idea of the king as a benevolent parent depended sometimes on the idea that the king's counsellors were evil men, for if they were not, it would be necessary to attribute the awful things he did to himself. That the king was badly counselled was the most common formula of what might be called a monarchic theodicy. It is, perhaps, a sign of the king's humanity that, unlike God, he can take bad advice. But the formula saves his love for his subjects, his good intentions, and his ultimate power to do the right thing. None of these were widely doubted, at least among the people, even at the outbreak of the two revolutions. Only gradually did the revolutionaries and their followers come to believe that the king was a bad father, and only after that did they deny that he was a father at all. No doubt, there is a long intellectual preparation for the second of these denials, the work (among others) of Calvinist clerics and French *philosophes*. Nevertheless, the benevolence of this particular man, Charles or Louis, had to be called into question – it was one of the purposes of the trials – before royal benevolence itself was finally rejected. It is interesting that in both cases, the definitive attack upon the king's person awaited the interception of his personal correspondence, a dramatic exposure of his private intentions and opinions. After his letters were seized at Naseby, Charles suggested (rightly) that 'men will now look upon me as my own counsellor and ... confine their anger to myself'.[2] The case is the same with body imagery: it was not until the king was clearly seen to have made war

---

[1] Michael Walzer, *The Revolution of the Saints* (Cambridge, Mass., 1965), pp. 196f.
[2] *Eikon Basilike*, p. 131.

against his own body, that it began to be said that the kingdom was not his at all and the political community not a body politic.

The king claims to look after his subjects because their care is his natural function (as well as his divine charge), because he is head, knower of the mysteries, father. And the vast majority of his subjects believe him because it is or seems to be a good thing, in nature as in divinity, to be looked after. A remarkable incident in the first year of the French Revolution suggests the extent of their faith. On 6 October 1789, a crowd of Parisians, many of them women, brought the king and his family from Versailles to Paris. As they marched, they chanted triumphantly of the return of 'the Baker, the Baker's wife, and the Baker's boy'. The titles have sometimes been thought derisive. But there was hunger in Paris, and to hungry people the baker is not a subject of derision. He is a provider. The chant of 6 October was one of the last tributes the children of France paid to their royal father: they thought he could give them bread. Nor was the tribute paid only by the Parisian crowd. Jean-Paul Marat wrote in his paper that same week that the king's 'presence will soon change the face of things'.[1] What mysterious power did he think Louis had? Whatever it was, Louis did not have it; he was a poor provider. He did not measure up to his pretensions, and in kings, though not in the rest of us, that failure is likely to be called a crime.

COURT POLITICS

When the state is represented by the king's person, political activity is restricted to his immediate vicinity. There is very little space within which to maneuver, agitate, and organize. The idea of a national politics is antithetical to the practice of kingship, for while the king may well build a nation and embody or symbolize its unity, he does not mobilize its members if he can help it. The claim to rule alone means that political mobilization is restricted to those persons whom the king literally summons into his presence. Rebels and traitors may organize outside, but legitimate public life takes place only within the royal circle. All activities properly called political – they will not always be recognizably so to the modern eye – are focused on the royal person.

But the royal person is also a particular man, for the 'body corporate is in the body natural', and so the private life of the king becomes synony-

---

[1]Louis R. Gottschalk, *Jean Paul Marat: A Study in Radicalism* (Chicago, 1967), p. 65.

mous with the public life of the kingdom. This is not true only because the king's policies are state policies, the king's wars state wars. Equally important, especially after the triumph of the monarchy over feudal disorder, the king's household is the central political arena. Politics is court politics – a very special kind in the study as well as the practice of which the king's passing moods and abrupt assertions as well as his deepest moral convictions are crucial data. Attention is focused on the king as if through a magnifying glass, enormously enlarging his person, his importance, and his sovereign willfulness. Everyone faces the king, though not everyone sees him, for the splendors of court life distance him from ordinary men and women, establishing with absolute clarity his position at the peak of the hierarchical system and greatly enhancing the public's sense of the power and mystery of kingship.

> Au fond de leur palais leur Majesté terrible
> Affecte à leurs sujets de se rendre invisible.[1]

In the depths of the royal palace, nevertheless, the king acts out the public life of the realm. His country is epitomized in his own household, and there he himself is constantly on display. Kings are not born, nor can they die in private; their illnesses are national crises; their celebrations, prayers, meals, even, in the France of Louis XIV, their daily *lever* and *coucher* are public occasions, spectacles in which the state itself is made visible and manifest. The courtiers are spectators, whose presence merely testifies to the importance of the royal person, until the king calls them to his side and shares his importance with them. They compete to whisper in his ear, and though the issues about which they whisper may be of the greatest national significance the competition is intensely personal. For what the courtiers seek from the king is not or not necessarily public agreement, but personal favor. And they whisper because only the king need hear. Whispering is to royal courts what public speaking is to democratic assemblies – which suggests one reason why the revolutionaries were so obsessed with conspiracies: the court is a world of conspiracy, of private intrigues with public effects.

The court is not, however, or not very often, or not for very long, the only political arena. The more complex the royal state, the more developed the government, the less it can be contained within the highly charged atmosphere of the king's household. The history of administration and justice in both England and France is in large part the story of how offices and

---

[1] Jean Racine, *Esther*, I, 3.

courts of law originally associated with the household were separated from it, one by one, and established on an independent basis. The king retained more or less control of these new institutions, depending on his success in controlling the appointment of their officials. Whatever his success, administration and adjudication did provide opportunities for public and even oppositional activity, at least in the king's absence. Thus the French *parlements* could defy the king up to the moment he appeared in person before them. Then the judges reverted, in effect, to the status of personal servants: *apparente rege cessat magistratus*.[1] Positions from which men might speak out loud to the king were also created whenever kings found it convenient or necessary to seek the consent of their subjects. This they could only do by recognizing in the nation a power (to consent or not, though the power to refuse consent was not always explicitly recognized) that was necessarily independent of themselves. The French Estates and the English Parliament met only when the king summoned them to meet; they nevertheless managed, the second far more successfully than the first, to establish a corporate identity and to assert corporate rights. Ultimately, it was they who summoned the king and organized his trial.

When English kings convened Parliament (or French kings called the Estates), they immediately expanded political space and opened the way for activities which were bound to stand in uneasy tension with all that went on at court. The expansion was obviously not unlimited; it was not the nation but a group of men representing the nation, in one way or another, who were invited to meet together. And even they were not permitted to meet outside the parliamentary chambers to discuss public business. Within those chambers, however, the members won the right to speak freely, not only to the king, but also to one another. Hence politics no longer focused so narrowly on the royal person; he was not the only person who had to be convinced. The king, who was followed everywhere by men eager to please, had to find a following in Parliament. Among English rulers, only Elizabeth seems to have been a (more or less) willing and truly adroit practitioner of this sort of politics. 'She converted her reign', wrote Harrington, 'through the perpetual love-tricks that passed between her and her people, into a kind of romance.'[2] The language here is significant. In describing the best of royal politicians, Harrington instinctively turns to

---

[1] In the sixteenth century, the *parlement* was still called '*pars corporis principis*' – Church, *Constitutional Thought*, p. 54; for a description of the *lit de justice*, the king's personal appearance before his judges, see p. 150.
[2] *Political Writings of James Harrington*, p. 97.

the metaphors of sexual relations and personal attachment. He does so in part because the ruler he is discussing was a woman dealing with men, but also, I think, because such metaphors were somehow appropriate to the courtly intrigue which constituted a large part of the everyday politics of kingship. The metaphors were inappropriate, however, to the king- (or queen-) in-Parliament. At court, the courtiers court the king. In Parliament, Harrington is suggesting, the monarch must woo his subjects, as if they might turn to another lover if they found him unappealing, much as the king in his household might choose another favorite. But it is just this possibility that the king cannot grant. He cannot agree that his regal authority depends on the success of his love-tricks. As Elizabeth's successor pointed out, the king and his subjects are already married.

Earlier English and French rulers had excelled in the kinds of intrigue and warfare required to survive among and eventually to overcome powerful aristocratic factions. But parliamentary politics was alien to them, or rather, it became alien whenever the members of Parliament ceased to be members also of aristocratic (or royalist) factions – the king's own men or someone else's. Then the king was inclined to withdraw to his court and, in response to Parliament's claim to represent the nation, to elaborate (intellectually in the England of James I, ceremonially in the France of Louis XIV) upon his own embodiment of the state. The French kings virtually destroyed the Estates by the simple expedient of never summoning them to meet: a success that made them the envy of their English brethren. They ruled from the midst of their court, after 1680 chiefly from Versailles, with no sense of having isolated themselves from their subjects, since the aristocracy followed them and obediently circled round the throne. It was the only place to pursue a political career. Cultural life too focused increasingly on the royal household. Indeed, the extraordinary cultural efflorescence of Paris in the middle years of the seventeenth century (as of London at the end of the sixteenth) was undoubtedly a triumph of monarchic centralization. And since the strength of a regime ought to be measured not only by its power to command soldiers, but also by its power to attract poets, the careers of Molière and Racine (as of Shakespeare and Jonson) can be taken as signs of the power of the king-in-his-court. They are signs also of the new importance of the capital city created by the ascendent monarchy, for the arts did not flourish so well in the marble palaces of Versailles. There Louis created the milieu within which the French monarchy slowly decayed.

The withdrawal of the king into his court and then of the court from the city took place in England also, though there was no similar physical removal. The story is best told by the literary critics and historians, who were also the first to apply the idea of decadence to the court culture of the pre-revolutionary years.[1] The story of court politics has not been told, or not explicitly told, in terms of the same idea, but it would be useful to try to do so. Decadence is, as it were, the 'secret history' of the latter-day court, its concrete expressions retailed to the nation by journalistic scandal-mongers and puritanical politicians. The period of decay was much briefer in England than in France (though in England the decadent court had a post-revolutionary afterlife), but the Jacobean court was a hothouse, and many similar features appear in the royal households of the two countries before their respective revolutions. And the same sorts of tales were told of the two, which may help explain why both revolutions were in part revolts of the country against the court.[2] The quality of court life also helps explain, I think, the personal response of the two kings to this revolt, from their first stubborn refusals of negotiation or agreement to the extraordinary grace of their last moments on the scaffold.

In a brilliant passage in his *History of the Russian Revolution*, Trotsky attempts a composite character of Charles, Louis, and Nicholas, 'the last-born offspring of absolutism'.[3] He points to striking similarities in the psychological traits and the mental and moral attitudes of the three, drawing largely upon the work of contemporary memoirists and historians. His description is worth repeating. Well-bred and self-restrained, tranquil under great pressure, wonderfully sure of their personal status and of their duties, the three last kings were at the same time, Trotsky says, 'absolutely deprived of imagination and creative force'. They all responded to the revolutionary movements that eventually destroyed them with an intellectual indifference that is really remarkable and then with a purely negative politics. 'His first word was usually *No*' – this was said of Louis, but it fits the others as well. They did not hesitate to lie to men in whom they saw nothing but personal enemies, but they all lied badly. What they did best was to die. Trotsky attempts, very hastily, a sociological explanation of the characters of the three or of the single character that he constructs out of the three. Such kings are produced, he argues, when 'the dynasty becomes

---

[1] See especially the essays of T. S. Eliot on the Jacobean and Caroline dramatists, *Selected Essays* (London, 1949).
[2] The tales are still told: see G. P. V. Akrigg, *Jacobean Pageant, or The Court of James I* (Cambridge, Mass., 1962), ch. 16 (on the Overbury affair) and Alfred Cobban, *Aspects of the French Revolution* (New York, 1970), ch. 4 (on the affair of the Queen's necklace).
[3] Leon Trotsky, *The History of the Russian Revolution*, trans. Max Eastman (Ann Arbor, 1961), I, pp. 91 ff.

isolated; the circle of people loyal to the death narrows down; their level sinks lower; meanwhile the dangers grow; new forces are pushing up; the monarchy loses its capacity for any kind of creative initiative; it defends itself, it strikes back, it retreats . . .'. In sum, the 'moral insignificance' of the three kings '[derives] from their dynastic epigonism'. It is a fine formula and highly suggestive, even if it makes the historical process sound rather tidier than it is. In fact, both the English and French kings were served at the end by men of quite remarkable ability. But there were few enough of them, and they were often moved more by a lingering sense of loyalty to the king than by any absolutist convictions. Even this is less true in England, where the ideological commitments of Laud and Strafford can hardly be doubted – no more than their ability can be doubted. Yet Trotsky is right, I think, to point to the isolation of the dynasty. Its social base had narrowed so that the court made up a great part of it, and the court, for all its symbolic importance, was by itself no bastion of strength. Nor were many courtiers loyal unto death, least of all in France, where the court had been most splendid. By 1791, Marie-Antoinette was complaining, *'personne ne vient a mon jeu; le coucher du roi est solitaire. . .'*.[1]

'The court is the tomb of the nation', wrote D'Argenson, some years before the revolution.[2] In fact, the court was the tomb only of the old regime. It was the crucial mediating institution in the making of those kings that Trotsky described, who died with such grace. What happened in the royal household of the last years was simply that the royal embodiment lost its mythic qualities, even before the king himself lost his power to command. The *Parlement* of Paris, in 1771, could still affirm, it had no choice but to affirm, that 'All authority in the political order emanates from the authority of the king; all magistrates are the king's officials; the right of making laws belongs only to the king'.[3] And the affirmation was accurate; the king was still absolute. But he could no longer act out the ideology that made absolutism credible. The reasons for his failure undoubtedly have to do chiefly with transformations in the society as a whole, but they have to do also with the inability of the court to reflect those transformations, to attract the new men or shape the changing opinions of the nation. Once court etiquette had epitomized social relations outside; now it lost its evocative quality and became an esoteric ritual. The court's

[1] Alfred Pizard, *La France en 1789* (Paris, n.d.), p. 33.
[2] Pizard, p. 30.
[3] Pizard, p. 5; see also, A. Esmein, *Histoire du droit français* (Paris, 1898), pp. 536–9.

withdrawal from the culture and politics of the capital city had turned the courtiers inward, focused their attention less on the sovereign, more on the man who was king and on all the other men and women surrounding him. Courtly pleasures grew increasingly refined and sophisticated, manners and discourse increasingly stylized. But refinement and style only masked activities devoid of political substance or of any larger meanings that could be translated to the nation. Personal relations, above all sexual relations, replaced every other sort of alliance.

The king's private life was no longer lifted to the level of a public action; public life was degraded instead to the level of a private intrigue. Hence the real political power of the beautiful young men of England and the royal mistresses of France – hardly unprecedented in the history of kingship (similar tales can be told, for example, of the court of Edward II, a deposed but not a 'last' king), but important nevertheless in understanding the revolution. The distribution of political power for sexual reasons is the clearest possible expression of courtly decadence. It helps account also for the patriotic virtue of the anti-monarchic forces. They were the new embodiment, or so their leaders claimed, of all that was healthy in the state.

The bizarre patterns of personal intrigue that characterized the court bred a kind of skepticism, first of human nature, then of divine beneficence. 'Atheism', Robespierre declared in 1794, 'is aristocratic.'[1] He was right, though kings themselves remained devout. Equally important, the court in its last days produced a kind of competition more direct and intense than the marketplace has ever generated, and court wits as a consequence were more ruthless in their exposure of their own and everyone else's egotism than the most clear-headed bourgeois theorist would ever be. Self-love and self-interest were also aristocratic: what did a man do at court but aggrandize himself? The animating principle of monarchy, Montesquieu argued, was personal honor, a sense of dignity and place appropriate to the hierarchical system over which the king presided. But he also described the more particular forms of honor in a decadent regime, where 'the actions of men are judged, not as virtuous, but as shining; not as just, but as great; not as reasonable, but as extraordinary'. Here, 'among the crimes that dishonor, there is always a way of committing them that does not dishonor' – a witty remark, a gesture of nonchalance, a graceful movement were often enough to insure that the criminal did not fall behind in the race for royal favor and

---

[1] A. Aulard, *Christianity and the French Revolution* (Boston, 1927), p. 113.

Regicide and Revolution

reward.[1] The honor of the courtiers consisted entirely in their reputations, and the more intensely committed they were to the court, the less their reputations depended on practical achievements or noble conduct in the external world. At court, they sought the notice of the king, so as to be noticed by everyone else. Outside, they simply defended their privileges. The king, who was born to be noticed, had only to defend his privileges. His honor also did not require any external achievements; above all, it did not require any imaginative or determined effort to recreate his representative role — itself the achievement, after all, of earlier kings. Once again, it was the revolutionaries who dreamed, impossibly perhaps, of a new embodiment and a national monarchy. The king was both politically and spiritually immobilized by the empty ceremonies, the obsequiousness, and the cynicism of his courtly household. When he said No with courage and refinement, he had done all that he had been taught to do. It remained only to mount the scaffold in such a manner that men might say:

He nothing common did or mean
Upon that memorable scene.[2]

The popular revolt against the king's household seized upon institutions that the king had created and then failed to dominate or manage. The Long Parliament was called by Charles and continued to act in his name even after it went to war against him. Louis did more than summon the Estates; he invited the courts and municipal corporations and 'tous les savants et les personnes instruits' to join in a national inquiry as to their character and organization.[3] He was no longer able to stipulate the form of the representative body, let alone himself embody the nation. Nor did he know the proper names of the wise men of his kingdom. They had not attended him in his court. And so he called into being a new political public, whose opinions he made painfully little effort to understand; he apparently did not even bother to read the cahiers. The state was reconstituted outside the body of the king, and the king was left with little more than his honorable pretensions and his courtliness.

[1] *The Spirit of the Laws*, IV, trans. Thomas Nugent (New York, 1949), p. 29; Robert Shackleton, *Montesquieu* (Oxford, 1961), p. 275.
[2] Andrew Marvell, *An Horatian Ode*.
[3] *Arrêt du Conseil* of 5 July 1788.

34

3

THE KING AND THE LAW

THE INVIOLABLE KING

It was not easy to clothe the revolt of the country against the king in the forms of law, for the country as a body had no legal standing under the old regime; it was not conceived to exist apart from its royal head. Nevertheless, the attempt was made and is of considerable importance, though it is usually ignored or dismissed by modern commentators. Indeed, the *forms* of law were adopted: the king was brought to trial. But in order to do that, the substance of the law or, more simply, the position of the king *vis-à-vis* the law had to be changed. For Charles and Louis lived within a seemingly impregnable legal fortress. Though there were major differences between English and French kings with regard to their legislative powers, there were none at all with regard to their standing before their own courts. They may or may not have been above the law when it came to making law, but they were clearly beyond its (worldly) reach. It was a legal maxim in both England and France that the king could do no wrong: *le roi ne peut pas faire mal*. This principle the revolutionaries were committed to deny, and their denial was a large part of the revolution they made.

To be a king was to be inviolable. That meant that no action of a reigning monarch, whatever its character, could possibly be construed as a crime. The status was, strictly speaking, a legal one only; it followed logically from the king's position as the source of law and justice. The king's inability to do wrong was no proof against sin — as even court preachers reminded him again and again. Nevertheless, royal inviolability was deeply rooted in the mystique of kingship, and it has important moral and political as well as legal implications.[1] The significance of the king's trial will hardly be un-

---

[1] English legal historians have tended to stress the narrowly legal character of royal inviolability, especially for the medieval period, and to deny that it had any mystical corollaries. See W. S. Holdsworth, *A History of English Law* (London, 1909), III, p. 357. The tendency is best represented by F. W. Maitland's robust assertion that 'The medieval king was every inch a king, but just for that reason, he was every inch a man, and you did not talk nonsense about him' *Collected Papers*, ed. H. A. L. Fisher (Cambridge, 1911), II, p. 246. Against this, it is useful to

derstood unless these are analyzed in some detail. The revolutionaries had to overcome two central difficulties in planning the trial: first, that there were no standards, that is, no conventionally specifiable legal rules or moral principles by which a king could be judged; and secondly, that there was no-one in all his kingdom by whom he could be judged, that is, no officer or magistrate (for they were all the king's men) who could exercise authority over him. The king answered to a higher court; he could be tried by God alone, and the judgments God delivered were never publicized on earth.

This did not mean, however, that the king was a law unto himself, subject to no legal or moral restraint at all. Royalist ideology suggested something very different. As divine deputies, kings were subject to the decrees of God; as heads of political bodies, they were bound by the laws of nature. In the Middle Ages and even until the end of the sixteenth century, the very structure of the universe was imagined in terms of legal harmonies, and the law itself was viewed as a reflection of the universal order. The world was lawful in the literal sense, and the king was subject to its laws even when his personal dignity, his political authority, and his legal irresponsibility were all unquestioned. He could do whatever could rightly be done, but despite the Roman Law maxim about the pleasure of the prince, he could not do whatever he pleased.[1] But this limit was very difficult either to specify or to enforce, since the king was the only effective spokesman within his kingdom for God and nature. The Pope, of course, claimed an alternative and superior representative position, and concerted opposition not merely to the power of this or that king but to royal authority itself was most often attempted from a Roman base. But this was opposition from a distance. Despite the moral unity of Christendom, particular conflicts between the king and Pope looked less like domestic disputes than like diplomacy and war. Except at the very height of papal power, when English kings were forced to acknowledge themselves Roman vassals, these were conflicts, for all effects and purposes, between two reigning monarchs. And since local bishops were usually forced into alliance with their own king, no internal ecclesiastical control

(Footnote 1 continued from page 35)

place Bloch's statement that 'Medieval men never resigned themselves to seeing in their sovereign a mere layman or a mere man'. *Rois thaumaturges*, p. 259. In fact, of course, a great deal of 'nonsense' was talked, though Maitland is right in insisting that it did not find its way into the lawbooks until a later period. The legal basis of the king's inviolability was the simple fact that no man (no feudal lord) could be sued in his own courts. But in the king's case, this freedom was but one aspect of a general untouchability, which was indeed of an essentially mystical kind.

[1] See Fritz Kern's summary statement, *Kingship and Law*, pp. 69ff.

over royal authority was ever won.[1] The Pope issued judgments and excommunications (which were also licenses to revolt), but the king's clerical subjects were faithful more often to their political than to their spiritual father. If court preachers called the king a sinner, they did not often dare to specify his sins.

In much the same way that the king could be a sinner, he could also be a tyrant. As he was subject to divine and natural law, so he was bound also, indeed, he was formally committed by his coronation oath, to respect the fundamental laws or the ancient constitution of his realm – which included the customary rights and liberties of his subjects.[2] A king who trampled on fundamental law was a tyrant: though the terminology is late, it came to be widely accepted, and on this proposition Charles I and Oliver Cromwell would not have disagreed.[3] But it was less easy, once again, to specify the content of fundamental law. Efforts to do so against the king were almost certain to fail, for as long as the old regime survived, kingship itself was the most fundamental law and the unquestioned basis of all subsequent disputes. What was at issue was the scope of royal prerogative, never its existence, and radical or extensive limitations of that scope could not easily be defended given the ideology of kingship and the available historical precedents. The constitution of the monarchy might be conceived so narrowly – as by James I, who limited it to the *jus coronae* – that tyranny became an entirely academic matter; the king could have little interest in violating fundamental law when it imposed so very little on himself.[4] Conceived more broadly, however, the constitution might appear to stand, not independently of the king, but at least as a bar to his own absolute independence. Even then, it was not necessarily a bar to absolutism, but only to what Bishop Bossuet called arbitrary government.[5] Thus the king of England could only legislate in and through his Parliament, and the king of France had to register his decrees with his own *parlements*. These were

---

[1] That is, neither the English Convocation nor the *Assemblée générale* of the French clergy ever exercised any significant political power. As late as 1752, to be sure, the French clerics still claimed the right to bring 'even kings to the judgment of God'. But this was mere declamation and corresponded to no political reality. Pizard, *La France*, p. 11.

[2] The English oath is referred to several times during the trial of Charles (Muddiman, *Trial*, pp. 117, 236); for a detailed history, see Schramm, *English Coronation*, pp. 179–227. In France, the oath was radically devalued by absolutist writers (beginning with Bodin) and played no part in the revolutionary debates, thought it had been cited frequently during the sixteenth century civil wars and the Fronde.

[3] J. W. Gouge, *Fundamental Law in English Constitutional History* (Oxford, 1955), ch. 5.

[4] McIlwain, 'Introduction', *Political Works of James I*, xxxviii.

[5] *Politique tirée*, pp. 92ff. The distinction was common among seventeenth century French writers.

nothing more than descriptions of the different institutional structures of the two monarchies, of arrangements and procedures that the king had no reason to modify so long as he got his own way when he most wanted to. What fundamental law could not specify was the right of Parliament or of the *parlements* persistently to oppose the king's will or to challenge his prerogative. Until the two revolutions, the name of tyrant was not successfully attached to any king who refused to tolerate such a challenge – or at least it was not attached simply because of such a refusal.

It was a serious matter to call a king a tyrant; the word had deep resonances in the history of the old regime. But it signified moral opprobrium only; it had no accepted political or legal content. The king who ruled willfully, arbitrarily, selfishly, without proper regard for the rights and liberties of his (more powerful) subjects – in sum, against the law, in the widest and vaguest sense of that term – was a common figure in medieval political thought.[1] He provided a dramatic contrast necessary to anyone attempting a convincing description of a good king or, for that matter, a convincing justification of a new king. But the word remained a party term, and it is difficult not to sympathize with Hobbes' dictum that tyranny was never anything more than 'monarch misliked'. There often seems terribly little difference between the kings called tyrants and those free from such reproach – except perhaps with regard to their political fortunes. By and large, in the chronicles and history books, only deposed kings are called tyrants, though we have no reason to believe and there would be no way of demonstrating that only those kings (or all those kings) who overrode the fundamental laws of their kingdoms were deposed. In effect, usurpers called their predecessors tyrants: hence the conventional portraits of the last two Richards of England. But such portraits suggest no substantive view of the limits on royal power. They have more to do with the moral temper than with the political actions of the deposed kings, and no doubt that is what the new rulers wanted.

In sixteenth century France and again in seventeenth century England, efforts were made to specify a constitution that severely limited the king's authority. The Estates General and then the English Parliament were written more deeply into fundamental law than any historical analysis could possibly justify (though historical analyses were offered), and kings who tried to govern without their active assistance and support were called

---

[1] See Oscar Jászi and John D. Lewis, *Against the Tyrant: The Tradition and Theory of Tyrannicide* (Glencoe, Illinois, 1957), ch. 2.

tyrants.[1] It was one of the offical charges against Charles I that, 'out of a wicked design to uphold in himself an unlimited and tyrannical power', he had sought to 'alter the fundamental constitutions of this kingdom'. Charles, however, directed the same charge against his parliamentary opponents, and probably with greater justice: they were working, he said, 'to subvert the fundamental laws and government of the kingdom of England'.[2] In any case, neither side could do anything on behalf of fundamental law except fight for it. The issue came quickly to war, for the disagreement was not over the particular actions of the king but over the general form of the regime, and no adjudication was possible. The king could not be judged in court until divine right monarchy had been broken on the battlefield. Even then, the charge of tyranny was not one that could easily be documented. Perhaps for this reason few details were provided by the High Court as to the acts that made it up; the Court elaborated on the treason, but not on the tyranny of the king.

In France, the notion of an 'ancient constitution' survived until the revolution, though it played no serious part in any of the revolutionary settlements. It had been the theme of Hotman in the 1570s, and it was still being argued in the pamphlets of the 1770s and '80s.[3] But the argument as commonly stated would have made virtually every French king since Francis I a tyrant, and the condemnation was too wholesale to carry much weight. It was possible to believe that royal authority should be limited; it was very difficult to believe that it *was* limited and that the limits had been brutally overridden by one king after another for hundreds of years. The truth was that absolutism had triumphed in France, intellectually as well as politically. That meant that there was no constitutional measure, no substantive measure of any sort, that any significant number of Frenchmen could imagine applying to monarchic government. It did not mean, again, that the king could do what he pleased. He could not leave his kingdom to his daughter, for example, however much he loved her; he could not sell Burgundy to the king of Sweden or to the merchants of Amsterdam; often enough, he could not even get his decrees registered without a *lit de justice*. When Louis XIV wrote a will to please his mistress, the *Parlement* of Paris set it aside — though it waited until after his death to do so, it having been neither necessary nor expedient to do so

---

[1] The important texts are collected and translated by Julian Franklin, in *Constitutionalism and Resistance in the Sixteenth Century* (New York, 1969).

[2] Gough, *Fundamental Law*, p. 78.

[3] E. Carcassonne, *Montesquieu et le problème de la constitution française* (Paris, n.d.) summarizes the pre-revolutionary literature.

before. Probably this is the sort of thing Bossuet had in mind when he said that the French king did not govern arbitrarily. He clearly did not have in mind any laws by which a living king might be judged by his subjects: there simply were no such laws.

Nor were there any subjects who might apply them. There had indeed been feudal opponents of the king who claimed a kind of equality with him and the right of legal self-help against him: I will take up their views later on. By and large, however, the recognition of a king was the recognition of a superior. Royalist ideology was not much more than a series of elaborations on the nature of that superiority, and it was a necessary conclusion of every one of the series that the king could not possibly be apprehended, accused, judged, or punished by any man who owed him loyalty. The king's person, his physical as well as his politic self, was sacred: he could not be touched against his will, let alone attacked or assaulted.[1] Legally, he was similarly unassailable: he could not be brought to justice in his own courts (or in anyone else's, for his own were the highest in the land). He could be petitioned and pleaded with, but there was no way to bring suit against him.[2] Nor did there exist any procedure by which a king might be impeached by some body of his subjects. At most, the English Parliament might 'recognize' the deposition of this or that king and offer reasons to justify it after the fact; they could take no initiatives.[3] The members did not possess the requisite authority, either moral or legal, for they did not participate in the king's divinity or headship. Even active rebels against the king regularly admitted his inviolability. Thus the pamphlet of a French *frondeur*, written on behalf of men actually at war with the king's armies (for it is easier to make war than to pass judgment): 'The person of the king is the body of the royalty; it is always holy and sacred.'[4]

There is a much-discussed sentence in the work of the medieval English jurist Bracton which suggests a legal process against the king that might have looked rather like impeachment had it ever been tried. For gross

---

[1] During the minority of Henry VI of England, the regent was permitted by the Council to 'chastise' the young king – a perfect example of the exception that proves the rule. Holdsworth, *History of English Law*, III, p. 356.

[2] On the 'myth' that the English king could once be sued, see Frederick Pollock and F. W. Maitland, *The History of English Law* (Cambridge, 1905), I, pp. 516–17. According to jurists writing as late as the 1570s, the French king could be 'called to justice' before his *parlements*, but this was possible only if he consented. See Church, *Constitutional Thought*, p. 132.

[3] See Lapsley, 'Parliamentary Title', for an assessment of Parliament's role in the depositions of Edward II and Richard II.

[4] Paul Rice Doolin, *The Fronde* (Cambridge, Mass., 1935), p. 137.

violations of the law, Bracton writes, the injured people need not wait for God's judgment, but can themselves seek remedy 'and may do it in the court of the king himself'.[1] But Bracton could cite no cases of such justice; there were none to cite before 1649, when the courts no longer belonged to the king. Impeachment was a parliamentary weapon against the 'high crimes and misdemeanors' not of kings but only of royal officials. It was used frequently, for example, in the fourteenth century and again in the early years of the revolution. But though it might strike close to home, no impeachment could possibly 'lie against the king', as Charles I reminded his judges, 'they all going in his name'.[2] The point was a logical one only, but it dramatically points to the purely personal character of monarchic authority. Only when the writs ran in the name of the state or of the people would the king be open to legal challenges, as distinct from mere rebellions, in his own kingdom. But then the kingdom would no longer be his own.

The king's inviolability is often described as if it were a function of his sovereignty. Then, it is a said, the revolutionaries transferred sovereignty to the people, the king was replaced by *la puissance publique*, and royal inviolability gave way to state immunity.[3] In fact, the story is far more complicated than that. Kings were inviolable long before they were sovereign in anything like the modern sense of that word, and the precise degree to which they achieved or failed to achieve absolute power has nothing to do with their freedom from accusation and judgment. James I wrote that he was 'above the law, as both author and giver of strength thereto'. Louis XV insisted that the law-making power belonged to him alone, '*sans dépendence et sans partage*'.[4] The English king was plainly wrong, the French king probably right; but the trials of their successors were equally innovative and equally surprising, for the inviolability of the two was exactly the same. They were both untouchable because 'there's such Divinity doth hedge a king'. Their inviolability was not only a legal status; it was also a personal attribute – or better, it was the legal form of that personal inequality which kingship (but not sovereignty) presupposed. The doctrine of state immunity that derives from it is something very different, crucially because the privileges it provides do not belong permanently or as a matter of right to a particular person. They are enjoyed

[1] Holdsworth, *History of English Law*, II, p. 256.
[2] Muddiman, *Trial*, p. 231.
[3] Paul Tirard, *De la responsibilité de la puissance* (Paris, 1906), pp. 117–18: 'The Revolution transformed the political and social order, but the theoretical concepts of the royal jurists have been maintained . . .' See also R. D. Watkins, *The State as Party Litigant* (Baltimore, 1925), ch. 12.
[4] *Political Writings of James I*, p. 63; Esmein, *Histoire du droit*, p. 348n.

by a succession of representatives, officials or functionaries of the abstract state. But the king alone represents God; he alone embodies the state, and the particularity of his embodiment cannot be overemphasized. It was what the revolutionaries most held against him.

The claims of James I and Louis XV reflect long-term transformations in the theory of law rather than any specifically new view of kingship. They fall more under the purview of legal than of political historians, though no doubt the spheres of these two cannot easily be distinguished. What was involved, most importantly, was the exaltation of positive law and the weakening of all moral restraints on legislative authority, the weakening, that is, of divine, natural, and customary or fundamental law. Or rather, as Hobbist and Austinian writers would say, the changes involved the growing recognition of what legislative authority *is*.[1] The king was only the most immediate beneficiary of this recognition, by virtue largely of his historical presence. The revolutionaries were the next beneficiaries, and undoubtedly found sovereignty a greater benefit. For the new doctrine was abstract and precise in a way far better suited to the collective people than to the particularity of the king. The king was necessarily more than sovereign. He was mysterious and sacred; his inviolability was a matter of personal right. The lawfulness of the universe was not, as I have tried to show, a significant restraint on him, for his person and his station were part of that universe, symmetrical with the macrocosm and the microcosm, with an omnipotent God and a supreme and rational head. The people were not similarly placed, which is probably why their leaders were forced to adopt the absolutist position that there was nothing they could not do. The Commons and the Convention claimed to be sovereign *sans dépendence et sans partage*: only then could they touch the untouchable king.

ROYAL TREASON

When Charles and Louis were finally brought to trial, the chief charge against them was treason. There is a special irony in this, for under the old regime no laws more perfectly expressed the king's embodiment of the state than did the laws of treason. Although the king could not be conceived to commit any crime, treason was peculiarly alien to him, for it was

---

[1] On the tangled question of just how *new* this recognition actually is, see Elton, 'Introduction', xxv–xxxii.

a crime against his own person. According to the basic English law of
1352, treason consisted in compassing the king's death, levying war
against him, or adhering to his enemies.[1] The personal pronouns in the last
two clauses are crucial for an understanding of what is at stake here. In
the French ordinances, the pronouns are always first person plural (*notre
personne, nos enfants et posterité*) and indicate even more clearly the specifically limited character of the crime of treason. Edward II of England
spoke in the same style when he refused to attend the proceedings at which
he was to be formally deposed: 'he would not come among his enemies or
rather, *his traitors*'.[2] The king, of course, stood for the kingdom: English
legislation sometimes referred to 'treasons against the king and the realm',
and an ordinance of Francis I (1539) spoke of '*aucune chose . . . conspiré
ou entrepris contre . . . le république de notre royaume*'.[3] But the crime was
usually thought to require an act aimed directly at the king's person (or
some member of his immediate family) or construed by the courts to be so
aimed. Treason, argued the judges in Calvin's Case (1608), that is, 'to
intend or compass *mortum et destructionem domini Regis*, must needs be
understood of his natural body, for his politic body is immortal and not
subject to death.'[4] The kingdom cannot be killed, or so it was believed,
and its enemies are by definition the king's own enemies. Hence no king
can possibly be a traitor, whatever actual harm he does to his subjects or to
his kingdom, unless perhaps he harms himself.[5] A king's suicide might
constitute treason, and Shakespeare's Richard II describes his acquiescence
in his own deposition as a traitorous act:

> I find myself a traitor with the rest
> For I have given here my soul's consent
> T'undeck the pompous body of a king. . . .

In practice, however, the issue never arose; reigning monarchs do not seem
at all prone to self-destruction, perhaps because they so acutely understand
their own importance. The same understanding is clear in the law: thus the
Second Treasons Act of Elizabeth I (1571) looked to 'the surety and preservation of the Queen's most royal person, in whom consisteth all the

---

[1]For an extended discussion of this important statute, see J. G. Bellamy, *The Law of Treason in
the Later Middle Ages* (Cambridge, 1970), ch. 4.

[2]Harold H. Hutchinson, *Edward II* (New York, 1971), p. 139 (emphasis added).

[3]G. R. Elton, *The Tudor Constitution: Documents and Commentary* (Cambridge, 1960), p. 63;
Répertoire du droit français, ed. M. Fuzier-Herman (Paris, 1890), VI, p. 313.

[4]Quoted in Kantorowicz, *King's Two Bodies*, p. 15. Cf. Bellamy, *Law of Treason*, p. 209.

[5]Thus Henry IV's first Parliament charged the deposed Richard with perjury – the violation of
his coronation oath – rather than with treason. Lapsley, 'Parliamentary Title', *English Historical
Review*, 49:577.

happiness and comfort of the whole state and subjects of the realm. . .'.
To call the king an enemy of the state (or of the people) represented a
monumental overturn. It was itself the ultimate treason, as Elton suggests
when he describes treason as 'the final denial of the divine order of things as
established in the body politic. . .'.[1]

In England, though not in France, this ultimate treason has a shadowy
kind of legal preparation. The notion that the realm is separate from the
king and can be betrayed as well as the king (hence, at least conceivably,
by the king) is not entirely new in 1649. But the only firm precedents
were barely a few years old, themselves revolutionary, and the resistance
of English law to such a view was considerable. During the reign of
Edward II, the argument had been put forward that it was sometimes
necessary, even obligatory, to defend the country and the Crown against
the king. This position, attributed to the Despensers and condemned
with them in 1321, rested ultimately on a feudal version of the theory of
the governmental contract: 'for he is bound by his oath to govern the
people and his Liege Subjects, and his Liege Subjects are bound to govern
in aid of him and in his default'.[2] I will discuss this and other contracts
later on. What is important here is the description of a body of men who
can go into action on behalf of the kingdom against the king. This suggests
a fairly radical division between the king and 'his' state, and the suggestion
was called treasonous in the fourteenth century and a 'damnable and
damned opinion' at the opening of the seventeenth: the memory of the
law is long. It was then effectively adopted by the revolutionary Parliament, whose members could hardly look for favorable precedents, however, in a history that contained nothing but condemnations.

In the early 1640s, the king's ministers were themselves charged with
creating a division in the kingdom – this time between the king and his own
subjects. They had acted, it was said, so as to make the king's power odious
to his subjects and so, by construction, to compass his death. But the construction was devious, since it virtually stipulated the treasonable
readiness of those Englishmen to whom the king's power had been made
odious, to kill him. The argument was explicitly put forward in the first
charges against the Earl of Strafford, with due citation of precedents,
but it was not very persuasive. Nor could it easily have been extended to
catch the king: 'it would have been ludicrous', writes a modern scholar,
'to execute Charles for constructively compassing his own death, and he

[1] *Tudor Constitution*, p. 59.
[2] J. C. Davies, *The Baronial Opposition to Edward II* (Cambridge, 1918), pp. 24–5.

had to be tried for offenses against the State'.[1] The major step on the way to doing that was the attainder of Strafford for having made war against the *subjects* of King Charles. The assumption underlying the charge, accepted by the Lords and, with whatever self-reproach, by Charles himself, seems to have been that levying war against the people was the same as, or was as serious as, levying war against the king. In the impeachment of Archbishop Laud, the Commons took the next step and argued explicitly that 'treason may be against the realm as well as against the king'. Here was a new victim for an old crime: the disembodied realm, the state conceived abstractly, the body of the people without its head. A monstrous entity in royalist ideology, its existence made it possible, at last, for the king to be a criminal. It also established a standard for his criminality, for everyone knew what sorts of actions might constitute treason. 'Levying war' was the chief of these, and it was the one on which the High Court focused its attention.

In France, the revolutionaries made an even more radical break with the legal past; they wrote a new constitution and a new criminal code. Yet the king remained inviolable up to the moment he was actually brought to trial, and there were no earlier trials which set any precedent for his. After the insurrection of 10 August an extraordinary tribunal was set up (elected by the Parisian sections), and a number of court officials were tried and several condemned to death.[2] But the particular legal issues raised by the king's trial did not arise in these cases. What made the king's trial difficult was that the Constitution, though it declared him impeachable, had specifically denied that he was justiciable – it was the drafters' only bow to the 'ancient constitution' of France. Even an impeached king was still described, in language more appropriate to the old regime, as one who was 'considered to have abdicated'. The 'consideration', however, belonged to the Assembly, and among the reasons for considering the king to have abdicated were two that looked very much like conventional treasons: his use of armed force *'contre la nation'* and his failure to oppose anyone else's use of armed force. Obviously, then, the revolutionaries conceived the nation to exist independently of the king, but they did not yet assert the nation's legal authority over his person. The Constitution maintained his inviolability for all acts previous to his formal 'abdication', and the new definition of treason in the Criminal

[1] Conrad Russel, 'The Theory of Treason in the Trial of Strafford', *The English Historical Review*, 80: 46 (1965).
[2] Edmond Seligman, *La justice en France pendant la révolution* (Paris, 1913), II, pp. 186–215.

Code of 1791 did not apply to the king while he was king.[1] The legislators opened up the possibility of a solemn national inquisition into the
political conduct of a reigning monarch, a legislative trial culminating
in deposition, but they meant to avoid actual criminal proceedings. It was
a vain hope, given the egalitarian thrust of the revolution, which is best
represented by Article VI of the Declaration of the Rights of Man: 'the
law must be the same for all'. If it was the same, how could the king be
deposed and nothing more for acts that would have been the death of any
other man?

On the other hand, there was still no basis in *the law* for trying the king,
no more in France than in England. Charles I insisted upon this point and
refused to recognize Parliament's High Court of Justice or to plead to its
charges. He was found guilty without ever having defended himself except
by denying the right of his judges to sit in judgment over him. 'He suffered
as the champion of the laws which his enemies were breaking . . .'[2] – as
the champion, anyway, of kingship itself, whose legal structure remained
intact until the ceremonial destruction which the trial represented. Louis
was more compliant, though he could have taken the same line, despite his
own consent to the Constitution and the Criminal Code. For there was
nothing in either that bound him to answer in court. The treason of kings
still belonged to political theory, not to law, at least not to statute law.
The theory on which the revolutionaries acted did, to be sure, have a legal
form: it held simply that royal government was the result of a contract
between the people and their ruler-to-be or that it was the result of an
agreement among the people themselves, of which the king was merely
the beneficiary. And protagonists of these views were always eager to
find legal sanction for their positions in Roman Law, feudal example,
coronation ceremonies, deposition proceedings, or whatever. But they
relied largely, if not always willingly or explicitly, on their own reasoning.
It is important to stress, however, that their reasoning, in both England
and France, antedated the revolution by a good many years. It provided
a crucial body of material to which revolutionary writers might turn, once
they had turned on the king, in search of those precedents and continuities
that the law itself did not provide.

---

[1]For the arguments within the Constituent Assembly, see R. K. Gooch, *Parliamentary Government in France: Revolutionary Origins, 1789–1791* (Ithaca, New York, 1960), pp. 201ff.
[2]G. M. Trevelyan, *History of England* (New York, 1926), p. 419.

4

THE REVOLUTIONARY ARGUMENT

KINGSHIP BY CONTRACT

Again and again at his trial, Charles I demanded to know 'by what lawful authority I am seated here. . .'. John Bradshawe, Lord-President of the High Court of Justice, attempted an answer: 'Namely by the authority of the Commons of England, assembled in Parliament, in behalf of the People of England, by which people you are elected King.' 'Nay, I deny that', replied Charles, 'England was never an elective kingdom; it was an hereditary kingdom for near this thousand years.' The king was right, or at least more right than the Lord-President. The election of kings had ceased in England at the time of the accession of Edward II in 1307, an accession formally dated from the day of his father's death, with no inter-regnum during which the barons might meet and confirm his authority.[1] For centuries before that, the monarchy had been hereditary in the ruling family and the choice of the electors (the Saxon Witan or the Norman barons and bishops) had been narrowly circumscribed.

Yet kings were once elected, and in France the ruling family itself dated its authority from the choice of Hugh Capet, whose father was no king, who was himself no conqueror. His successors could, of course, claim that he derived his power in the same way as French kings since Charlemagne had taken their crowns, from no-one's hands, symbolically from God alone. Still, he had in fact been chosen by his peers, and the election was no doubt accompanied by intrigues, bargains, threats, and promises – and but for these might have gone differently. Ceremonial and even legal vestiges of this electoral process lingered long after monarchy in both England and France was firmly hereditary. Above all, the oath of the king and the sub-sequent acclamation of the people were lasting reminders that kingship had not always been a matter of birth and blood. But all this was grist for the theoretical, not the legal mill. The precedents were too old for Brad-

---

[1] Schramm, *English Coronation*, pp. 166–7; for France, see Charles Petit-Dutaillis, *The Feudal Monarchy in France and England*, p. 27n.

shawe's purposes, or they had been formally repudiated, or drained of any serious content.[1] John Cook, the lawyer entrusted with the prosecution of the king, was probably wiser, though more extravagant, when he referred only in passing to the law, basing himself instead on the 'unanimous consent of all rational men in the world' to the theory of kingship by contract.[2]

Here too there were historical precedents, far more recent than the last royal election, reflecting the long struggle of kings and barons. But these, again, were of little legal value, since the kings had so decisively won out. In the recurrent wars of the feudal age, periods of truce or of relative stability had often been marked by solemn agreements between the king and his 'liege subjects' — the most famous of these being the oath of the Aragonese nobles, with its final threat of renewed warfare: '*and if not, not*'. Victories of the barons had sometimes led, as in the days of Magna Carta or during the reign of Louis XI of France, to the creation of aristocratic 'committees of resistance' designed to watch over the exercise of the royal prerogative and if necessary to restrain or even fight against the king. When it came to war, the barons regularly pointed to the king's violation of the pact between him and themselves as their justification. This was still the argument used in the seventeenth century to justify the rebellion of ordinary men — though the shift from 'liege subjects' to commoners entailed changes also, as we will see, in the structure of the theory. I cannot, however, attempt to trace its intermediate history here. It is enough to say that it is a rich history. Bradshawe and Cook were able to point to a considerable body of literature, the work of men of different countries and different religious faiths, who had found themselves at one time or another in opposition to their king and who had defended themselves by working on, that is, elaborating and distorting, the feudal tradition. Buchanan, Mariana, Mornay, and the English Jesuit Parsons were Bradshawe's immediate references, but the list could have been longer had he been a more scholarly man or had he had more time to work up his arguments.

Because these arguments drew on the feudal tradition, however, they justified war but not judicial proceedings against the king. For feudal kingship seemed to rest on an agreement between two parties of very nearly equal

---

[1] The accusation of some revolutionaries that the English coronation oath had been weakened by Archbishop Laud at the command of Charles was false: the crucial phrase, *quas vulgus juste et rationabiliter elegerit*, had fallen into disuse many years earlier. See Muddiman, *Trial*, p. 236n. and Schramm, *English Coronation*, pp. 218–19.

[2] Muddiman, *Trial*, p. 246: Cook's speech, prepared for the trial, was never delivered owing to the king's refusal to plead, but was subsequently published as a pamphlet.

status: the king on the one hand and the baronage, pretending to represent the community as a whole, on the other. If the king defaulted, the body of barons or any individual member could rightly resist him, and the two parties were then in a state of war. An individual baron might appeal for help to the baronage in general, or to some specified group of his peers, or only to his relatives, but all that any of them could do was to join him in his war. 'A formal condemnation of the monarch by legal proceedings was unknown' in the feudal period.[1] It was unknown because of the nature of the contractual tie, which presupposed neither an encompassing community nor an external superior. Hence while both parties possessed the right of self-help if the contract was violated, neither possessed the legal or moral authority needed to terminate the conflict between them by means of a 'formal condemnation'. To be sure, the king, if he won, might use legal proceedings against particular barons; his courts were superior to theirs.[2] Against the baronage itself, he had no legal recourse; nor was there any such recourse against him. Given his own violation of the contract, the king could legitimately be assaulted, even, some writers said, assassinated; he could not legally be charged or punished.

This was still the implicit conclusion drawn by most of the writers to whom Bradshawe referred his listeners. Certain Jesuit publicists especially had made themselves the mortal enemies of kings by the open defense of assassination, but they never recommended judicial proceedings against the monarch. Mariana suggested that a tyrannical king might be deposed and declared a public enemy by some representative assembly, and then legitimately killed by any private man; but a formal execution lay beyond his ken.[3] Even in the Protestant *Vindiciae Contra Tyrannos*, where the superiority of the people over the king was clearly stated, the possibility of trying the king in the name of the people was never raised. The tyrant was condemned by the very decision to resist him, when that decision was made by the appropriate magistrates, and the actual resistance constituted the only punishment that Mornay could imagine.[4]

Deposition was a common theme of Huguenot writers, but the fact that it had in the past almost always been followed by a secret murder was not something they discussed. Nor did they ever ask why the murder was

---

[1] Kern, *Kingship and Law*, p. 86.

[2] Holdsworth suggests that until the Treason Act of 1352, noblemen who formally defied the king and then made war against him could not be charged with any crime: *History of English Law*, III, 353.

[3] Juan de Mariana, *The King and the Education of the King*, trans. G. A. Moore (Washington, D.C.. 1948), I, v (p. 148).

[4] Franklin, *Constitutionalism and Resistance*, pp. 189–97 (*Vindiciae*, 'the third question').

so crucial to the deposition, or why the long history of murder and deposition to which they referred themselves had never actually reduced monarchy to what were now regarded as its proper proportions. These men were not revolutionaries, and that is why Protestant aristocrats, acting on their principles, did no greater harm to kingship than did Catholic assassins — though particular kings were indeed resisted and killed. Their failure is especially clear in the French civil wars: Henry of Navarre had little difficulty in reasserting both royal mystery and royal absolutism once the struggles were over.[1] Henry was, of course, the legitimate heir, but the Catholic claimant, had he won out, and in the face of all that the radical priests of Paris said about the rights of the people, would have had no greater difficulty.

Only George Buchanan, in his philosophical dialogue on Scottish kingship, broke with this tradition and launched a more direct attack on royal inviolabilty. He had been involved in the 'first trial' of Mary Stuart of Scotland, an experience which undoubtedly accounts for the break and explains the form it took.[2] Mary having been accused of adultery and murder, Buchanan attempts first to distinguish a form of trial appropriate to such crimes, private rather than public acts, fundamentally different, he thought, from treason and tyranny.

Buchanan: What if the king stands accused of parricide; what name is appropriate to that king at his trial?

Maitland: The name of parricide only, for he is not in court on any question respecting his government, but only as respects parricide.[3]

But in a hereditary monarchy (such as Scotland then was), parricide is surely the political crime *par excellence*! A royal parricide is, one would think, a usurper also: the question respects his government in the most urgent way. It is indeed hard to imagine any crime for which a reigning or even a deposed monarch might be brought to trial as a mere private man. The king's private acts necessarily had public effects; his crimes might destroy the state, even if he committed them as a man rather than a monarch. That is why 'something is rotten in the state of Denmark', when the king is a murderer. In any case, Buchanan did not shrink from trying the king as king:

[1]Bloch, *Rois Thaumaturges*, pp. 342, 356ff.

[2]Gordon Donaldson, *The First Trial of Mary, Queen of Scots* (London, 1969).

[3]George Buchanan, *The Powers of the Crown in Scotland*, trans. C. F. Arrowood (Austin, Texas, 1949), p. 141.

Buchanan: . . . if there should arise a question as to whether Hiero be king or tyrant, or if there is any question which belongs particularly to the duties of a king, then the king is judged in terms of his kingship.

The issue came to war, he went on, only if the king refused to stand trial, and only then might any of his subjects (Buchanan actually said, any member of the human race, reflecting an internationalism that reappeared during the two revolutions) take up arms against him.[1]

It would be almost seventy-five years before this argument was acted out. Two things were necessary if a king was actually to be brought to the bar, face to face with men who claimed to be his peers and were morally and politically prepared to judge him. The first was the new sense of opposition rectitude which the English Puritans seem first to have introduced into political life. Righteousness is far more important than mere equalitarianism: feudal lords had sometimes thought themselves the king's equals, and so they had resisted him when he challenged their rights. But the revolutionaries of the seventeenth and eighteenth centuries were not only asserting their rights but also doing their duty. Once again, the case of Mary of Scotland marks a significant change. After her second trial and condemnation in 1586, Elizabeth wanted her secretly killed, done away with in the old style, so that she could publicly repudiate the act. The horror she would have expressed (and perhaps even have felt) on hearing of the assassination was the tribute she wanted to pay to sacred kingship, to Mary's regality and her own. It was her Puritan ministers, Walsingham especially, who pressed for a formal trial and a public execution.[2] This was no doubt easier for them to do in that Mary was not their own queen. The legal argument against her held that in England she was an alien and a mere private person: regality does not travel. But it was not the legal argument that triumphed; nor was political necessity decisive, for that required only that the Scotswoman die. When Sir Amias Paulet, Mary's prison keeper, wrote to Elizabeth that he would not make 'so foul a shipwreck of my conscience' as to murder her (though he eagerly sought her execution), he suggested a new element in English politics. Monarchy would be destroyed by men in whom conscience had triumphed over mystery.

Even men of conscience, however, could not bring their king to trial until they had convinced themselves that they might (or might have to)

---

[1] Buchanan, p. 143.

[2] A. Francis Steuart, *Trial of Mary Queen of Scots* (Edinburgh, 1923); Conyers Read, *Mr Secretary Walsingham and the Policy of Queen Elizabeth* (Cambridge, 1925), III, pp. 63–5.

do without another. And this did not happen until the revolution was well-begun. For years, both Puritans and Jacobins were widely thought to have a royal successor in mind. Charles himself told his youngest son 'that he heard the army intended to make him king . . .'. In France, there were persistant rumors that the Jacobins planned to raise Phillipe Egalité to the throne.[1] But these were clear misconceptions of what the revolutions were all about. No royal heir could possibly embody revolutionary principles in the same way that Navarre until his conversion embodied the hopes of the Huguenots. The struggle with the king, the mobilization of the people, the pressure of their own doctrines (multiplied a hundredfold by the sudden appearance of 'mechanic' preachers and radical journalists) – all this had carried Puritans and Jacobins far beyond the point where they could trust their achievements, or their own lives, to any king. The trial was the outcome of revolutionary practice. There was still no theory to justify it, however, except that of the opposition publicists cited by Bradshawe. By asserting the sovereignty of the people, they had prepared the way for a kind of justice they themselves would never have attempted.

The subordination of the king to his subjects was founded by Bradshawe and Cook on a supposed contract of government. This was the 'election' to which the Lord-President referred, an ideal rather than an actual event. Instead of an exchange of feudal vows, <u>Bradshawe described</u> <u>an agreement explicitly naming the king as a mandatory of the people</u> – <u>without, however, explaining how the people itself came to be constituted.</u> Whatever the origins of their own unity, the members of political society, on this view, chose a ruler in order to enjoy certain specific advantages of being ruled. They gave the sword to a particular man, as Cook said, for their own protection and preservation. They cannot be conceived to have done so to their own detriment.[2] The very invention of kingship, logically if not historically, presupposes a purpose in the mind of the inventors, and that purpose could hardly have been any injury to themselves. Hence kings are limited by the ends of their subjects; they accept this limitation when they accept their office, whether or not they are actually elected to it. As Condorcet argued at the trial of Louis, 'any citizen who accepts a position of public trust enters into a contract with the entire nation . . .'. That contrast is mutually obligatory only so long as the king or other

---

[1] *Eikon Basilike*, p. 194 (appendix 9); Seligman, *La Justice*, II, p. 474.
[2] Muddiman, *Trial*, p. 246.

officer fulfills the task set for him (or, Condorcet adds, until the office itself is abolished by the people).[1]

It is an interesting question whether, on this view, the people can betray the king. Perhaps they can, for resistance or deposition without cause might constitute a breach of faith. I cannot imagine what else Bradshawe had in mind when he told Charles that 'the people of England might have incurred [the charge of treason] respecting you, if they had been guilty of it . . .'.[2] Given the view of the governmental contract that he and Cook expound, however, it hardly seems possible that a breach of faith with the king could be called treason, for it is no longer the king but only the people who constitute the state. Even individuals cannot really commit treason against the king: if they violate the terms of the mandate or attack the person of the mandatory whom the people have established, then it is the people alone who have been betrayed. The king's own treason was a crime of the same sort. Charles I, Cook claimed, had used against the people that sword 'which was put into his hand for their safety'. Whenever a king does that, he 'becomes an enemy to that people and deserves the most exemplary and severe punishment that can be invented'.[3] *Most* exemplary and severe, because he has been trusted as no other man; the king's powers for evil are greater than anyone else's.

This is the doctrine implied by the formula the High Court adopted in its charge: 'Charles Stuart being admitted King of England and therein trusted with a limited power to govern . . .'. The terms clearly point to the position that John Locke later defended and turned into a liberal commonplace, but Locke never suggested that they might appear in a formal accusation. He would have done so, perhaps, had he been a less politic writer or had he ever faced the realities of revolutionary (as distinct from oppositional) politics. In any case, the argument of the revolutionaries is more consistent than that of Locke. For if the king is merely 'trusted' with his office, it cannot be the case, as Locke claims, that his violation of

---

[1] *Archives Parlementaires*, 54: 149; below, pp. 148–49. In his *Tenure of King and Magistrates*, published immediately after the execution of Charles, John Milton also claims that 'free-born' men can change the form of their government as well as judge their governors, but nothing like that was said at the trial. *Complete Prose Works*, ed. Don Wolf (New Haven, 1962), III, pp. 236–7. The 'Introduction' to this volume by Merritt Y. Hughes surveys the extensive pamphlet literature on the king's trial.

[2] Muddiman, *Trial*, p. 122. Cf. Cromwell's reported statement 'that if any man moved upon this design [trying the king for treason], he should think him the greatest traitor in the world, but since providence and necessity had cast them upon it . . .', etc. Christopher Hill, *God's Englishman: Oliver Cromwell and the English Revolution* (New York, 1970), p. 233.

[3] Muddiman, *Trial*, p. 246.

that trust can only be countered by an 'appeal to heaven'.[1] That famous phrase is a euphemism for a war such as the barons might fight against the king, in which God, if he can distinguish the sides, might or might not give victory to the righteous. But why should the struggle of the people against a defaulting (or even allegedly defaulting) trustee be called a war? It may come to fighting, but insofar as judgment is possible, surely it lies with the people – who pre-exist the king and who have trusted him. That at any rate was the claim upon which the High Court based its authority. It did not lead at the time to any full exploration of the nature of the people's pre-existence, that is, to a theory of the social contract, in part because Charles in responding to the charge never attempted to exploit the possibilities of his trusteeship. He simply reasserted the anti-contractualism of royalist ideology: 'I have a trust committed to me by God, by old and lawful descent. . . .'[2] By contrast, Louis at his own trial claimed the rights granted him under the terms of the most recent governmental contract, the Constitution of 1791. And so he forced his opponents to describe the subordination of kings in an even more radical way. Marat did this most succinctly:

> There was never a contract between the people and their agents, although there was a binding one between the sovereign and its members. A nation which delegates its powers to agents does not contract with them; it assigns them some function in the general interest.[3]

Before examining the consequences of this argument, it is necessary to look for a moment at the Constitution of 1791 itself. For this document combined in a very curious fashion features of both the feudal and the governmental contracts. Since it was never submitted to any kind of popular ratification, but took effect as soon as it had been approved by the king and the Assembly, it stood, in effect, as an agreement between those two parties. Its text reflected this fact by according the two an exactly equal status. Both the Assembly and the king, though the one was elected and the other not, were called representatives of the people. 'The French Constitution shall be representative: the representatives shall be the legislative body and the King.' Overriding Robespierre's objections, the members of the Constituent Assembly refused to specify the superior-

---

[1] John Locke, *Second Treatise of Government*, para. 168, where Locke seems to be explicitly preferring this 'appeal' to any more regular judgment.
[2] Muddiman, *Trial*, p. 82.
[3] *Archives Parlementaires*, 54: 246; below, p. 159.

ity of their successors over the king and his successors.[1] The king could be impeached, as we have seen, but only for causes listed in the Constitution, to which the assembly could not add. He could not be judged. His legal inviolability followed not from his superiority, but from his equality. And it was to this inviolability, derived, however distantly, from the status the king had once enjoyed as divine deputy and natural head and father, that Louis' supporters and his lawyers pointed in his defense. This was the argument bravely offered to the Convention by the provincial conservative Morisson on the first day of its debate. He insisted that the king could have been killed at the Tuilleries during the fighting of August 10 – he would have killed Louis himself, he said, though his colleagues probably found the act hard to imagine – but the Convention had no legal standing or authority to organize a trial. They were bound by the governmental contract of 1791.[2]

The case for legal proceedings against Louis was put forward by two groups of deputies: the Girondins, most of whom apparently hoped to follow the English precedent and establish a special court of justice, and a centrist majority, who were prepared to bring the king to the bar of the Convention itself. The Jacobin leaders opposed the trial; they were ready, like Morisson at the Tuileries, simply to kill the king, and his eventual execution was, in fact, a party victory for them. I shall not attempt to review here the political struggles that preceded and accompanied the trial, important as these were for the later history of the revolution. They have been discussed at length by a number of historians, while the theoretically crucial debate over the trial itself has largely been ignored.[3] In outlining the arguments in favor of trying the king, I shall focus chiefly on the Girondins, since they among all the delegates were most deeply committed to the forms of justice and legality. Modern scholars, examining their arguments, have tended to convict them of incoherence and opportunism, and indeed, the Gironde was not in any sense a disciplined political party or even a strikingly resolute group of men.[4] Nevertheless,

---

[1]Gooch, *Parliamentary Government*, pp. 225–6.

[2]*Archives Parlementaires*, 53: 387; below, p. 117.

[3]Jaurès, virtually alone among modern historians, addresses himself to the larger issues raised by the trial; Seligman's is the most detailed account available, but, despite its title, is less concerned with justice than with party conflict: *La Justice*, II, pp. 378–488. Aulard, Mathiez, Lefebvre, the best of French historians, are similarly limited and have, indeed, very little to say about the trial. For a documentary survey, see Albert Soboul, ed., *Le procès de Louis XVI* (Paris, 1970).

[4]M. J. Sydenham, *The Girondins* (London, 1961); Alison Patrick, 'Political Divisions in the French National Convention', *Journal of Modern History*, 41: 421–74 (1969).

Condorcet, Vergniaud, and their associates deserve more sympathetic attention than they have usually received. They represent, like the English lawyers who, with different theoretical tools at their disposal, managed the trial of Charles, an important conception of what the shape and character of revolutionary justice ought to be.

The Constitution of 1791 set the king apart from all other members of the nation by stipulating that only after he had been deposed would he enter 'the class of citizens'. Before that, he inhabited and entirely filled a class of his own, a fact seized on by the defense lawyers, Malesherbes and de Sèze. The king was once not a citizen, they argued; now he is a citizen 'liable to accusation through the ordinary forms'. He cannot, however, be tried as a citizen for acts committed while he was a king.[1] This argument was answered in three different ways, which are best taken up in ascending order of importance, for the course of the Convention debate was often confused. Condorcet first attempted a strictly legal reply, aimed at maintaining the king's citizenship in the face of the constitutional provisions that seemed to deny it. He argued that the Constitution protected Louis only for acts within the scope of his legal functions. It protected him as king against political prosecutions, but not as a man against prosecution for such crimes as murder and treason — *for as a man he was also a citizen.*[2] The distinction between the two kinds of liability goes back, as we have seen, at least to Buchanan, but it unfortunately has no firm basis in the text from which it was drawn. In any case, Condorcet went on (joined here by a considerable number of delegates) to argue that the constitutional provision was irrelevant since Louis had never really been a constitutional king. He had never accepted his new status in good faith, as a long series of actions, beginning with the flight to Varennes, forcefully indicated.[3] Another delegate, following the same line of argument, painted a dramatic but unlikely picture of Louis coming before the Convention to proclaim his stubborn and faithful royalism:

I have been forced to subscribe to your Constitution . . . but I have never thought myself obligated by my oaths: when one gives way to force, even the most solemn promises form no bond. I declare to you that I have always remained committed to my ancient prerogatives . . . and I have continually struggled to re-establish the old monarchy.[4]

[1] Raymond de Sèze, *Défense de Louis*, ed. André Sevin (Paris, 1936), pp. 14–18.
[2] *Archives Parlementaires*, 54: 149; below, p. 142.
[3] *Archives Parlementaires*, 54: 149–50; below, p. 148.
[4] Speech of Jean-Nicolas Méaulle, *Archives Parlementaires*, 54: 251.

There may well be moral truth to this description: Louis probably did feel this way. But he never spoke this way, at least not in public, and his kingship had in fact been widely recognized – not least by those Girondins who served as his constitutional ministers. They could hardly claim that they did not think him a true king or the Constitution a valid document.

What had to be said was that Louis had indeed been a king, had been recognized as a king, and could be tried as a king. This is what Jean-Baptiste Maihle argued for the Convention's majority and Pierre Vergniaud most clearly for the Gironde. Reporting on behalf of the committee that planned the trial, Maihle sought to cut through the legal worries of many of his colleagues with a simple assertion of popular sovereignty: the right to judge kings was 'a necessary condition, inherent in the social act which placed them on the throne'.[1] Vergniaud argued in the same way, claiming that 'the promise of inviolability made to Louis by the people was not binding on them . . . '. He did not mean that the people are never bound by the promises they make; he meant that their right to judge their rulers is inalienable. 'The people [can] never validly renounce their right to punish an oppressor.'[2] They may choose not to exercise that right for a period of time, but they can resume its exercise whenever they like. For all practical purposes, then, there is no governmental contract, for there is nothing of any importance that the people can contract away. The 'social act' by which kings are designated is the election or appointment of a functionary, nothing more, and the rights of that functionary can never be greater than those of any other citizen. Before the law they are all equal, their equality recognized and fixed by the social contract that necessarily precedes the designation of a king.

Maihle concluded that the inviolability of kings was a fiction, and it was on the basis of this conclusion that the trial of Louis went forward. Chiefly for party reasons, Vergniaud argued that Louis had in fact been granted a special status, which could, however, be withdrawn at will by the people. He thus provided the theoretical foundation for the Girondin proposal that the entire nation be polled on the fate of the king. Though they did not agree among themselves on the precise form the poll should take, the Girondins insisted that a direct exercise of sovereignty was the only way to override the Constitution – which the Jacobins argued had already been overridden by the insurrection of 10 August – and to strip the king of his

[1] *Archives Parlementaires*, 53: 278; below, p. 101.
[2] *Archives Parlementaires*, 56: 91; below, p. 197. The notion of inalienable rights cannot, obviously, be deduced from the original contract, but requires an independent foundation. This Vergniaud never describes; probably he is thinking along lines similar to Rousseau, *The Social Contract*, I, iv.

inviolability.[1] Louis' life probably hung on the outcome of this dispute, for it is generally thought unlikely that he would have been condemned to death in a free referendum. Nevertheless, the argument for the referendum was not the most interesting feature of the Girondin position. It was at best an argument peripheral to the deepest convictions of lawyers like Vergniaud, forced on them by the course of party disputes. Far more important was their insistence that Louis in some crucial sense was a citizen of France and the trial therefore at least a possible act of justice. From this fundamental proposition, they worked out an impressive picture of the sort of trial that was legally and morally required. Here was the crux of their theoretical disagreement with both the king himself and with the Jacobins, both of whom thought any sort of trial impossible: Louis claimed that he had once not been a citizen; the Girondins that he had always been a citizen; the Jacobins that he had never been and could not be a citizen.

Louis, Vergniaud conceded, '*n'est pas un accusé ordinaire*' – a sentence which recalls Charles' insistence that he was not 'an ordinary prisoner'.[2] The only conclusion the Gironde was willing to draw from this, however, was that Louis' inviolability could only be revoked by the sovereign people. They would have had him tried before a tribunal elected expressly for that purpose or, that failing, they would have submitted the verdict of the Convention to a popular vote. In every other sense, they wanted to treat the king as much like an ordinary prisoner as they could: 'what justice truly demands', Condorcet argued, 'is that ... the general principles of jurisprudence in favor of the accused should be preserved or even extended.' Louis crimes must 'be judged and punished like crimes of the same sort committed by any other man'.[3] There was a powerful strain of equalitarianism in the Girondin position, and it must have had great appeal. What a splendid spectacle: the king judged by his subjects, his peers! Louis Capet, *ci-devant roi*, standing before the court, exposed as a man, all the mythic masks of kingship torn off: it could not help but be, Condorcet imagined, a great movement in the education of the human race.

The lesson he and his friends wanted to teach was not only that kings were citizens, but also that citizens (including traitors) had rights that could not be taken away even by the will of the people. They would pretend that the king really was an ordinary prisoner so as to preserve for other prisoners some democratic portion of the respect once accorded to kings.

---

[1]The debate can best be followed in Seligman, *La Justice*, pp. 434ff.
[2]*Archives Parlementaires*, 56: 93; below, p. 204.
[3]*Archives Parlementaires*, 54: 149; below, p. 147.

As if they foresaw the judicial terrorism of the next eighteen months, they laid enormous stress on the formal procedures of the trial, and they worried a great deal over their own status as judges. The Gironde had opposed a trial by the Convention, for the addition of judicial to legislative functions seemed to its partisans, as one of them said, 'a monstrous accumulation of powers'.[1] The sincerity of their opposition cannot be doubted. It followed from other doctrines associated with the Girondin leaders; above all, it represented an effort to maintain standards of judicial behavior that were widely accepted among French lawyers, and which drew on the theories of the *philosophes*, Anglo-Saxon precedents, and the new Criminal Code. Here was the Girondin world: they sought a trial consistent with it, an act of regicide (if it came to that) that did not mark a total break with previous history. The trial should at least be familiar, they argued, even if the defendant was not. So they fought for the right of the accused to legal counsel, for the distinction between the jury that indicts and the jury that judges, for the right of the defense to reject particular jurors, and so on.[2] Revolutionary justice was to be as much like justice itself as it could possibly be, given the need to override the Constitution and to impose upon the king a status that kings had never before enjoyed.

Finally, some members of the Gironde wanted to save Louis' life. Here again there were party reasons: such an act of 'magnanimity' by the people or their representatives would, they thought, visibly call a halt to Jacobin success — a success already associated in men's minds with proscription and violence. It would represent a victory for moderation at a time (after the August rising and the September massacres) when the moderates desperately needed a victory. It would represent also a victory for the provinces, where the Girondins were strong, over the city of Paris, where they were not. It would hardly have been a victory for equality, however, and more than one delegate argued angrily that no-one would have called for magnanimity had Louis been a common traitor. Yet there was, once again, a kind of equalitarian idealism in the argument for the king's imprisonment or exile. Thomas Paine, a close friend of Condorcet's, who shared his opposition to the death penalty, suggested that the king be banished to the United States, and the idea behind this proposal, though not the proposal itself, played a part in the speeches of many other delegates.[3] Having been en-

---

[1] L. A. J. Vardon, during the *appel nominal* on the fate of Louis: *Archives Parlementaires*, 57: 393.
[2] These are all stressed by Condorcet. In the Convention debate of 11 December 1792, Marat and Robespierre both opposed Louis' request to be allowed counsel, but the deputies were almost unanimous in granting the request. *Archives Parlementaires*, 55: 15.
[3] *Archives Parlementaires*, 56: 523; below, p. 212.

rolled at last in the class of citizens, they urged, Louis should be forced to live, rather than made to die, in that class. This could hardly be called punishment by other members of the same class, but it might be called reformation. And was it impossible to imagine Louis Capet, a good bourgeois and a saved citizen, mending clocks in Philadelphia or Bordeaux? Another educational spectacle, even less likely, I am afraid, than the trial the Gironde hoped for. Let us execute the king but not the man, Paine pleaded; he would have reversed exactly the old politics of assassination. But could monarchy be killed if the most recent monarch was allowed to live? Perhaps, some of the delegates thought, if he lived quietly as a citizen. But what if he refused? 'A king cannot be so low but he is considerable', Charles I had written, 'adding weight to that party where he appears'.[1] It was the 'considerableness' even of Louis Capet, as much as the rising power of the Jacobins, that stood in the way of magnanimity and moderation.

In England in 1649, virtually no-one who advocated trying the king wanted to spare his life. No-one that I have encountered had a vision of Charles Stuart living as a commoner in Bristol (let alone in Boston). The equalitarianism of the seventeenth century was very different from that of the eighteenth, more rooted in notions of spiritual brotherhood, less directly social in its implications. And the ideology of kingship was concomitantly much stronger in the first than in the second revolution. Many of Charles I's judges undoubtedly expected that there would be kings again in England, and though the formal abolition of monarchy was only a few weeks off, the greatest enemies of the king had too strong a sense of his personal prestige and of his royalist convictions to imagine him alive and themselves at peace. At the same time, no-one in England who sought to have Charles killed sought to do so without a trial. Cromwell and his friends wanted 'to bring [the king] to justice with some plausible appearance of legality . . .'.[2] Like the French moderates, they wanted a trial that would make the king's crimes clear to the nation. But they also brought Charles to the bar because they really thought he was a criminal. Louis was brought before the Convention for the same reason. Whatever penalty they hoped for, most of the deputies firmly believed that the people's quarrel with the king could be represented and was represented by the adversary proceedings of the courtroom. They believed, that is, that Louis was a defaulting functionary, a criminal magistrate, whose moral responsibility was clear. Their republicanism was satisfied by the equalitarian spectacle of

Is this a difference between Puritans and Catholics?

[1] *Eikon Basilike*, p. 153.
[2] C. V. Wedgwood, *The Trial of Charles I* (London, 1964), p. 83.

the king face to face with his peers; their sense of justice was satisfied by the fact that this dramatic confrontation was shaped and molded by the forms of the law. But the English trial offered another kind of satisfaction, which the French could not provide. For at least a few of the judges and for more of the onlookers, it had larger meanings than a lawyer's brief could possibly suggest, meanings provided by the religious content of English radicalism. Among Puritan sectaries, Charles I was thought to be an ally, if not an incarnation of the Antichrist. And even more moderate men lived and acted in anticipation of the last days. The High Court of Justice, suggested John Cook, 'was a resemblance and representation of the great Day of Judgment when the saints shall judge all earthly powers . . .'.[1] It was, to be sure, an uncharacteristic moment, for Cook doubtless knew that the saints would pay little attention to all his arguments about the secular purposes of kingship. The 'resemblance and representation' points toward a politics of ultimate struggle against kings and their supporters – who described their own connections with heaven in exactly the same terms. Among the French, this kind of politics was not even suggested by the procedures of the courtroom. These had, for the revolutionaries at least, no implications of ultimate judgment. That is why the Jacobins, who thought themselves at war with kings, opposed the trial altogether.

THE KING AS A PUBLIC ENEMY

The Jacobin argument was powerful indeed, for it had the great advantage of taking royalist ideology seriously and of surrendering absolutely the fictions of royal citizenship and legal continuity that the Gironde required. St Just's speech of 13 November 1792, setting it forth in bold outline, is probably the most brilliant of all the speeches at the king's trial, and in analysing the argument, I shall attend chiefly to his formulation of it. One point should be made first, however: St Just's argument did not carry the day. It has colored much of the later discussion of the trial of Louis, but its central proposals, reiterated at greater length but with less originality by Robespierre, were not adopted by the Convention. Had they been adopted, there would have been no trial at all.

The Jacobins played on certain ambiguities in the notion of treason –

---

[1]Christopher Hill, *Antichrist in Seventeenth Century England* (London, 1971), pp. 108ff.; Muddiman, *Trial*, p. 258.

ambiguities not so much in the legal tradition, which had undergone no such development in the French case as was marked in England by the trials of Strafford and Laud, but in the moral idea. Treason involves making war against the king (under the old regime) or against the state or people (under the new) or it involves adhering in some overt way to the enemies of any of these three. Though he makes war, however, the traitor is not simply called an enemy, or regarded as a soldier subject to international law, or when captured recognized as a prisoner of war entitled (according to the theories of Montesquieu and Rousseau) to life, if not to liberty. Because he was and is a citizen, his treason is not an act of hostility but a breach of faith, and that breach constitutes a crime for which the usual penalty, throughout much of political history, has been death. The idea of treason, then, depends upon a theory of membership, for only the member of a community can be a traitor to it. Under the old regime, this theory was clear enough. In the language of royalist ideology, the king's subjects were his members in the most literal sense, parts of his politic body. He might cut off a corrupt arm or leg, but they could not separate themselves or dismember him. Having received sustenance and protection from the royal head, that is, having been born within the kingdom, they are subjects forever. The allegiance of a natural-born subject, wrote Blackstone, 'cannot be forfeited, cancelled, or altered by any change of time, place, or circumstance'.[1] Hence membership had nothing whatsoever to do with volition; there was no way to renounce one's loyalty to a king, and to make war against him was treasonous on the part of any man born within his kingdom.

The feudal version of the theory of the governmental contract was elaborated in large part as a defense against this charge. It specified conditions under which hostile acts against the king were not treasonous because, the contract having lapsed, membership or allegiance had lapsed with it, and the king and his subjects were simply in a state of war. The theory of the king as trustee or mandatory made possible an entirely new kind of treason, a crime of the king against the people. But this crime depended upon the king's membership, just as traditional treason depended upon the subject's membership. The all-important innovation of St Just's speech was his dramatic denial that the king had ever been a member of the French people. If he had not been a member, he could not be a traitor, and there was no point in arranging a trial. The king, St Just argued, should be dealt with as an enemy of France; his death need not wait upon a legal condemnation, and it was the height of foolishness to

[1] William Blackstone, *Commentaries on the Laws of England*, I, 10.

raise him to the rank of citizen merely in order to condemn him.[1] Revolution was a war against the old regime, and it was a difficult and arduous war because the old regime had deep reserves of strength. Even in captivity, the king was a dangerous man; the republic would not be safe until he was dead.

But how had Louis Capet missed out, as it were, on the social contract that constituted the French people? The great advantage of the social contract, one would have thought, lay precisely in its inclusiveness. Once he had shared in the common life, a man could not be denied the rights that the contract established and guaranteed – or, at least, he could not be denied them without a fair trial. Only because he was a contracting member could he ever be called a criminal, and because of his membership he had rights, including the right to a trial, that must be respected whatever his crime. But St Just knew nothing of citizen Louis Capet. He addressed himself to the case of King Louis XVI, and he drew out the implications of the king's own claim to be inviolable. For if the king was inviolable, then he was formally irresponsible; he could not be called to account by any earthly body; to all effects and purposes he was without political obligations. The king claimed that his subjects were bound to him, not he to them. Such a contract, St Just insisted, is null and void, that is, it can be broken or set aside whenever the people chooses to free itself from servitude. Nevertheless, royal inviolability has moral consequences; St Just was not ready, as were Vergniaud and the other Girondins, simply to set it aside. By ruling irresponsibly, the king had excluded himself from the body of citizens and therefore from the enjoyment of civic rights. As king (even under the Constitution of 1791) he had denied his own citizenship; he had opted out of the social contract, for 'a contract affects only those whom it binds. As a consequence, Louis, who was not bound, cannot be judged in civil law'.[2]

St Just was an apocalyptic historian: if he described monarchy at anything less than the height of its own pretensions, he thought he would diminish the revolution. The grandeur of the popular struggle depended upon the grandeur of the overthrown king. So one by one, he repeated the age-old claims of French monarchs. Did they insist that they governed France without consent? St Just agreed: that is exactly how they ruled. He would not pretend that they were ever entrusted with their office: *they were*

[1] *Archives Parlementaires*, 53: 390; below, p. 125.
[2] *Archives Parlementaires*, 53: 391; below, p. 123. A number of prominent Jacobins had called for civil judgment in the months before November; now most of them adopted St Just's position: see Jacques Guilane, *Billaud-Varenne: l'ascète de la révolution* (Paris, 1969), p. 118.

In short, his crime was not to be an evil king, but to be a king at all. And this not so much a crime as an act of was.

masters then. But to be a master, to rule without consent, is usurpation and tyranny. Hence St Just's most famous sentence: 'No man can reign innocently.' The line has often been turned into an ironic commentary on his own career. 'When St Just made this remark', writes Camus, 'he did not know that he was already speaking for himself.'[1] But the young Jacobin would have missed the irony, even later on, and not only because of his zeal and humorlessness. He and his friends did not rule innocently, no doubt, but they did not *reign* at all. They were always responsible to the Convention, and they were overthrown and condemned by a single vote of its members. To reign is to command as a king; it is to lay claim to the privileges of divine authority and natural headship; it is to occupy all alone the heights of power, out of reach of one's own subjects. A man who reigns, St Just meant to say, can only be overthrown by revolutionary war. War is, in fact, the last token of respect that one pays to his exalted position. He cannot be voted down, for he was never elected king. He cannot be judged, for he does not acknowledge or consent to the bonds that make judgment possible. 'To judge is to apply the law; law supposes a common share in justice; and what justice can be common to humanity and kings? What has Louis in common with the French people?'[2]

If these rhetorical questions receive the expected answers, then there is another question that must be asked: if the king is beyond justice, as he and his ancestors claimed to be, then what does it mean to call his innocence into question? What is the nature of his guilt? All the Jacobins use and use freely the language of moral condemnation, even while insisting that the language of legal condemnation is entirely inappropriate. Since the two languages share the same vocabulary, Jacobin speakers often fall into verbal confusion, but their doctrine, I think, is sufficiently clear. To say that it is impossible to reign innocently is not to say that kings are criminals and traitors and certainly not that they are born criminals and traitors. Kings are enemies of the people; their guilt consists in reigning, hence in tyranny, oppression, and what might today be called aggressive war (against their own subjects). None of this is a crime, however, since it involves no breach of faith — they never pledged their faith — and no violation of the law — kings were not bound by the law. Royalist ideology, in the eyes of the Jacobins, had publicly proclaimed the tyranny of kings, though without ever calling it by its proper name. The appropriate popular response was insurrection, and the revolt of the people was the only judgment to which

[1] *The Rebel*, p. 118n.
[2] *Archives Parlementaires*, 53:391; below, p. 124.

64

the king was susceptible. It was not a judgment in any legal sense but simply a declaration of war, sufficient in itself to justify the killing of the king. He cannot be tried, argued Robespierre, without putting the people's revolt into litigation, an especially absurd procedure for the Convention, whose only title to legitimate authority was the triumph of 10 August.[1] It has a mandate which requires it not to judge the king (again), but simply to kill him.

St Just believed that the climactic moment had come in the long struggle of kings and peoples. This was the only class conflict he understood: the monarch and his corrupt court on the one side, the people, simple, virtuous, pure, though at the same time degraded and enslaved, on the other. Now the triumph of the people was at hand, but it could not finally be won unless the people themselves were savagely intent upon winning it. For centuries they had acquiesced to tyranny. The illusions of royalism were, the Jacobins knew, popular illusions. But now the revolution depended upon the strength of the people's hostility to kingship. 'The spirit in which the king is judged is also the spirit in which the Republic will be established.'[2] That spirit must be passionate, angry, vengeful, or else the insidious corruptions of royalism and servitude would win their way again. Above all, the people must be made to understand that it is the king who is their enemy, not Louis Capet, who will tremble on the scaffold, but the inviolable, all-powerful, divine, and unreachable king. This is the man who must be denounced and destroyed — but not tried, for a trial would suggest that there were doubts about his guilt, as if he had never been king! 'We invoke forms', said Robespierre, 'because we lack principles'.[3] This is the classic radical argument against the liberal preoccupation with legality. Though Robespierre said 'we', he meant 'they' — his reference was to the Girondins, who had revealed, he thought, by their insistence on a fair trial that they did not really hate kings. For the trial put Louis once again, however briefly, in the center of public attention, made him the focal point of a ritual world where he would be accorded respect, listened to, even praised by friendly attorneys. When all this began, the Jacobins thought the worst had happened: the orators of the Convention, Robespierre solemnly declared, have embarked the nation 'once again on the course of mon-

---

[1] *Archives Parlementaires*, 54: 74; below, p. 131.
[2] *Archives Parlementaires*, 53: 392; below, p. 125. Robespierre makes the same point more sharply: to talk about the king in 'religious' terms, he argued, was to insure that he remained a danger to liberty — 54: 74.
[3] *Archives Parlementaires*, 54: 75; below, p. 133.

archy'.[1] The equalitarianism of the spectacle was lost on him, as it was on St Just; the two of them obviously believed that only the guillotine could establish the equality of kings and other men.

Yet the trial that Robespierre called 'counter-revolutionary' went forward. The king had his lawyers, despite Jacobin protests, and he and his lawyers were listened to in profound silence — a sign of that 'delicacy' that Robespierre thought demonstrated nothing more than a lack of revolutionary energy. 'Among us', said St Just, 'subtlety of spirit and of character is a great obstacle to liberty'.[2] Given these views, it is obviously false to argue, as a recent historian has done, that 'the Montagnard argument was ultimately irresistable . . . This was the terrible logic which . . . sent Louis to the guillotine'.[3] Jaurès is much closer to the truth when he says of the famous speech of St Just that it was 'too strong for the hesitant and troubled conscience of France'.[4] The most effective argument of the Jacobins was not their dramatic denial of the king's moral membership, but their more prosaic assertion of his political danger. Doubtless, the two were connected: Tom Paine did not think Louis a danger to the republic; Robespierre did; and these perceptions were deeply rooted in their opposing political creeds. The Jacobins demanded Louis' death because they thought he was an enemy of themselves and of all mankind, and the fanatical vigor with which they pressed their demand had a lot to do with its success. But they had to endure the trial of the king before they could kill him.

In the course of the trial, one senses among those centrist delegates who wavered uneasily between the Mountain and the Gironde a growing conviction not only that Louis was a guilty man but that he was indeed a dangerous one. Not that he could possibly have looked dangerous sitting in the Temple: indeed, more than one speaker argued that if Louis was an enemy at all, he was palpably a captured enemy, a prisoner of war. 'When opposition ceases', said one delegate, following Rousseau, 'there is no longer an enemy to kill; the conqueror does not have the right of life and death over the conquered'.[5] True enough, the Jacobins responded, for any ordinary prisoner. But Louis only looked like an ordinary prisoner — who does not, when he stands in the dock? In fact, he was a king, 'the last king', Jacobin speakers called him, but not, like the Girondins, 'the former king'.

[1] *Archives Parlementaires*, 56: 17; below, p. 182.
[2] *Archives Parlementaires*, 53: 390; below, p. 122.
[3] Sydenham, *The Girondins*, p. 136.
[4] *La Convention*, p. 859.
[5] Méaulle, *Archives Parlementaires*, 54: 252; see Rousseau, *The Social Contract*, I, iv.

It could not be said that his opposition had ceased merely because he had been captured. He remained the center of all counter-revolutionary activity even in his prison and whatever his personal intentions (and the evidence found in the secret cabinet hardly suggested that his intentions were good). His kingship would be a living reality for many of his subjects so long as he was himself alive; his name was a rallying cry even while he was locked up. The king's name alone, Robespierre said, 'draws the scourge of war on the restless nation: neither prison nor exile can render his existence indifferent to the public welfare'.[1] One can hardly put a man on trial for his 'name', but if the name cannot be changed — as the king's name could not be — one can take defensive measures against the man who bears it. That is what the Jacobins urged upon the Convention. It fell to them to remind their fellow revolutionaries of the power of the king's title. Because he was called king, St Just said, 'this man must reign or die'.[2]

But the Jacobins could not be satisfied to kill the king as an act of military necessity — out of fear of his possible restoration or of the wars waged in his royal name. There was, to be sure, something in their argument of the old maxim, *If you strike a king, you must kill him.* To found the republic of virtue, however, it was necessary that Louis be killed not out of fear alone but also out of respect, that is, in the plenitude of his kingship, by a people in arms, who knew what a king was and why he was their enemy. The problem was that such a people did not exist in France in 1792 (anymore than they existed in England in 1649, as Charles knew when he challenged the High Court actually to seek out popular consent). The insurrection of 10 August had been entirely a Parisian affair. The nation as a whole was still under the royalist spell; even the Jacobins believed that a national referendum would probably save Louis' life. Hence Robespierre's extraordinary declaration of 28 December, when the trial seemed to drag on interminably and the delegates worried over the legal arguments of the king's lawyers: 'Virtue is always in the minority on this earth'.[3] The king was an enemy of the people, but the people were not finally and single-mindedly enemies of the king. If the Girondin case involved the pretense of Louis' citizenship, the Jacobin case required another fiction: that Louis was 'an alien among us'.[4] In truth, he was a familiar; he was not or not yet a peer.

---

[1] *Archives Parlementaires*, 54: 76, 77; below, p. 138. Against this argument, the Girondin Salle pointed to the dangers of civil war if the Convention sentenced Louis to death — 55: 715ff.

[2] *Archives Parlementaires*, 53: 391; below, p. 123.

[3] *Archives Parlementaires*, 56: 22; below, p. 192.

[4] *Archives Parlementaires*, 53: 392; below, p. 125.

The strength of the Jacobins' position lay in their persistence in calling Louis a king, a persistence in which they were joined, however weakly, by the king himself. When he was summoned to the bar of the Convention, he answered the summons and appeared at the bar, but he told the delegates nevertheless: 'I am not called Louis Capet'.[1] Indeed, he was not; he was known throughout France by his royal title and his title still called to mind a world of images and ideas. That was a reason for killing him, but it also helps explain why most of the men who were determined to kill him were determined to bring him to judgment first. They felt that they had to make their case: against a king who could do no wrong, it was necessary to present evidence of wrong-doing. So the centrist majority insisted on a trial and found the king guilty not of kingship but of treason. We must now consider whether their judgment was justified.

---

[1] Soboul, *Le procès*, p. 111. Apart from that brief defiance, the king said virtually nothing: he stood before the Convention, as Jaurès writes, 'without an idea'. *La Convention*, p. 883.

5

A DEFENSE OF THE TRIAL AND
EXECUTION OF LOUIS XVI

REVOLUTIONARY JUSTICE AND TERRORISM

'The king's head was not taken off because he was king', Cromwell told the London aldermen in 1653.[1] He is right as regards the verdict of the High Court, though he may or may not be reporting accurately his own views at the time. Nor was Louis killed simply because he was king, but rather because men called him king, because he acted like a king, because he intrigued and conspired, like Charles, to 'be really king again'. Charles was convicted as the man chiefly responsible for England's civil wars, and of that responsibility, especially in the case of the second war, there can be little doubt. Louis was convicted for his support of rebels inside and émigrés outside revolutionary France and for his negotiations with foreign powers planning and then actually engaged in an invasion of the country. Once again, there is no doubt of his guilt, that is, of his actual engagements with enemies of the new French state, though the evidence collected by historians is more telling than that discovered in the king's secret cabinet in November 1792. The treasons of the two kings are clear enough, if one agrees that it is possible to act treasonously against the Commons of England or the People of France and if one agrees that it is possible for a king to be a traitor.

The difficulty with the trials is simply that these agreements had not been written into the law at the time the two kings acted. For this reason, neither the High Court nor the Convention could possibly meet the high standard suggested for the trials of kings by Condorcet: 'when [an entire nation] judges a king, then kings themselves, in their inmost hearts, must feel moved to approve the judgment'.[2] Though one knows as little about the inmost hearts of kings as of other men, it is unlikely that they were so moved. The kings of Europe still believed in their personal dignity and their royal inviolability, as Charles and Louis still believed when they struggled

[1] Hill, *God's Englishman*, p. 108.
[2] *Archives Parlementaires*, 54: 146; below, p. 139.

69

with the revolutionaries. If they had not believed, they would not have struggled. But there is a difficulty also with the consciences of other men, who must judge both the king and the judges of the king, and it is on their behalf (there being no kings of any importance left to convince) that I want to raise the general question of revolutionary justice. Regicide is only one example of what Kirchheimer calls 'trial by fiat of a successor regime', but it is an important example, both because the fate of the king is intrinsically interesting and because it poses in a dramatic way one of the hardest questions faced by the leaders of a new regime. How are they to settle with the leaders of the old? Some settlement there must be, to terminate, if that is possible, the ongoing struggle between the two and to establish the legitimacy of the victors. But in what sense can this be, in what sense (if any) ought it to be, a legal settlement?[1] The king is brought to trial in violation of the laws of the old regime, the only laws that he acknowledges; he is judged in the name of political or legal principles to which he never consented. He is judged, moreover, by a court whose authority he does not recognize (or which he recognizes only under duress), a court composed in large part, if not entirely, of his political opponents. How can this be justice done?

The Jacobin argument solves the problem, and it does so with the appearance at least of theoretical neatness. St Just's speech amounts to a demand for the proscription of the king. He is to be set beyond the law or rather, the Convention is to decree that he has set himself beyond the law, and so no trial is necessary. Justice need not be done in any legal way; the summary proceedings of the executioner are enough. Louis' enemies do not pretend to be his judges; the seriousness and solemnity of the courtroom are not exploited for political purposes; every sort of legal sham is avoided. All this must be very appealing to realistic and toughminded historians (and revolutionaries).[2] And yet what would have resulted had the Jacobins had their way is precisely what Camus believes, wrongly, happened in any case: 'the public assassination of a weak but good-hearted man'.[3] Without a trial, there would have been no way of recognizing in Louis the tyrant or the traitor. Jacobin theory may serve to justify revolutionary action against the king, including, as I have already suggested, the killing of the king at the height of his power by an aroused populace, perhaps even by an anti-

---

[1] Two books are especially helpful here, and my own discussion owes a great deal to both of them: Kirchheimer, *Political Justice*, and Judith Shklar, *Legalism* (Cambridge, Mass, 1964), esp. part II.
[2] It is appealing to conventional political leaders too: thus British leaders in 1945 opposed the trial of Nazi war criminals, preferring that they be proscribed and then shot upon capture.
[3] *The Rebel*, p. 120.

royalist martyr. But when a helpless man is dragged to the scaffold and placed into the hands of the executioner, more arguments are required than the Jacobins provide. It is not enough to say, as one of their delegates does, that the people and the king fought, the king lost, and therefore he is the traitor. Here is another example of realism: if the people had lost, their leaders would undoubtedly have been called traitors. But such an argument leaves entirely open the question of right. Indeed, as long as the war goes on, both sides have a right to fight, and the king's proscription does not terminate the war. Proscription is final only with regard to its victim, but not with regard to the political community itself which still waits upon some determination of what is just and what unjust. That is a determination that revolutionary realism cannot provide.

The mere outlawing of the king does not constitute the republic; it does not even tell us who are the citizens of the republic. 'The revolution begins', said St Just, 'when the tyrant ends'.[1] A curious sentence, since he had already said that the triumph of the revolution was the only judgment the king required. In fact, he did not believe that the revolution had triumphed – yet. For him, Louis' proscription pointed toward a society not yet constituted, from which many other men and women would have to be excluded. The revolution was an ongoing war against the enemies of the French people. The king was only the first enemy, embodiment and representative of all the others, who would be left naked and exposed by his death. Who were the others? The courtiers of the king, his ministerial accomplices, active supporters, faithful followers: 'the basest and most corrupt men,' said Robespierre, ' . . . proud bourgeois and aristocrats, all the former privileged classes hidden behind the mask of civic virtue, all those born to grovel before a king' – in a word, the human remnants of the old regime, neither a state nor a party, but in 1792 a very substantial number of Frenchmen.[2] These are men and women with whom the revolutionary regime uneasily and inevitably co-exists.

It is, I think, the great fault of the Jacobins that they found that co-existence intolerable. For it could not be avoided short of civil war, and in that war (as in the civil wars of ancient Rome, with which St Just and Robespierre were so familiar), proscription was not a weapon that could be used just once. Once the Jacobins were firmly in power, the lists of proscribed persons got longer and longer, in part because revolutionary zeal

---

[1] *Archives Parlementaires*, 55: 710; below, p. 176. He was responding to arguments that the revolution was over and it was now necessary to consolidate its gains.
[2] *Archives Parlementaires*, 56: 19; below, p. 186.

came to be identified with the discovery of enemies, in part because there were so many enemies to discover. The whole enterprise was given some degree of credibility by the Austrian invasion of France and by counter-revolutionary risings in the West. The trial of the king must also be viewed against a background of domestic and international struggle. Yet the Jacobins were not willing to convict Louis of intrigue with foreign powers; in their eyes, he was an alien whether he had intrigued or not. Nor were the later victims of the Terror soldiers or subjects of states at war with France, though they were often enough denounced as the hired agents of such states. Jacobin orators took a peculiar delight in describing all their enemies, real and imaginary, as engaged in one great war against the revolution. Proscribed and outlawed Frenchmen were, however, different from their supposed foreign allies in this important respect: they lacked the protection which soldiers and subjects ordinarily receive; they were men without a state, deprived of civil rights. The war against them was wholly terrorist in character. Its purpose was not to defeat an organized enemy, but to deter every sort of opposition to the revolution, particularly, though not exclusively, that opposition which derived from royalist sentiment.

The proscriptive zeal of the Jacobins has its philosophical source, Camus tells us, in Rousseau's *Social Contract*: there St Just and Robespierre found the dogmas of their revolutionary religion.[1] The truth is harder to discover than that formula suggests. Yet it is worth looking at the Jacobins' Rousseau, if only in order to understand the difficulties and dangers of the word 'enemy' – which Rousseau indeed uses – when applied literally to domestic politics. The passage which comes nearest to anticipating the argument of St Just occurs in Book II of the *Social Contract*, in the chapter on life and death:

> . . . every malefactor, by attacking social rights, becomes on forfeit a rebel and a traitor to his country; by violating its laws, he ceases to be a member of it; he even makes war against it . . . in putting the guilty to death, we slay not so much a citizen as an enemy. The trial and the judgment are the proofs that he has broken the social treaty . . . he must be removed by exile as a violator of the compact, or by death as a public enemy; for such an enemy is not a moral person, but merely a man; and in such a case the right of war is to kill the vanquished.[2]

It should be noted first, against the Jacobin view, that Rousseau explicitly assumes the necessity of 'trial and judgment' before an accused man is

---

[1] *The Rebel*, p. 114.
[2] *The Social Contract*, trans. G. D. H. Cole (New York, 1950), II, v (p. 33).

declared an enemy. The violation of the compact must be proven, and that requirement is an absolute bar to legislative proscription as it is a clear sign that the contract has established standards of right binding on everyone. But it might be argued that men who oppose the revolution are not violating the contract at all, but rather refusing to join in making it and actively opposing those who do join – for the state is only at that moment being formed. In that case, as in the case of the tyrant himself, no proof is required to establish enmity, and the revolutionaries can presumably proceed to exercise 'the right of war'.

Rousseau's more particular comments about the right of war, however, do not support the domestic application of the term. 'War', he argues in Book I of the *Social Contract*, 'is constituted by a relation between things and not between persons ... [the] war of man with man can exist neither in the state of nature, where there is no constant property, nor in the social state, where everything is under the authority of the laws'. It is for this reason that 'the supposed right to kill the conquered is by no means deducible from the state of war'.[1] War cannot rightly be waged against men, but only against hostile states – and then against individuals only insofar as they are the active agents of hostile states. Clearly, then, no man can stand toward his own (or any other) people as an enemy. Rousseau does say that if a king claims to rule by the right of conquest, he must grant the people's right to renew the struggle: his victory has settled nothing; nor, however, would the people's victory. All such claims, he insists, are absurd and meaningless.[2] If one were to derive a theory of revolution from the arguments of the *Social Contract*, the terms of the derivation would have to be those of the contract itself and its enforcement, not of ongoing war. Royal absolutism is best described as the triumph of a particular will over the general will; a successful revolution would re-establish the supremacy of the general will and force the king to be free, that is, to live in obedience to the law like any other citizen. If the king refused this obedience, he might be called a rebel, perhaps even a traitor, but he would remain, whatever he was called, under the authority of the laws. Under that authority, he would be tried and judged, and under it again, he would be punished. The trial, the judgment, and the punishment all imply a close connection between the king and other 'moral persons', for the king, like all the rest of us, ceased to be a 'mere man' a long time ago.

[1] I, iv (p. 9).

[2] I, iv (p. 12); see I, iii (p. 6): 'Force is a physical power, and I fail to see what moral effect it can have.'

But it ought not to be surprising that one can oppose the Jacobins out of Rousseau. In fact, their view of the revolutionary state is their own, though they refer themselves to Rousseau (and to other writers) when they can. What we must do now is to imagine with them a republic where every 'malefactor' and more importantly, every political opponent, is a public enemy. Then law would be for the law-abiding only, and civil rights only for the politically committed. Anyone who broke the law would simultaneously renounce his commitments and actually free himself from all obligations to the state. Against such men law enforcement would be impossible; it would be necessary to wage war; and they would find it necessary, presumably, to fight back. Relations between virtuous citizens and their enemies would be essentially lawless: *inter arma silent leges.* Even if the citizens were to win, or rather, were to go on winning, their victory or victories would create no new right binding on the men they had defeated and no stable social order. No society can survive for long if its members can opt out of the obligations it imposes merely by reneging on the social contract or violating its terms. Nor will the members endure for long a social system that drives them into the state of war every time they break the law or, worse, every time they are alleged to have broken the law. It is precisely at such moments that men (and kings too) need to be able to claim the rights of membership.

The republic permanently at war with its internal enemies is a certain formula for defeat. Perhaps some sense of this fact accounts for the underlying pessimism of St Just's and Robespierre's speeches. They embody, as Camus says, the despair of virtue and of virtuous men forced to confront the deep corruption of the people. The problem is not only that royalism lingers on as a profound nostalgia – like that of the Children of Israel in the desert – for fleshpots and servitude. That is only the particular historical form of popular corruption. When Robespierre imagines the Jacobins as a permanent minority, he suggests that corruption can and will take other forms. What use is it then to kill the king? 'The others are too many; they cannot all be killed.'[1] Camus is not referring here to the practical difficulties of success – today we can kill more men more quickly than the Jacobins thought possible – but to the moral certainty of failure. So long as the war continues, there is no victory that can even conceivably be final. To found the republic it is necessary to make peace, and to make peace precisely with the enemies of the republic, with all those men and women

[1]Camus, *The Rebel*, 129.

on Robespierre's list. That does not only mean to negotiate settlements of this or that issue, for not all issues can be settled through negotiations. It means something much more important: to treat the republic's enemies as individual human beings, some of whom (including the king) are guilty of particular crimes under republican law for which they must be punished, all of whom (including the king again) are entitled to the rights and protections of republican citizenship. Foundation must be an act of inclusion, and this is best symbolized by the equal application of the law. That equality no doubt represents a compromise with corruption, with the old regime, and above all with the king. It gives the king what he never knew he had, his republican rights. But at the same time, it establishes, as Jacobin proscription could never do, the higher right of the republic itself.

The higher right of the republic consists in the sovereignty of the people, a claim to legitimate authority that can and often must be asserted against hostile powers aiming at conquest and domination, but which has first of all to be asserted (as Rousseau makes clear) over each individual member of the people itself. It represents a denial of every sort of personal authority except that which derives from the people by election, and it is vindicated against the king only when the king is required to answer to the people like any other member. That this vindication requires a trial is forcibly suggested by a curious passage in Immanuel Kant's *Metaphysics of Morals*, the only major philosophical work to deal explicity with the question of regicide. Kant recognizes that regicide can take two very different forms, which he calls assassination and execution. His preference for the first of these is clear enough, and it has been taken by Jaurès as an expression of support for the Jacobins.[1] But since Kant writes from a standpoint profoundly hostile to revolution in general (despite his 'sympathy' for the French Revolution), readers who are moved by his particular arguments but who do not share his general hostility will have to reverse his preferences. In any case, his support for the position of St Just and Robespierre is certainly indirect: 'Of all the abominations in the ... Revolution', Kant writes, 'the murder or assassination of the monarch is not the worst. For that may be done by the people out of fear, lest if he is allowed to live, he may again acquire power and inflict punishment upon them; and so it may be done, not as an act of punitive Justice, but merely from regard to self-preservation.' It is 'the formal execution of the monarch', he goes on, that is truly abominable, for 'the accompaniment of a *judicial process* ...

[1] Jaurès, *La Convention*, p. 857.

implies a principle which would necessarily make the restoration of a state when once overthrown an impossibility'.[1] Kant presumably means that the restoration of any state would be made impossible, since he regards the king as a legitimate sovereign and believes that the sovereign, in any conceivable constitution, must be inviolable. But it is precisely the claim of the revolutionaries that no single person can be inviolable as a matter of right, and it is their intention to make the restoration of monarchy impossible. They insist that the claim of the people as a whole to be the source of justice, hence beyond the law, is radically different from the pretension of the king to a similar status. If they are right, then it follows from the distinction Kant makes that the king must be put on trial. To kill him simply because he is a danger is not to assert a moral or legal superiority over him but only to invoke, as Kant says, a right of necessity (or, as the Jacobins argued, to act in accordance with the laws of war). The assassination of the king would represent only a 'divergence' from the rule of royal inviolability, and there had been many such divergences before. But his execution overthrows the rule; it symbolizes the new equality of kings and citizens and their mutual subjection to the community as a whole. 'It makes the people, who owe their constitutional existence to the legislation [of] the sovereign, to be the ruler over him.'

Given that result, the trial can clearly be defended politically, but it does not follow that it is morally justified. The trial founds the republic, but it seems at the same time to do a specific injustice to the king. He did not know that his actions were (or might be called) criminal; he never chose to be a traitor, for he never imagined that he could be one; he thought in all good faith that he was inviolable. There is, I think, nothing to do but accept this criticism. The legalist explanations of Girondin leaders like Condorcet are unconvincing; they all assume an understanding of the governmental contract and of the Constitution of 1791 that was certainly not shared by the king, nor by many other people, before the final overthrow of the monarchy. The judgment of the king was *ex post facto* justice. It is not the case, however, that the king's crime was invented to fit the things that he had done; his actions were of a kind long thought to be criminal in any other man. What the revolutionaries invented after the fact was not the crime but the possible criminality of the king. That is a more radical invention, but it does the king less of an injustice than is done by *ex post facto* justice of the sort that had been common enough under the old regime.[2] For

---

[1] Kant, *The Philosophy of Law*, trans. William Hastie (Edinburgh, 1887), pp. 120–21.
[2] Its principal means were the bill of attainder and the *lettre de cachet*: for France, see André Chassaigne, *Les lettres de cachet sous l'ancien régime* (Paris, 1903),

it is not personally vindicative in the same way; it is not narrowly designed to catch the king and to destroy him; it aims instead at asserting and vindicating a general principle, and a principle too that continued to be applied after the king was condemned. Nor was it necessary that the judges be personal enemies of Charles or Louis in order to get a conviction. All that was required (in theory, at least) was that they be committed to the special kind of equality that follows from the idea of popular sovereignty: because every man is a citizen, every man can also be a criminal; because no man is without peers, no man is exempt from judgment. Such notions were entirely alien to the mind of the king, and therein lies the unfairness of the trial. One might plausibly ask, of course, whether it was fair of the king to call himself inviolable in the first place. But the more immediate question is this: does a trial founded on the revolutionary invention of equality, without a firm legal base, differ in any important respect from the proscriptive justice of the Jacobins?

The first and most obvious difference is that the decision to try the king was also a decision to adopt the formal rules of the judicial process. The adoption was, to be sure, considerably less complete than Girondin deputies had urged. The king was not tried by an ordinary tribunal, nor even by a special tribunal (as in England), but by the revolutionary assembly itself. The members of that assembly were judges and jurors (and many of them, prosecuting attorneys as well); they first indicted and then condemned the king. Louis was not granted the right to bar any of them, even his foremost opponents among them, from participation in the trial. At the same time, however, specific charges were brought against the king and evidence was collected to substantiate them; the king and his lawyers were informed of the charges and of the evidence; and Louis was permitted to defend himself in detail and in public against them. That is hardly a sufficient description of legal fairness, but it is a partial description. Similarly, the formal rules of the courtroom are not in themselves an absolute barrier to political persecution — as the justice of kings had long ago made clear — but they are a partial barrier. And they are well worth maintaining, especially in revolutionary situations, for they have a universal quality that transcends the immediate conflicts of the revolution itself. Men who meet under their aegis meet in conditions of at least minimal peacefulness and civility. Fullscale political terror almost certainly requires their overthrow: thus the so-called trials of the Girondins in 1793, which make the judgment of the king look like the most perfect justice. The charges brought by the Jacobins against the proscribed deputies 'were scarcely susceptible of proof, and the Montagnards did not seriously attempt to substantiate them'.[1] Nor did they permit their prisoners to defend themselves in open court. I think it is fair to say that honesty in accusation and freedom in defence are incompatible with terrorism (and their maintenance therefore a significant defense against it), even if they are not incompatible with more subtle forms of political repression. In this (admittedly limited) sense, the Girondin deputies who urged that the king be tried like any other citizen can rightly be called 'representatives of the Rule of Law'.[2] Mr Sydenham's capital letters probably exaggerate the case, but the case is a good one still. The trial of the king is in no sense the beginning of the terror; nor are the advocates of a trial the organizers of the terror. In fact, the first group of men were the mortal enemies of the second and among their first victims.

It is also not the case that the principles on which the king was tried are the principles of the terror. The truth is quite the opposite. The principles of the trial, though they were not yet established in the law, are nevertheless fundamental to the very idea of a legal system as we have come to understand it, according to which equality before the law is the precondition of justice. England and France under the old regime had legal systems of a very different sort, systems of considerable complexity and sophistication, but based on a different understanding. No doubt justice was sometimes done within them, but equal justice was not done. The privileged position of the king was a bar to equal justice, both because it set the king beyond the reach of the law and because it justified the privileges of lesser men, though not of commoners, throughout the two societies. The king's body politic was clearly an organism composed of unequal parts. Insofar as the trial of the king represented a political attack on this organism, it pointed the way to equal justice. That is the only defense that can be offered for the specific injustice done to the king. It is the same as the defense that might be offered for the revolution itself, for the trial was nothing other than the acting out in legal form of the overthrow of divine right monarchy.

No trial would have been necessary had the king yielded to revolutionary politics, acceded, that is, to the principles of popular sovereignty and equality before the law. Then the new principles would have been established, as it were, by unanimous consent. The king did not yield, however, and so they were established first by mass action and then through the adversary proceedings of the courtroom. Only with the second

---

[1] Sydenham, *The Girondins*, p. 30; see also Donald Greer, *The Incidence of the Terror during the French Revolution* (Cambridge, Mass., 1935).
[2] Sydenham, *The Girondins*, p. 210.

of these was the king subjected not merely to the power but to the sovereignty of the people and treated, so far as possible, as the equal he never was. It is true that he was subjected at the same time to his political enemies, but it is important to remember that he could not have been brought to trial at all by his faithful followers. Given the mysteries of kingship, the only way to bring Louis to justice was through adversary proceedings in which the whole court was in effect the adversary of the king or at least of kingship. For such a court, legality is no doubt only a form of self-restraint, but it is important nonetheless because that restraint suggests as nothing else can do that the principles being established are at least potentially principles of justice.

Revolutionary justice is defensible whenever it points the way to everyday justice. That is the maxim that marks off morally legitimate trials from proscription and terror.[1] The legitimacy of the king's trial lies first in its resemblance to an ordinary judicial proceeding. Condorcet was entirely right to argue that the nearer the resemblance, the better the trial: the more just to the king and, not inconsistently, the more effective for the revolutionaries. But justice in revolutions cannot be measured in a purely formal way, for what is usually at stake is not the validity of this or that procedure — there was no disagreement in the Convention as to what constituted a fair trial — but the status of the men and women involved. In the case of the king, what was at issue was whether he was entitled to a trial of any sort and whether he was justiciable at all. Here the whole purpose of the revolution was to change the law, not merely to apply it, and it is obvious that the proposed changes have to be defended in political and moral, not in legal, terms. Hence the second and more important defense of Louis' trial is simply the claim that to turn kings into citizens is to advance the cause of justice.

Had the king been known to be an innocent man, of course, the transformation would have had to be signalled in some other way. I do not intend a purely utilitarian defense of the trial, for both the principles which the trial asserts and the arguments for asserting these principles *in a courtroom* may well have other foundations. A criminal trial presupposes a crime: in 1792 there were good reasons for thinking that the king, if he could be a criminal, was guilty of a crime. There actually was an organized

[1]Shklar, *Legalism*, p. 151: 'Ultimately it is the political results that count.' Yes, but only with the qualification that I suggest immediately below. One of the classical arguments against utilitarianism involves the construction of a case where great advantages follow from the trial and execution of an innocent man. Assuming an innocence that is not merely legalistic, the trial and execution can surely not be justified. See Sir David Ross, *The Right and the Good* (Oxford, 1930) pp. 56–7, and E. F. Carritt, *Ethical and Political Thinking* (Oxford, 1947), p. 65.

attempt to overthrow the revolutionary regime and re-establish monarchy with the help of foreign armies. It may well be that Louis' participation in this attempt was a tribute to his integrity as a king. To his followers he was guilty only of an incompetent attempt, of political irresolution, of a failure to assert his prerogative with the boldness and force that were required. His actions were nevertheless a betrayal of the French people, who had elected the assemblies against whose authority Louis conspired and who cannot be supposed to have sought a foreign invasion. And that was a betrayal for which Louis as a man and a citizen might justly be punished.

THE PUNISHMENT OF THE KING

In May of 1919, the czar of Russia and his wife and children were shot by Bolshevik guards fearful of the approach of counter-revolutionary troops. Trotsky later justified the slaughter, arguing that 'the czar's family fell victim to that principle which constitutes the axis of monarchy: dynastic succession'.[1] Nicholas' children had to die so that none of them might be proclaimed czar by the White armies and so become a rallying point for the disorganized forces that opposed the Bolshevik regime. Here was an example of that military necessity to which the Jacobins had earlier appealed. It suggests immediately how limited was the eighteenth century sense of what was necessary, for none of the Jacobin speakers in the Convention proposed killing the brothers of the king or the *dauphin* of France – for the crime, they might have said, of being potential kings. The *dauphin* died in prison, but he was not killed; nor was he, while alive, a threat to the revolution or even a crucial factor in counter-revolutionary politics. Why might Louis not have been imprisoned also, after he had been found guilty of treason? The immediate answer is that he might well have been imprisoned: the vote on the death penalty was very close. Just how close it was is not absolutely clear, since the delegates were permitted to make short speeches while they were voting, and some of the votes that were thus cast were highly ambiguous. The number of delegates explicitly voting for immediate death constituted a majority of one in the Convention, no more.[2] Greater unity and tactical skill among the Giron-

---

[1] *Trotsky's Diary in Exile: 1935*, trans. Elena Zarudnaya (Cambridge, Mass., 1958), p. 82. The Bosheviks 'had intended to let the revolutionary tribunal try the czar as Charles I and Louis XVI had been tried; and Trotsky had chosen himself for the role of Chief Prosecutor.' Isaac Deutscher, *The Prophet Armed: Trotsky: 1879–1921* (London, 1954), p. 418.

[2] For a detailed account of the voting, see Arthur Conte, *Sire, ils ont voté la mort: la condemnation de Louis XVI* (Paris, 1966).

dins could probably have saved Louis' life. Danton's prediction that if the king were brought to trial, 'he is dead', was only barely borne out. It fits the English case more closely, where the trial itself was widely opposed, but none of its organizers fought for indulgence. Perhaps that was because Charles was still formally a king when he stood before the High Court (and still regarded as a king when he met his executioner, who explained to him how he must place his head, adding 'and it please your Majesty'), while Louis had already been deposed and was thought by at least some of his judges to be a citizen. In both cases, however, essentially the same reasons pressed the revolutionaries to kill the king, and in both cases, these reasons had a great deal to do with the nature of kingship.

Death was, of course, the normal punishment for traitors in seventeenth century England as in eighteenth century France, and once the two kings had been found guilty of treason, their judges did not have a great deal of latitude in deciding what to do with them. In England, the practice of locking a man up as a way of punishing him did not exist. Debtors and vagabonds were locked up; noblemen were detained while awaiting trial, often for many years, but all punishments properly so called were corporal in nature. It was hardly possible to whip or brand Charles like some ordinary thief; nor were the English revolutionaries sufficiently equalitarian or sufficiently brutal to mete out to their king the punishment he ordained for traitors and rebels (such as many of them were, in his eyes), hanging and quartering.[1] There remained only the ax; here they followed the precedent of the king, who had usually commuted the sentence of aristocratic traitors and permitted them to die at one blow. The case in France was different and, in one sense, even more restrictive. By 1792, Dr Guillotin had succeeded in establishing a single mode of execution, common for all citizens. Some of the delegates to the Convention had, however, adopted the views of Beccaria and Voltaire and declared themselves absolutely opposed to the death penalty. (Robespierre, who was one of them, made an exception in the case of the king and eventually, it appears, in the case of most other people.)[2] Hence there was a growing interest in imprisonment, even though under the old regime the general rule had still been that of Roman Law – 'prisons are for confinement, not punishment' – and the actual development of a prison system awaited the work of nineteenth

---

[1] According to Muddiman, only one of the English regicides was actually hung and quartered after the Restoration; twelve others were hung only; and fourteen died in prison after having been sentenced to death. *Trial*, pp. 183–8.

[2] See his explanation of his willingness to kill the king, *Archives Parlementaires*, 54: 77; below, pp. 137–38.

century reformers. Rousseau's writings and then the nationalist fervor of the revolutionaries made banishment seem at least a possible way of punishing criminals, perhaps especially political criminals. On the other hand, the extent of the aristocratic emigration suggested that there were still significant numbers of Frenchmen who agreed with Hobbes' dictum that 'a change of air is no punishment'.[1] To punish a criminal still seemed to require some corporal injury, some infliction of physical pain, and when the time came for deciding Louis' fate, only a minority of the delegates cast their votes in favor of imprisonment (for the duration of the war) and banishment (once peace had been restored). This was the only alternative to death that emerged with any force during the Convention debates, however, and so it remains to ask whether, given that alternative, the execution of the king was justified.

Curiously enough, detention and exile seem to follow naturally from the Jacobin theory of kingship, though the Jacobins themselves argued most vehemently for death. What, after all, does one do with prisoners of war but detain them for the duration and then return them to their friends and relatives? Why should not Louis have been allowed to rejoin the international community of kings and noblemen, if that community still existed after the war was over? This is surely a solution easier to recommend on behalf of captured enemies than on behalf of convicted traitors, despite the growing sense that prison and exile were possible forms of punishment. The logic of the trial itself pressed the revolutionaries toward the death penalty. In this sense, Danton was right. It would be difficult to defend the trial without defending also the sentence of the court (though this is just what some of the Girondins did, for reasons which had little to do with the logic of the case against the king). Nevertheless, I do not want to rest the argument for the king's execution at this point, for if Louis was not killed solely because he had been king, he was also not killed solely because he had been found guilty of treason.

The argument that the king posed a danger to the revolution and would do so as long as he remained alive undoubtedly weighed heavily in the minds of the delegates. The precise extent of the danger is problematic – as the case of the *dauphin* suggests – and was debated at the time. What is more important is that the danger posed, whatever its extent, was a function of Louis' kingship and not of his actual or predicted behavior: more exactly, it was a function of the predicted behavior of other people responding to Louis' kingship. This anticipated response has to do with very nature

[1] *Leviathan*, Ch. XXVII.

of monarchy, and it raises a hard problem. Killing Louis because of what kingship is sounds frighteningly like killing X (an aristocrat) because of what aristocracy is or Y (a Jew) because of what Judaism is. It seems utterly to overthrow the rule of law when men are punished not for what they have done but for what they are — or worse, for what other men think they are. But there is a clear distinction between taking into account what a man is in determining the extent of his punishment and punishing him for being what he is. Obviously, some description of those identities that can rightly be taken into account and those that cannot is necessary. It seems to me certain that a man's kingship can be, yet the qualities of kingship may be unique and consideration of them not terribly helpful in producing a general rule. The king is unique both in the claims that are made on his behalf and in the mystic attraction that he holds for his subjects. If we imagine the aristocracy as a class of absolute rulers, who have dominated for centuries over other men, each of whose members is held in awe and dread by his subjects, then it might well make sense for rebels against that class to kill some member of it, *once he had been found guilty of a specific crime for which death was or was once the conventional penalty.* If a new convention is to be established, it would be best to begin with a shoemaker or a peasant. For otherwise, the aristocracy will seem once again to have exercised its magical grip, and the new punishment may not fulfill its minimal task of rendering the criminal harmless. War might still be waged in his name and men moved to action by his name, and that is not tolerable (it might be said) when the name is that of a convicted criminal. In fact, however, it is hard to imagine a class all of whose members actually share such a mysterious and frightening authority. Historically, authority of this sort has tended to lodge more specifically, precisely in that single person called a king. Kingship describes a class with only one member, or only one member in one state at one time: Louis was not *a* king, but *the* king of France. Surely no court could be morally bound to overlook that fact in fixing on an appropriate punishment for him.[1]

The nature of the king's uniqueness, however, raises doubts about the more conventional justifications that might be offered for his punishment: the deterrence of tyrants and traitors or the moral satisfaction of an oppressed and betrayed people. Boswell's father is said to have told Dr Johnson

---

[1] It might also be said, of course, that Louis' kingship was grounds for mercy: having been raised as a king, he knew no better than to try to maintain his ancient prerogatives, and he undoubtedly felt more closely allied to the kings of Austria and Prussia than to the revolutionaries at home (he was allied by marriage to the Austrians). But this was hardly an argument that he would have, or that his followers could have, made on his behalf.

that Cromwell made 'kings ken they had a lith [joint] in their neck' — a knowledge without which deterrence is hardly possible.[1] It can certainly be argued that the executions of the two kings had at least a short-run deterrent effect, that the image of the scaffold made an appreciable difference in the behavior of the restored Charles II (though not of his brother) and perhaps even of those French kings who are usually said to have learned nothing and forgotten nothing, Louis XVIII and Charles X. More importantly, the executions played a vital part in a long process of constitutional change that fixed limits on the exercise of sovereign power, and they played a part also in the transformation of popular ideas about kingship. But I do not think they had any of these effects by associating the idea of punishment with the idea of absolutism. Men who find themselves placed so that they can reach for absolute power are in a position so extraordinary, their ideas about themselves are likely to be so inflated, their followers so sycophantic, that they are almost certain to be closed to the patterns of calculation through which criminal deterrence works. Nor could the two executions have added greatly to the probability that if they lose out, they will be killed. It was always dangerous to be a king, even when assassination, not execution, awaited the king who failed.

The groan that went through the crowd when Charles' head was cut off suggests that the execution, if it had no deterrent effect, was also not in any simple sense retributive. There were undoubtedly some men who took moral satisfaction in the deed — the soldiers who had called Charles a 'man of blood', for example. In the case of Louis the number may have been greater. The Jacobins tried to picture the killing of the king as an act of popular vengeance, but there is little evidence to suggest that anything more than a party among the people actually demanded revenge and it is not at all clear that they had any special claim to it. Moreover, the argument from military necessity seems to stand in flat contradiction to the argument from retribution — though the Jacobins made both — for the first rests on the strong support the king was said to have among the people, the lingering sense of him as a sacred and untouchable figure, while the second appeals to the virtually unanimous outrage of the people against the king as a tyrant and traitor. If the nation sought vengeance upon the king (for crimes he had actually committed against its members), then it might

---

[1] Boswell, *Life of Johnson*, ed. G. B. Hill (New York, 1891), v, 382, n. 2. Among the delegates to the Convention the trial and execution of Louis was more often seen as a way of educating and inspiring peoples than of deterring kings: see especially the letter of Thomas Paine, read to the Convention by Maihle, *Archives Parlementaires*, 53: 498–9. In the older defense of tyrannicide, however, deterrence played an important part: see Mariana, *The King*, I, v (p. 149).

well be desirable to kill him, but it would no longer be necessary to do so. If it was necessary, it could not be desirable — as that strange (and unverified) story suggests which has Cromwell standing late at night over the coffin of the king and muttering, 'Cruel necessity'. [1]

The revolutionary courts had another reason for killing the king: to convey to the people the new idea that what he had done was a crime and that he could be a criminal. The two executions were expressions of abhorrence at the treasons of the two kings, and I think it is fair to say that that abhorrence could not have been expressed in any other way.[2] Had the kings been punished in some lesser fashion or not punished at all, it would have seemed as if the courts were saying that royal treason was less serious than the treason of subjects or that royal traitors were privileged criminals. Their members clearly did not believe this, and it was especially important that they find some way of communicating what they did believe since the beliefs of the two kings were still so widely shared. Punishment is always an expression of public abhorrence and communal condemnation, but in the case of revolutionary justice the expression takes on a special significance. It focuses not only on the crime that has been committed, but also on the institutions and ideologies that inspired or supported the criminal act. Ordinary justice assumes the personal character of criminal motivation, but the king had motives as a body politic, not only as a body natural, and the revolutionary courts condemned simultaneously the treason of his royal self and of his royal state. To judge the treason of a king was also to judge kingship, if only because the king's royalist pretensions and the encouragement of his courtly entourage led directly to his wars against the republican regime. Perhaps some formula of words or actions could have been found that would have expressed the same condemnation as well or better than public execution. But it is not easy to find such a formula; nor can one be invented on the spot. Punishments must have resonances; they depend upon hierarchies of value and symbolic systems already well established. Given the established hierarchies and systems of eighteenth century France, it is unlikely that either the imprisonment or the banishment of Louis XVI would have expressed that extended condemnation of royal treason and of royalism that the scaffold successfully symbolized.

It is this extended condemnation that radical historians like Kropotkin and Jaurès have in mind when they say that the principle of monarchy or

[1]Wedgwood, *The Trial of Charles I*, pp. 234–5.
[2]For an analysis of the 'expressive function of punishment', see Joel Feinberg, *Doing and Deserving: Essays in the Theory of Responsibility* (Priceton, New Jersey, 1970), pp. 95–118.

monarchy itself was done to death along with the king.[1] A political execution was coupled with a legal execution: this is surely what many of the revolutionaries had in mind, and it describes with some accuracy also the effects of what they did. And then the argument can be made, again, that this coupling, like the trial which preceded it, merely exploits for party purposes the solemnity and decorum of the law. It uses the symbols of the legal system to deliver a political message. I shall leave aside the response that the law is often used in this way, even by established regimes; that is in part what the law is for. The coupling of king and monarchy at the trial and on the scaffold, however, has a history quite its own, and it sets precedents only for men who hold power in that peculiarly personal way which royalist ideology specifies. For the double execution in which the two trials culminated was a function of the king's embodiment of the old regime and of his claim to be inviolable. It was not possible to bring Louis within reach of the law without attacking both his person and his pretensions. The punishment of the king was necessarily a revolutionary act as well as the proper conclusion of a legal proceeding. But it does not lose the attributes of punishment merely because it was revolutionary. To argue that it does is to demand that revolutionaries always act outside the law, and that is surely a foolish demand to make. Lawfulness served the revolutionaries well until Cromwell and the Jacobins cast it aside, but it did not serve them only. Because of the solemnity and decorum of the law, the two kings were able to speak out at their trial – as Charles especially did with such eloquence – and they were able to die with grace and dignity. They were not hurried out of existence as were the victims of the proscriptions of 1793 and '94. They did not die ignominiously or obscurely as countless victims of political terrorism have done since. Though they were condemned as men and citizens, they died as they had tried to live, as bodies simultaneously politic and natural, symbols of a regime, gods incarnate: greater justice could not have been done them.

REGICIDE AND REVOLUTION

'The condemnation of the king', writes Camus of the trial of Louis, 'is at the crux of our contemporary history. It symbolizes the secularization of our history and the disincarnation of the Christian God.'[2] That is true, I

---

[1] Jaurès, *La Convention*, p. 962; Peter Kropotkin, *The Great French Revolution*, trans. N. F. Dryhurst (New York, 1971), p. 335.
[2] *The Rebel*, p. 120.

think, at least insofar as no subsequent claim to political authority can rest on divine right. God is no longer represented within our political systems, and our leaders must share the divine image with the rest of us and represent or pretend to represent our will and not His. But Camus goes on to make a further argument that is not true and that radically misconstrues the nature of the justice that was done to Charles and Louis. He suggests that regicide leads men on to deicide, a crime that cannot have the same precise historical location, but which represents for Camus the deliberate attack upon the moral structure of the universe or the denial that any such structure exists. The killing of the king stands, in his view, at the beginning not of republican or democratic rule, but of revolution simply: the permanent revolution of modern history, terrorist and nihilist in character, against which he holds out the limiting principle of existential rebellion.

This argument seems once again to presuppose a particular idea of historical development, an idea presented and elaborated with great power, but one which bears little relation to the actual histories of England and France. That the trial of Louis and the subsequent Jacobin terror were radically disconnected I have already sought to demonstrate. But it is necessary to say more than this. In the two countries where kings were publicly condemned and executed, revolutionary nihilism as Camus describes it has had no triumphs. Of other kinds of injustice and crime, there have certainly been no lack. But the specific horrors to which he points have been avoided. Not so in countries where kings fared better — as in Germany, where the kaiser went into exile — or worse — as in Russia, where the czar and his family were shot. I can hardly attempt here to explain why this is so. Any explanation would have to take into account the previous histories of the four countries as well as the special character of their revolutionary crises.[1] But it is surely worth pointing out that the politics of England and France have been dominated throughout recent history by men faithful in their fashion to the principles which underlay the two trials: that political leaders are 'trusted' with their power and responsible for its exercise to the people they lead. And it is not merely

---

[1] One would have to write a book of the scope of Barrington Moore's *Social Origins of Democracy and Dictatorship* (Boston, 1966), but distinguishing, as Moore does not, between different kinds of revolutionary violence. It is indeed 'very difficult to deny that if France were to enter the modern world through the democratic door she had to pass through the fires of the Revolution, including its violent and radical aspects' (p. 105). But this is not to justify every act of revolutionary violence; it is still morally necessary to make distinctions, looking to the future — and to other things as well. Neither the proscription of the Girondins nor, even more obviously, the murder of prisoners in the *Vendée*, had much to do with opening the 'democratic door'. The killing of the king, I think, did.

fanciful to suggest that that faithfulness has something to do with the fact that the two trials took place.

Monarchy was a political structure of large dimensions, and men lived within it for a long time. Whatever the different forms it took, the exaltation of a single person and the denial of the political rights of ordinary men and women were its consistent features. Its ideology taught a kind of political piety; its subjects learned to worship authority, and they worshipped for so long that the attitudes and postures of subservience came to be thought natural to them. The political history of mankind was the history of its kings: reigns and dynasties marked its periods. That was not a history that could be abruptly sloughed off; no more could men simply walk out from under their kings as if they were taking a stroll. The destruction of kingship was a long and a difficult process, and the sense of adventure and of danger that it frequently entailed should never be forgotten. Much of this process remains hidden from view: the erosion of royalist ideology, for example, still awaits its historian. Nevertheless, there are clearly a number of decisive moments, which we know about in part because they were marked off, like the two regicides I have been discussing, in a ceremonial fashion. This is obviously not just a matter of emphasis. In an important sense, the ceremonies make the decisiveness. Without the public acting out of revolutionary principles, not merely in front of the nation, but in ways that involve and implicate the nation, those principles remain a party creed, the revolution itself nothing more than a seizure of power. The revolutionaries must settle with the old regime: that means they must find some ritual process through which the ideology it embodies (and the man who embodies it) can be publicly repudiated.

The principle of kingly authority, writes Clifford Geertz, 'was destroyed long before the king: it was to the successor principle that he was, in fact, a ritual sacrifice'.[1] But this is only partly true. Geertz points rightly to the long process of erosion, but that process was far from complete in 1792 (let alone in 1649); kings were still magical figures for large numbers of their subjects and royalism was still a popular ideology. And so the trial was an act of destruction as well as the vindication of a new political doctrine; it represents the symbolic disenchantment of the realm as well as the establishment of a secular republic. Precisely how effective it was in either capacity is very hard to say. It is striking how little attention English

---

[1] 'Ideology as a Cultural System', in David Apter, ed. *Ideology and Discontent* (Glencoe, Illinois, 1964), p. 75n. Against this, one might set Marat's comment after the execution of the king: 'I believe in the Republic at last!' Gottschalk, *Marat*, p. 131.

historians have paid to the trial of Charles: mostly, they express their hostility to this 'illegal' proceeding and then move quickly on, averting their eyes. And while the French have dealt with the trial of Louis far more extensively, the event remains marginal to most histories of the revolution; nor has it figured significantly in the fierce controversies that have been waged over the meaning and value of revolutionary politics. This avoidance might be justified on the principle that executions should never be celebrated. They should sometimes, however, be remembered. We must surely come to grips with an event that seemed so central, that was so shocking to contemporary men and women, and that was marked at the time, as Camus says, 'by hysterical scenes of suicide and madness'.[1] When we do, we shall discover, I think, that the renunciation of magical authority and political servitude is not easy, and that it approaches finality only when the revolutionary attack is raised to the level of symbolic action. The mere establishment of a new regime or the adoption of a new constitution does not have the same effect. The former subjects of the king must witness the destruction of kingship; they must somehow share in the renunciation of their own servitude. Otherwise, it is far more likely than it ever was in England or France that the mysteries of government will outlast the 'last' king and will be re-embodied in men who make up in brutality what they lack in divine right.

Similarly with semi-feudal landlords in China?

Is the same true of military dictatorship?
In this sense, is Argentina pursuing (1984) a more sensible path toward democratizing its society than the more conciliatory process under way in Brazil?

---

[1] *The Rebel*, p. 120.

THE SPEECHES

1. MAIHLE

7 November 1792

After weeks of uncertainty in the Convention and agitation in Paris, the Committee on Legislation was asked on 1 November to consider the legal problems of trying the king, and if they thought him justiciable, to propose a form for the trial. Jean-Baptiste Maihle, a lawyer from Toulouse, was draftsman and *rapporteur* for the Committee. His report begins the serious debate and points the way the *conventionnels* eventually followed. Though sometimes identified by historians with the Mountain, Maihle was an able and characteristic figure of the Plain — that middle group of deputies, a majority of the Convention, whose members were unconnected even to the disorganized factions of the time. His proposals were quickly attacked by St Just, who spoke for the Jacobin leadership, and, a few weeks later, by Condorcet, whose views were typical of the Gironde. But they found wide support nonetheless, for they seemed to resolve many difficulties. 'Here comes Deputy Maihle', writes Carlyle, 'with a legal argument very prosy to read now, very refreshing to hear then . . .'

On the roll-calls of January 1793, Maihle voted for the appeal to the people, though that proposal is rejected in his report: perhaps he spoke in November for a committee majority which did not, on this issue at least, include him. He then voted for death, with a proviso adopted by 25 other deputies (Maihle's was the first name called on that dramatic roll-call): if death obtained a majority, he said, there should then be further discussion on whether it was in the public interest that Louis be executed immediately or that the execution be deferred. There was a majority for death, in which Maihle and his 25 followers were included, and then a final vote (though with little debate) on 'reprieve'. Here Maihle stood with the minority, against the culmination of the long proceeding his report had begun.

Louis XVI has been charged with crimes committed while he reigned under the Constitution: shall he be subject to judgment for them? By whom should he be judged? Shall he be brought before an ordinary tribunal, like any other citizen accused of treason? Will you delegate the right to judge him to a tribunal formed by the electoral assemblies of the eighty-three departments? Is it not more natural that this Convention itself should judge him? Is it either necessary or proper to submit the decision for ratification by all the members of the Republic, gathered in communal or primary assemblies?

These are the questions which your Legislative Committee has debated long and well. The first is the simplest. Nevertheless, it is also the question which demands the most seasoned judgment, not for you, not for that great majority of the French people who understand the extent of their sovereignty, but for that small number who think they glimpse in the Constitution a pledge of impunity for Louis XVI and who await the resolution of their doubts; not for you, but for those nations still governed by kings, which it is your duty to instruct; not for you, I say, but for the entire human race which watches you, which desires and yet fears to punish its tyrants and which will not act, perhaps, until it can weigh your justice.

When I open that Constitution which consecrated despotism under the name of hereditary monarchy, I see that, 'the person of the king', was 'inviolable and sacred'.[1] I see that, 'if the king has not taken the oath, or if, after taking it, he retracts', that, 'if the king put himself at the head of an army and direct the forces of it against the nation, or if he do not oppose, by a formal act, any such enterprise undertaken in his name', that, 'if the king, having gone out of the kingdom, do not return to it, after an invitation by the legislative body, within the space which shall be fixed', 'he shall be held', in each of these cases, 'to have abdicated the royalty'. I see there that, 'after abdication, express or legal, the king shall be in the class of citizens, and may be accused and tried like them, for acts posterior to his abdication'.

Does this mean that the king, if only he is adroit enough to avoid those acts that would force his abdication, could abandon himself to his most savage passions? Does this mean that he could have used his constitutional powers for the overthrow of the Constitution? If, after having secretly called to his cause a horde of foreign brigands; if, after having caused the slaughter of several thousand citizens, he failed in his enterprises against liberty, his only punishment would be the loss of that scepter which, as it was not of iron, was odious to him. And the nation so long oppressed, so long betrayed, would have no right at its reawakening to avenge itself upon him and set an example for all mankind.

Perhaps that was in the hearts of those who urged these articles which Louis XVI will surely cite in his favor. Yet, pressed to explain their motives, they will respond only with evasive subtleties. They would have blushed to admit that they intended this grant of impunity as a bait to draw Louis XVI back to despotism. They remind us, in part, of the senatorial aristocracy of Rome, who by their frequent resort to a dictator prepared

[1] The relevant sections of the Constitution of 1791 are printed in the Appendix.

the people for slavery, and who did it cloaked by the shadows of night, 'as if there were something shameful', says Jean-Jacques, 'in setting a man above the laws'.[1]

Let us see what motives and what ends drew men to make their king inviolable, the better to judge, knowing its full meaning, if that inviolability can be opposed to the interests of the nation.

France, they said, cannot stand without a monarchy, nor can the monarchy stand outside the fortress of inviolability. If the king could be accused or judged by the legislature, he would be subject to its control. From that time forward, either the monarchy would soon be overthrown by the legislature which, usurping power, would become a tyrant, or it would be without energy, without strength to execute the laws; in either case, there would be an end to liberty. Therefore, it is in the interest not of the king but of the nation that the king be inviolable. Those who held this view agreed that there was also a certain danger to liberty in it, but they claimed to counter this difficulty by holding ministers answerable.

These are the sophisms by which they sought to mislead the nation. Did they not know that monarchy long existed in Sparta, as well as among other ancient peoples, without the dangerous shield of inviolability? that there kings were subject to tribunals of the people, that these constraints, even their trial and condemnation, far from hindering liberty, assured it?

Wiser than the Spartans, the French nation began by striking down monarchy without examining if the king was innocent or guilty. And already, France has proven how greatly it was slandered by those who claimed that monarchy was vital to its power and its glory.

But let us return to royal inviolability. We should note that it was not, in fact, absolute as regards the legislature. The Constitution required the abdication of the king if, for example, he did not oppose, by a formal act, the efforts of a force directed against the nation in his name, and a perfidious king might protest, yet never officially declare, his opposition. It would then be necessary to decide if that opposition had been genuine or feigned. To this end, an examination of the conduct of the king, a trial, a judgment would be required. In the state of things at that time, this right could only belong to the foremost of constituted authorities. There were, then, cases in which the Constitution placed the inviolability of the king before the legislature for judgment.

Did the king have to guard against those acts alone for which he might

---

[1] The passage is from Rousseau's *Social Contract*, Book IV, chapter 6; trans. G. D. H. Cole (New York, 1950), p. 124n.

be deposed? And was impunity assured him for all other crimes he might commit or conceive? We have already answered this. Those who wish to defend him admit that the sole aim of royal inviolability was the interest of the nation, its tranquillity and its liberty. And this, they argue, could never be harmful since the king was condemned to execute only those orders which had been signed by a minister, who might answer with his head for any breach of law.

If Louis XVI had considered this argument and acted in accordance with it, he would have had this specious rejoinder: 'In all I have done, I have had in view the welfare of the nation. Perhaps I have erred, but the knowlege of my inviolability encouraged me to try my ideas for the public good. I submitted them all to my agents; I ordered nothing which does not bear their seal. It is with them alone that you must deal, for they are the sureties for my errors.'

How far is he from being able to make such a claim if he violated the law which required him always to have an agent ready to answer for his error or his crime, if he turned against the nation the prerogative which he received on its behalf, if he studiously eluded this safeguard of individual and public liberty! We have long since suspected that the grave of the nation was being dug, but the hands which did the digging remained unseen. Treason hovered, invisible, above the heads of all citizens. Monarchy was meant, like the thunderbolt, to strike before it could be seen.

And Louis XVI, who, the better to deceive the nation, worked ceaselessly to cast suspicion on the purest members of the legislature; Louis XVI, who not long since stood poised to gather the fruit of his perfidies, and caused this august hall to echo with his hypocritical protestations of devotion to liberty; this same Louis XVI, is he not personally responsible for the ills of which he personally was the cause?

He will say that his person could not be separated from the functions of king; since as king, he was inviolable for administrative acts, as an individual he was equally so for personal acts. We will reply that he is accused of having justified only too well the possibility of such a distinction. His inviolability had as its only basis a fiction which transferred the crime and the punishment from the king to his agents. But did he not in fact himself renounce this fiction if it is true that he hatched his plots without the aid of his ordinary ministers, or other apparent agents, or if he put them out of reach of effective surveillance? As it is contrary to the basis of the Constitution, accepted by Louis XVI, that there be an infraction of the law without a responsible agent, Louis XVI was naturally and necessarily liable for all those crimes with which an agent could not be charged.

By whom might he then be accused or judged? By the legislature?

Doubtless reason would have it so, yet the Constitution is opposed. We exercise a ministry of truth; we should be culpable were we to disguise this, either in principle or in fact.

The true power of the legislature, with respect to the king, was limited by the Constitution to judging specific cases of deposition. Even in these cases, it could pass only a sentence of deposition. Apart from these cases, the person of the king was independent of the legislature. Apart from these cases, the legislature could assume no judicial functions. It could only bring forth an indictment, and even if it could have brought one against Louis XVI, to what court would it have been referred? Placed by the Constitution parallel to, and beside, the legislature, the king was above all other constituted authority. Therefore he could neither be accused, nor be judged, except by the nation itself.

Yet was the legislature so tied by the principles of royal inviolability that it was obliged, in a moment of crisis, to sacrifice the public safety to them? Was it obliged to imitate those soldiers of a superstitious race, who, seeing animals they held sacred fill the first line of the enemy army, dared not shoot, and let liberty forever die among them? Shall we call to account the men of the tenth of August, for the dike with which they opposed the torrent of treachery? Shall we call to account the legislature for the decrees which suspended Louis XVI from his functions and transferred him to the Temple? They will all answer, 'We have saved Liberty. Give thanks for our courage.'

This legislature, which the partisans of depotism accused with all the art of recrimination of debasing royal authority to glorify and perpetuate its own, this legislature had no sooner struck those blows which caused it everywhere to be proclaimed the savior of France, than it said to the nation: 'We return to your hands the powers with which you entrusted us. If we exceeded them, we did so provisionally, and for your safety. Judge us, judge your Constitution, judge the monarchy, judge Louis XVI, and see then if you wish to maintain or to reconstruct the foundations of your liberty.'[1]

Citizens, the nation has spoken; the nation has chosen you as the organ of its sovereign will. Here all the difficulties disappear; royal inviolability might never have been.

We shall not cease to repeat: that inviolability had, for its sole aim, to assure the strength of the executive power by assuring its freedom from the legislature: whence it followed that that body did not have the right to judge the king in cases unspecified by the Constitution. Equally it followed

---

[1] The Legislative Assembly, which had suspended the king in August, 1792, then dissolved itself and called for new elections.

that in no case could the king be judged by the other constituted authorities, since he was their superior. It did not follow, however, that he could not be judged by the nation, since to come to such a conclusion would be to claim that by virtue of the Constitution, the king was superior to the nation or independent of the nation.

Perhaps Louis XVI will reply: 'In ratifying, in enacting the Constitution through its representatives, the French people recognized the inviolability there accorded me. It recognized that I could be accused only of crimes committed after my abdication. By this disposition, the people bound itself, as it bound its constituted authorities, since it failed to reserve for itself the power, by right of its sovereignty, to prosecute me for earlier crimes.'

No, the nation was not bound by royal inviolability, nor could it be. There was no reciprocity between the people and the king. Louis XVI was king only by virtue of the Constitution: the nation was sovereign regardless of constitution or king. Its inalienable sovereignty proceeds from nature alone. This eternal principle is recalled in the Constitution itself. Yet would it not have been an alienation of sovereignty had the nation renounced its right to examine or to judge all the actions of a man whom it placed at the head of its government?

The legislature was inviolable as well. It too was independent of the king and of all other constituted authority. None of its members were subject to prosecution without a warrant. Yet if it had abused that inviolability, misused that independence, and if the nation had risen to question its malversations, would it have sufficed, do you think, to plead a prerogative granted not for the sake of the legislature itself but for the sake of the nation?

The inviolability of the king, like the inviolability of the legislature, was intended to prevent each from intruding on the authority of the other; it was meant to create a balance of powers supposed necessary to maintain liberty. For this reason, had the king been faithful to his duty, he could have called upon the nation for aid against any enterprise which might menace his inviolability. Yet, called before a national tribunal, under what pretext might he invoke an inviolability granted him to defend the nation and which he had used only to oppress it?

If the example of the Constituent Assembly could add anything to the authority of reason, we remind you that the Constitution was completed in June of 1791, and that in the first order of constitutional articles, article three declared the person of the king inviolable and sacred. Louis XVI had solemnly accepted all these articles, one by one, when he fled with such speed and secrecy as announced his intention to join the despots who already menaced liberty in France.[1] The Constituent Assembly therefore called him to account for his flight and his intentions, whereupon Louis XVI replied with claims proven false by his letters. Thus the Constituent Assembly was recognized to have the right to judge and punish Louis XVI, for a judgment was passed. His partisans cited the article granting royal inviolability. They exhausted all their zeal and all their efforts to prove inviolability needful to liberty, but they applied this argument only to the pretended necessity of retaining the mutual independence of the legislative and executive branches. They made no claim that this inviolability, already sanctioned, could be opposed to an assembly invested with all the powers of the nation. How could they have made such an assertion without contradicting the actions of the Constituent Assembly itself, which had arrested the king at Varennes, which had suspended his powers, ordered him to respond in writing as to the motive of his flight, and which would not have had the right to take any of these measures had it not judged that the inviolability of the king should bow before the tribunal of the nation?

Yet has not the National Convention already punished Louis XVI by taking from him the scepter granted by the Constitution? Can he be placed in double jeopardy?

That objection, were it to be made, would be mistaken. If the Constitution were to have continued in force, and if the legislature had pronounced the abdication of Louis XVI, in conformity with the provision of that document which provided for a successor, abdication might be regarded as a penalty. Even so, is it certain that the Constitution would have prevented the legislature from pronouncing further sentence? But the nation was not bound by the Constitution. It retains, inalienably, the right to alter its Constitution. Whether Louis XVI were guilty or innocent, the nation retained at any moment, the right to cause him to descend from the throne and to crown, in his stead, any other citizen. Should he be innocent, the right of the nation would be limited to resuming the powers which it had delegated to him; should he be guilty, if he forced the nation to rise and quell the course of oppression, the loss of a crown would not be punishment enough. He must then suffer also the penalty due his crimes.

---

[1] On 20 June 1791 the king and his family had escaped from the Tuileries in an effort to reach the Austrian army. They were recognized, stopped at Varennes, and brought back to Paris under guard. Louis was suspended by the Constituent Assembly, but eventually reinstated: after which he 'accepted' the Constitution and became an inviolable king! It is this anomaly of legislative power and monarchic status on which Maihle here builds his argument.

Here what has the nation done? It has charged its representatives to construct a new Constitution. Invested with its powers, you have not said that Louis XVI was unworthy to be king. You have said that there would no longer be a king in France. It is not because of the guilt of Louis XVI that you have abolished the monarchy, but because you are convinced that there is no liberty without equality and no equality without a republic. You have neither judged nor punished Louis XVI; you have not even, in this matter, considered his person. He was king only by the grace of a monarchical Constitution. Quite naturally, he ceased to be king at the nation's first impulse toward a republican Constitution.

Yet some will oppose the very idea of sentencing Louis XVI; they will invoke the Declaration of Rights; they will tell you that: 'No man shall be punished save by virtue of a law established and promulgated previous to the offense in question, and legally applied.' They will ask what law can be applied to the crimes of which Louis XVI stands accused. What law? In the penal code there is a law designed to punish breach of trust by public officials and, as you know, Louis XVI was in the words of the law itself no more than the first among public officials. That is the law which strikes down traitors and conspirators; that is the law which lays its heavy sword on the head of any man base or rash enough to make an attempt against social liberty.

In vain you will be told that these laws, passed after the Constitution, did not apply to the crimes of a king declared inviolable by that Constitution. No doubt, they could not be applied by those authorities that the Constitution had placed beneath the king; but before the authority of the nation, royal prerogative is clearly null.

Moreover, is it only in the new French code that these laws are found? Have they not existed through all times and in all lands? Are they not as old as society itself?

Everywhere kings were created only to execute the laws which govern us all, to direct the social forces for the protection of property, liberty, and the lives of each of their fellows in society, to assure freedom from oppression to society as a whole: they must everywhere have been inviolable in the sense that to strike against them would have been to strike against the nation they represented. Yet if they broke their vows; if they themselves trespassed against their nation in its supreme rights, or in those of its members; if instead of protecting, they stifled liberty – did not the nation itself have an undying right, rooted in nature, to call them before its tribunals and to cause them to suffer the punishments due to oppressors or brigands? Among our forefathers the Celts, the people were ever ready to assert their ancient rights against the prince. And why? Is not the right of every nation to judge and to condemn its kings a necessary condition, inherent in that social act which placed them on the throne? Is this not an eternal, inalienable consequence of national sovereignty?

When a French citizen, on the banks of the Seine, stopped the casket of William the Conqueror, accusing him of having stolen his field, and permitted the corpse of that prince to be taken to its tomb only after his property had been restored him; when don Henry, judged by the Estates of Castille, underwent first in effigy, then in reality, the most ignominious degradation; when Jeanne of Naples was formally accused of murdering her husband; when French kings, summoned before those assemblies of bishops and lords which called themselves representative of the people, were deposed and condemned to have their hair cropped and to pass the rest of their lives in a cloister;[1] when don Alphonso and a son of Gustavus Vasa were pronounced deposed from their thrones and forever deprived of liberty, the first by the Estates of Portugal, the second by the Estates of Sweden; when Charles I lost his head on the scaffold; when all these princes, and so many others expiated their crimes by a shameful or tragic end, there were no written laws to declare the punishment of a guilty king. Yet it is in the very nature of national sovereignty to supplement, if need be, the silence of written law, to invoke the sanctions entailed by the king's breach of the social contract, or to apply to the crimes of kings the punishments which apply to other citizens.

All the kings of Europe, relying on the credulity of nations, claim they hold their crowns from heaven. They have schooled the people to regard them as agents of the deity who governs men, to believe that their person is inviolable and sacred and beyond the reach of any law. Well then, if the Spanish nation, for example, enlightened by the spirit of France, were to rise and say to its king: 'Originally I gave myself over to kings so that they might execute my will. They abused the power with which I entrusted them. They became despots. Yet I was able to regain my sovereignty. I made them bow before a Constitution, guarantor of my rights. Every year, in representative assemblies, I detailed my plans for peace or for war, for taxation, and for all the branches of administration. At other times a magistrate presented a perpetual barrier in my name against the extension of royal authority. A tyrant overturned all those laws meant to preserve

---

[1] A number of French kings of the Merovingian and Carolingian lines were deposed by their bishops and barons in the course of what appears to have been virtually permanent warfare. The cases are cited at greater length in Huguenot literature, but they hardly provided plausible *judicial* precedents either in the sixteenth or in the eighteenth centuries.

my sovereignty. I sought to reëstablish them, and was crushed by the foreign forces of the Emperor Charles V. After his line ended in Spain, I would have been able to recover my liberty, but the great strength of two rival houses left me only a choice between tyrants. Finally, I am free. Come before my tribunal. Come to give an account of all your royal actions.'

Citizens, do you think that the impunity which Charles IV enjoyed until that day would shield him before a national tribunal?

If the Austrian people, if the Hungarian people, rose up and said to Francis II: 'Not content to perpetuate the despotism of your ancestors, you have gone forth to attack liberty in its native land. The French had declared themselves friend to all peoples, and you have exposed me to their hate, to their execration. For fear that liberty might reach even to me, you sought to banish it from the face of the earth. To this unspeakable project you have prostituted my wealth and my blood. O base king who would infringe on the rights of nature, the rights of men, the eternal rights of peoples, you have nothing but the shame of your aborted attempts. But do you think that, awakened at last from my slumber, I could desire to share your infamy? I must cleanse myself of the shame with which you have covered me in the eyes of the French, in the eyes of all nations, and I can be cleansed only with your blood.'

I ask again, citizens, do you believe that the despot of Hungary would have the right to counter this national justice with the phantom of his inviolability or with the silence of written law about the crimes of tyrants?

Yet would Louis XVI be in a position more favorable? His constitutional inviolability was as nothing before that nation. Further, we could ask him if he was ever truly constitutional king of the French. We could ask him if he did not always have to be false while his right to rule was, like the rights of those kings who still remain, the right of force or violence? We could ask him if all his actions as constitutional monarch prove more, in fine, than that he was able to add blackest ingratitude to the other crimes of tyranny? How had he not transgressed or plotted against the very basis of society, against property and against individuals; what villainy had he not committed or abetted when the French nation awoke for the first time in '89? Instead of punishing him as it could have, as it should have, the nation had the goodness to retain him on the throne and even, by its goodness, sought to make him just.

What was his response? After having accepted all the articles of the Constitution, he made his well-known protestation of the twenty-first of June: he declared that he was not free; that his acceptance had been forced. That was a signal for foreign powers to come to his aid. They did not come soon enough. He sought to join them, to speed their preparations and their progress. Once again, the nation forgave him. The Constitution, newly revised to favor him the more, was offered once again for his approval. He approved it. Yet to foreign lands he said nothing to undo the effects of his earlier protestation. Instead of calling back, containing, and thwarting his brothers and the other émigrés, who since the start of the Revolution begged in his name for a coalition of despots, he continued to support them with the favors and the money of the nation and paralysed all precautions of the legislature. Instead of forestalling the Prussian and Austrian invasion, he organised treason in all the border towns and districts.

Must we not, then, conclude that his general acceptance in September was no more sincere than his partial acceptances, that they were all a feint to keep him on the throne, to let him await the brigands there, the more readily to reëstablish despotism on the ruins of the Constitution? Then he would always have continued his protestations. He would never have truly accepted a constitutional throne. He would have been in a state of constant war with the nation. And today, brought before the justice of the nation, he would come forward to appeal to that Constitution by which he himself would never willingly have been bound, that Constitution which he would have used only to flood France with blood and to assure the success of his own plots against liberty.

What! If a tyrant had stabbed your wife or your son, there is no Constitution which could punish you for yielding to that first impulse of your soul which drove you to answer their cries for vengeance with the death of their assassin; there is no Constitution which could prevent you from calling down upon his head the censure of divine and human laws: rights and duties of nature are of an order higher than human institutions. And a people, whose rights are equally founded upon nature — would an entire people have no right to avenge itself for the treachery of one man who, having agreed to execute its supreme laws, having been granted the power to do so, abused that power and made himself their oppressor and their murderer? Citizens! Do you think that you can depart from the great principles of natural and social justice? Is not your duty clearly marked on all the objects which surround you, near and far? marked in the still smoking cinders of the brave city of Lille? on the gates of Longwy and Verdun stamped with the seal of treachery and infamy? on the unwonted atrocities practiced by a flood of cannibals unable to bear even for an instant the gaze of the soldiers of liberty, yet who for a few days had been strong with those treacheries of which Louis XVI stands accused? Do you not still have before your eyes the image of the deadly bullet which, during the tenth of August, menaced the nation in the very sanctuary of its laws? Do you not, deep in your hearts, hear the echoing voices of the citizens who died at the doors of the palace of the Tuileries and the cries of many a new Decius, patriots who, in giving their lives for their country, have carried to the grave the hope of being avenged?[1] Do you not hear the republic, with one voice, remind you that vengeance is an object of your mission? Do you not see all the nations of the world, all present and future generations press about you, waiting in silent impatience to learn if he who was originally charged with executing the laws could ever make himself independent of the people who made those laws. Is royal inviolability the right to oppress or murder citizens and society with impunity? Is a monarch a god, whose very blows must be cherished or, if a man, must we bless his crimes?

Louis XVI can be judged. He can be judged for crimes which he committed while constitutional monarch. But by whom, and how should he be judged? Will you refer him to the tribunal of his home district, or to the tribunals of the places in which his crimes were committed? Those who have suggested these methods to the Legislative Committee maintained that he should enjoy no sort of privilege.[2] Since constitutional inviolability, they add, cannot shield him from judgment, why should he be distinguished from other citizens, either by the method of his trial or by the nature of the court? The answer is that all our present courts were created by the Constitution and that the effect of the king's inviolability was precisely that he could not be judged by any such authority. His inviolability ceased to exist only before the nation. The nation alone has the right to arraign Louis XVI for his crimes against the Constitution. Consequently, the National Convention itself must either judge his crimes or refer the matter to a tribunal formed by the nation as a whole.

The Committee therefore weighed only these two propositions. Those who did not wish the Convention itself to judge Louis XVI presented a proposal which gave rise to long debate. They proposed that the National Convention should serve as grand jury. It would appoint six of its members,

[1] On 10 August 1792 the Tuileries were stormed by national guardsmen and Parisian *sans-culottes* organized by the Commune. Louis took refuge with the Assembly, but his Swiss Guard remained behind to fight. In the ensuing battle, the popular forces suffered some 500 casualties; the Swiss were defeated and massacred. Publius Decius was a Roman consul who died heroically in battle (340 B.C.): see Livy, *History of Rome*, Book 8, section 9.

[2] Unfortunately, no records have survived of the Committee's discussion. These suggestions, as well as the proposal that Louis be judged by a national tribunal, presumably came from members sympathetic to the Gironde. The case for a national tribunal is made in detail in Condorcet's speech below.

two to present the case to them and four to prosecute should an indictment be found.

Louis XVI would be brought to the bar. In his presence, the two members so appointed would detail the grounds for indictment, would analyse the evidence, and would present the bill of indictment. Louis XVI, either personally or through counsel, could reply with anything he might judge helpful to his defense. Finally the Assembly would approve or disallow the indictment.

If the bill of indictment was approved, the four members of the Convention appointed prosecutors would continue the trial before a tribunal and a jury which would be composed in the following manner: The electoral body in each department would return the names of two citizens so as to form a panel of jurors. These names, 166 in all, would be presented to Louis XVI, who would have the right to challenge 83 of them. If he did not make full use of this right, the number would be reduced by lot.

The tribunal would be composed of 12 judges, chosen by lot from the chief justices of the criminal tribunals of the 83 departments.

The jury's decision would be based on an absolute plurality. The tribunal would pass sentence. It would be necessary to provide for the case in which the judges were equally divided.

The Legislative Committee rejected this proposal, preferring to let Louis XVI be judged by the Convention itself. But how should this be done? A way has been suggested which would approximate within the National Convention the divers forms that the law provides for criminal trials.

First, the deputies who would present the case to the jury, those who would act as public prosecutors, and those who would act as judges, would be chosen by lot. Next, the remaining members of the Convention would be placed, again by lot, either in the grand or in the petit jury. This system has but one merit, that the defendant, in the course of his trial, will not find one person exercising two functions.

Yet is it true that the National Convention, should it decide to judge Louis XVI, must submit to the forms prescribed for criminal trials?

The English Parliament is reproached for having violated those forms. Yet on this subject there are misunderstandings, and it is essential that these be dispelled.

Like Louis XVI, Charles Stuart was inviolable, but like Louis XVI he betrayed the country which had placed him on the throne.[1] Independent

---

[1] This is the most common historical reference in the speeches: an account of the trial of Charles was being sold in Paris in 1792.

of all the authorities established by the English Constitution, he could neither be accused nor judged by any of them: that could be done only by the nation. When he was arrested, the House of Lords was all of his party. It sought only to preserve the king and royal despotism. The House of Commons seized all parliamentary power; and doubtless this was justified by the circumstances. But Parliament itself was only a constitutionally established body. It did not represent the nation in the plenitude of its sovereignty, but only in those functions specified in the Constitution. The Parliament, therefore, could neither judge the king, nor could it delegate the right to judge him. It ought to have acted as the legislature acted in France; it ought to have asked the English nation to form a convention. Had the House of Commons followed this course, the bell would have tolled for monarchy in England. That celebrated writer who would be the greatest of men had he not prostituted his pen to apology for monarchy and nobility, would never have had grounds to say, 'It was a fine spectacle to see the vain efforts of the English to reestablish the republic among them, to see the astonished people seeking democracy and finding it nowhere, to see them finally, after many jars and much tumult, forced to rely once again on the government they had but lately proscribed.'[1] Unfortunately, the Commons was ruled by the genius of Cromwell, who himself desired to be king under the title Protector; and the ambition of Cromwell would have been crushed beneath the heel of a national convention.

It was not, then, the violation of the forms prescribed in England for criminal justice, but the default of national power, the protectorate of Cromwell, which cast over the trial of Charles Stuart that odium with which even the most detached accounts are suffused. Charles Stuart deserved death, but this punishment could have been ordered only by the nation or by a tribunal chosen by the nation.

In the ordinary course of events, judicial procedure may be considered the safeguard of the fortune, liberty and life of citizens. The judge who departs from it may, with good reason, be accused either of ignorance of the principles of justice or of wishing to substitute his own passions for the will of the law. Yet all the complicated apparatus of legal procedure would plainly not be needed if society itself passed sentence on the crimes of its members. For a society which makes its own laws must surely know the principles of justice by which it wishes to be ruled, and must know as

---

[1] The passage is from Montesquieu, *The Spirit of the Laws*, Book III, section 3. Maihle has altered the text somewhat, but has not changed the meaning. Cf. the translation of Thomas Nugent (New York, 1949), p. 20.

well, that to wrong its members through disorderly passion is to wrong itself. Particular tribunals, distributed in the divers parts of an empire, may be moved by local interest, personal motives, or the grudges of private men. It is to avoid these drawbacks as much as may be done that the law has distinguished and detailed the means of administering justice: changes of venue, formal objections, and all other procedures set bounds to the power of tribunals. But these considerations, though valid for private persons, disappear in the case of a society. If society has an interest in punishing its guilty members, it has an interest greater still in finding them all innocent. Its pride, as well as its strength, lies in preserving them all, embracing them all with its love and protection, unless they prove themselves unworthy of it, provoke its vengeance through actions hurtful to the general interest. A society which, in sentencing one of its members, would not consult the interests of all, would clearly be moving toward its own destruction; and a political body can never be assumed to desire its own harm.

The National Convention entirely and perfectly represents the French Republic. Those men whom the nation has given Louis XVI as judges are the very men whom the nation has chosen to debate and decide its own interests. These are the men to whom it has entrusted its peace, its fame, and its happiness, the men whom it has called to chart its destiny, that of the citizens, and that of all France. Unless Louis XVI insists upon judges susceptible of corruption by foreign gold, could he wish for a tribunal more imperturbable or less suspect? To reject the National Convention or any of its members would be an attempt to reject the nation; it would be to attack the basis of society. Here we need not question the opinions or actions which prepared the fall of monarchy. All Frenchmen share your hatred for tyranny, they all equally abhor monarchy which differs from despotism only in name. Yet this sentiment is foreign to Louis XVI. You are to pass judgment on the crimes of a king, but the accused is no longer a king. He has resumed his original title; he is a man. If he is innocent, let him prove it, if he is guilty, his fate should serve as an example to the world.

Need your verdict for or against the former king be ratified by all the citizens gathered in communal or in primary assemblies? The committee has debated this question too, and recommends that it be dismissed.

In Rome, the consuls judged all criminal cases. Yet when they passed upon an offense against the sovereignty of the people, or any capital crime, the verdict had to be submitted to the people, which was the court of last resort.

In Sparta, when a king was accused of breaking the laws or of betraying the interest of his country, he was judged by a tribunal composed of his college, the senate and the ephors: and he had the right to appeal their decision before the people assembled.

But neither the consuls of Rome, nor the kings, the senate and the ephors of Sparta, truly represented the nation. How far they were from having or meriting that full exercise of popular sovereignty with which the National Convention is invested! Moreover, that which was called the people of Rome or the people of Sparta was but the people of a single city, ruling all the provinces of the republic. However numerous were the people enclosed within common walls, they might yet assemble to discuss, to deliberate, to judge; and it is this which is no longer possible for the people of France. And if the French people cannot meet together, how can a verdict be submitted to them? How could they render a verdict? The French people have no need to assemble to accept or reject the Constitution with which you will present them. Each citizen will look into his heart and will find his answer there. But to pass on the life of a man, one must have the documents, the evidence of guilt, before one. One must be able to hear the defendant, should he claim his natural right to speak directly to his judges. These two elementary conditions, which cannot be violated without injustice, are so incapable of fulfillment that we will dispense with considering all those other conditions which equally would force us to dismiss any plan to submit your verdict to the members of the Republic for ratification.

Of Marie-Antoinette we have said nothing. She was not in the charge that directed the report which I now make to you in the name of the committee. She neither should nor could have been. By what right could her case be treated like that of Louis XVI? Have the heads of those women who bore the name of Queen in France ever been any more inviolable or more sacred than the heads of the mob of rebels and conspirators? When you come to consider her case, you will decide if there are grounds for bringing charges against her, and it is only to ordinary tribunals that those charges then can be sent.

Nor have we spoken of Louis-Charles. The child is not yet guilty, for he has not had time to share in the iniquities of the Bourbons. However, you must weigh his fate against the interests of the Republic. You will have to judge the great sentiment that sprang from the heart of Montesquieu: 'In countries where liberty is most esteemed, there are laws by which a single person is deprived of it . . . [and] I must own . . . that the practise of the freest nation that ever existed induces me to think that there are cases in which a veil should be drawn for a while over liberty, as it was customary to cover the statues of the gods.'[1]

The time is perhaps not distant when the precautions of free people will no longer be necessary. The tottering of thrones that once seemed most secure, the active and happy prosperity of the armies of the French Republic, the political current which is electrifying all humanity, everything announces the imminent fall of kings and the reëstablishment of all societies on their original foundations. Those kings who have escaped the vengeance of the people, or whose exemplary punishment was not necessary to the interests of the human race, can privately parade their shame. For then, these tyrants and all those who might have been tempted by ambition to replace them will be no more to be feared than Dionysius at Corinth.[2]

Here is the plan of the law which the committee has asked me to present to you.

The National Convention enacts the following:

Article 1. Louis XVI can be judged.

Article 2. He will be judged by the National Convention.

Article 3. Three commissioners chosen from the Assembly and appointed by a roll-call vote, requiring an absolute plurality of all votes, will be charged to gather together all evidence, documents and proofs relative to the crimes with which Louis XVI is charged, and to present this material to the Assembly.

Article 4. The commissioners will conclude their report with a bill listing all the crimes with which Louis XVI has been charged.

Article 5. The report of the commissioners, the evidence on which it is based, and their bill will be printed and distributed.

Article 6. Eight days after the distribution of the report, discussion of the bill of indictment will open. This bill will be accepted or rejected by roll-call vote, and will require an absolute majority.

Article 7. If this bill is accepted, it will be communicated to Louis XVI and any defenders he may see fit to choose.

Article 8. Similarly a copy of the report of the commissioners and all the documentary evidence will be given to Louis XVI.

Article 9. The original of these documents, should Louis XVI ask to see them, shall be brought to the Temple and afterwards returned to the

[1] *The Spirit of the Laws*, Book XII, section 19; trans. by Thomas Nugent, p. 199.
[2] Dionysius the Younger, tyrant of Syracuse, for whose instruction Plato was brought to the city, was exiled to Corinth in 343 B.C.

National Archives by twelve commissioners who may not relinquish them nor lose them from view.

Article 10. The originals will be taken from the National Archives only after a copy, not to be taken from those Archives, has been made.

Article 11. The National Convention shall fix a date for the appearance before it of Louis XVI.

Article 12. Louis XVI, either himself or through counsel, shall present a written defense, signed by his own hand.

Article 13. Louis XVI and his counsel may also furnish, should they wish, a verbal defense which will be duly recorded by the secretaries of the Assembly and presented for the signature of Louis XVI.

Article 14. After Louis XVI has presented a defense, or after the time accorded him to provide such a defense has expired, the National Convention will pass judgment by a roll-call vote.

2. MORISSON

13 November 1792

No one in the Convention spoke for sacred kingship, though it has been said that Charles-François-Gabriel Morisson, a lawyer from the Vendée, oldest of the men represented in this book (he was in his fifties in 1792), was a believer in his heart. The first deputy, and one of the only ones, to defend the king, he worked out the line of argument used by Louis' attorneys in December: an appeal to the Constitution of 1791, where the ancient inviolability of kings still found a place. It is distinctly a lawyer's argument, and it includes, no doubt for political reasons, a repudiation of Louis' conduct that was probably insincere. Morisson faced an agonizing choice on the final roll-calls. He finally decided not to vote at all, since he did not believe a king could be judged, though he knew that his abstentions meant one less vote for life and then for reprieve.

In August of 1793, Morisson was denounced on the floor of the Convention for intrigues with royalist agents – an accusation usually fatal in those months of Jacobin supremacy. But he somehow survived the Terror and was elected later on to the Council of 500, where in 1796 he successfully carried a decree of amnesty for the royalists of the Vendée. Under Bonaparte, this man who refused to judge the king judged more ordinary citizens in the court of appeals in Bourges.

Citizens, since we have before us a question of the gravest importance, a question which touches the essence of polity as well as the principles of justice, any decision we make ought to follow only after the fullest discussion. And if, among the speakers there is one who presents an opinion at variance with the majority, it is precisely he to whom we should listen with the greatest attention. Error is often useful to make the truth more clearly felt. It is the shadow in a painting which defines the forms.

Citizens, I invoke these truths on my own behalf. My opinion appears isolated. It is in opposition to that of the majority of delegates. But in this assembly, the love of approbation must yield to duty; in this assembly, too, my very errors may have their use. I beg of you then, in the name of France, hear me out in silence, however shocking some of my reflections may appear.

Citizens, like you I am overcome with the greatest indignation when I consider the many crimes, the atrocities, with which Louis XVI is stained. My first and doubtless most natural impulse is to see this bloody monster expiate his crimes by the cruelest torments that can be devised. I know that he has earned them all. Yet I must deny my impulse: before this tribunal, representing a free people who seeks happiness and prosperity in acts that are just, in acts that are humane, generous, and kind, because only through such acts can happiness be found, I must deny my impulse, and heed instead the voice of Reason, consult the spirit and the disposition of our law, seek only the interest of my fellow citizens, for that alone must be the single goal of all our deliberations.

Your legislative committee, of which I have the good fortune of being a member, has proposed for discussion three questions: Can the king be judged? By whom ought he to be judged? In what way may he be judged? Without departing from the principal object of our present discussion, Citizens, I would like to propose to you another series of questions, a series of which only the first is to be found among those proposed by your committee.

Can Louis XVI be judged? Is it in the interests of the Republic that he be judged? Do we not have the right to take, with respect to him, measures for the general safety? Finally, what ought these measures to be?

I will undertake to discuss in succession each of these questions: and if the Convention finds itself in accord with me, it will not entertain the report of the committee, but will adopt the measures I propose. In general terms, that is the end I seek.

Can Louis XVI be judged? Citizens, I approach this question among a people exercising, without constraint, the plenitude of its sovereignty. I have no intention of contesting their rights: I shall always respect them.

But these rights have limits, limits all the more sacred in that nature herself has fixed them for the happiness of the entire human race.

Citizens, we all come into this world susceptible to diverse passions which act upon us, often in opposition to one another. We should be continually agitated and continually unhappy did we not have the power to resist some of these passions, and rather to give ourselves over to those which will lead us most surely toward our happiness.

We have this power and yet to exercise it we must sometimes compel ourselves to consider before we act. What is true for each man is true for the nation as a whole. To determine a course of action, we must do more than ask if we have the power to carry it out. Sometimes we must resist our most natural impulses and suspend all action the better to weigh the consequences. If these few mild precautions are taken, our judgment always has a faithful governor: benevolent acts lead to personal happiness; just acts alone can bring honor and prosperity to nations.

Thus a sovereign people has no other rule than its supreme will. Yet as the will of any people must be that it flourish, and as nothing save justice can promote this end, its rights and its powers have as their limits such duties as justice dictates. Citizens, it is by these principles that I will be guided in examining whether Louis XVI can be judged.

I know well that kings, as they were first conceived, were no more than delegates of the people; that their function, their duty, was to execute the general will and to guide it for public prosperity by all the means at their disposal. He among them who was guilty of treason or of some other crime was, in fact, answerable for it. This is clear, as in their original societies men could seek only their mutual advantage, and it was certainly in the interest of all to punish the traitor and the miscreant.

Yet this right to judge kings, irrevocable from its source in the sovereignty of peoples, may nevertheless receive modifications in the manner of its exercise. For example, a nation might establish by a precise article of its social contact that despite its inalienable right to pronounce sentence, given a crime and a conviction, the accused person will not be judged, will not be sentenced, unless before his crime there existed a statute which he has contravened. Thus our neighbors, the English, have for many years acquitted their criminals in those cases unprovided for by statute law. Thus, since the establishment of juries among us, the greatest scoundrel would be acquitted if our penal code had no statute which could be applied to him.[1]

[1] Juries were first introduced in France, for all criminal cases, by a law adopted in the Constituent Assembly, 30 April 1790.

I would go further, for it is a consequence of my principles that a nation, be it by superstition, ignorance, or reasons of interest well or ill considered, can declare a magistrate inviolate: that is, he cannot be indicted while in office, and if he commit any crime, he can suffer no punishment but discharge.

I fully agree of course that such a declaration can bind only a people who wish to hold to it. To claim the contrary would be to challenge the sovereignty of the people. That, I repeat, has not been my intention. Yet when a nation has promulgated a law, although it be a bad law, although that nation have the right to change the law at will, nevertheless, that changed law cannot have a retroactive effect, and the previous law must apply to all events which took place while it was still in force. One cannot dispute this truth without doing injury to the most basic principles of justice, principles sacred to all orderly nations, principles unknown only to tyrants.

Let us return to Louis XVI. In order to judge him according to our institutions, there must be a statute which can be applied to him. Yet no such law exists. The penal code, which takes precedence over all previous criminal law, decrees that those who betray their country be put to death. It is evident that Louis XVI has betrayed his country; he has been guilty of the most horrid perfidy; again and again he has forsworn himself; his aim was to enslave us beneath the yoke of despotism; he caused part of Europe to rise against us; he delivered up our positions and those of our brothers; he sacrificed our bravest defenders; he sought everywhere to create anarchy and disorder; he sent the coin of France to her armed and united enemies; he ordered the slaughter of thousands of citizens who committed no crime against him but that of loving liberty and their country. The blood of these unhappy victims still runs warm in the streets; they call upon all France to avenge them. But here we are religiously ruled by law; coolly, as impassive judges, we consult our penal code. Well, that penal code has no provision which may be applied to Louis XVI, since when he committed his crimes, there was a written law which carried an express exception in his favor; I refer to the Constitution.

Citizens, when I open that work, a work that is without question disorderly and unreasonable, a work that contradicts the first principles of social order, but nevertheless, a work which governed us all at the time when these crimes which we now lament took place among us, I find within it these articles:

'The person of the king is inviolable and sacred.

'If the king put himself at the head of an army, and direct the forces of it against the nation, or if he do not oppose, by a formal act, any such enterprize undertaken in his name, he shall be held to have abdicated.

'After abdication, express or legal, the king shall be in the class of citizens, and may be accused and tried like them, *for acts posterior to his abdication.*'

'The person of the king is inviolable and sacred.' That inviolability was, we were told, introduced only in the interest of the people, and not as a privilege for the king. And no doubt, this was the purpose, as the interest of the people is the sole purpose of all social institutions. But the king found advantages for himself as well, just as magistrates find some little advantage in the exercise of the functions with which they are entrusted. Surely no one would seek to deny so self-evident a proposition.

The king, you will reply, was inviolable only by virtue of the Constitution; the Constitution is no more and his inviolability has ceased with it.

Citizens, here I must remind you of a truth without which we would have been plunged long since into all the horrors of anarchy: laws that have not been abrogated by other laws continue to exist, and every citizen is obliged to obey them, for his own good and for the good of all. What holds true for laws in general is true for the Constitution. With the exception of those portions which have been negated by laws or acts posterior to it, such as the elimination of the monarchy and the establishment of the Republic, the Constitution stands.

Yet I will concede that the Constitution no longer exists. But, I ask, should a law which existed at the time of a crime, and which established a penalty for it, be ignored when the punishment for that crime is later deliberated, even if that law has been abolished in the interim? I cannot believe that anyone acquainted with the first principles of equity would dare answer this question in the affirmative.

What! you will reply, Louis XVI constantly violated the Constitution; by all possible means he sought to destroy it and with it the liberty which should have followed from it. And now you wish to permit him to take advantage of that same Constitution which he himself never sincerely adopted!

Yes, citizens, yes. That is what I propose. The Constitution was the law of my country without the consent of the king; it was law by the will of the sovereign, the people, who swore to maintain it until such time as, by the exercise of their sovereign powers, they might make laws in greater harmony with their love of liberty and equality. Yes, if I broke the laws of the land, albeit I had never approved them, I ought nonetheless to suffer punishment according to those laws. And if they contained some clause favorable to my position, I would have the right to ask for that benefit, to ask it of the sovereign which would have no right to refuse since my right sprang only from its supreme will, a will which it can change only for the future. Fortunately these maxims are incontestable. Fortunately for us, we practice them daily.

Finally, you will say to me that the Constitution declared inviolability only for those acts which were essential to monarchy, and for which ministers were, in fact, responsible. Citizens, I hope you will accept my response to this objection.

The king was only, so to speak, the head of his council; everything was done in his name, yet he answered for nothing since the ministers, his subalterns, were independently responsible, each for his own department. Thus he could not be punished for his exercise of executive power since, as I have said, his agents were in fact the ones responsible.

Yet he could commit crimes which were independent of his position as the foremost public official. Like any other citizen, he could form an alliance with the enemies of his country, furnish them aid, send them the coin of the realm. He could place himself at the head of an army; he could cause the slaughter of his fellow citizens; he could, in other words, like any other corrupt and evil man, attempt to commit all those crimes of which he stands accused. Therefore the sovereign people which is always the arbiter of justice did not wish that he escape punishment, nor that his inviolability should protect him, since for these crimes there was no other responsible agent, there was no one to pay the penalty to society or to offer society any satisfaction.

Yet by formulating its supreme will into statute, the people determined what punishment would be inflicted upon him, and that punishment was merely the forfeit of his throne, a punishment which it judged to be perhaps more rigorous a penalty for a despot than all those now meted out by our penal code. If some still doubt these truths, these doubts can be easily allayed by the text of the Constitution itself. Here it is: 'After abdication, express or legal, the king shall be in the class of citizens, and may be accused and tried like them, for acts posterior to his abdication.' The proposition is evident. Citizens, that was the will of the sovereign. We must now reverently respect that will.

You say, we cannot avoid passing judgment on Louis XVI because our mission demands it absolutely. You are mistaken, citizens, you do not have before you now the task of judging Louis XVI. I call my conscience to witness, I call upon all my colleagues in the legislature, I call upon all the citizens of the Republic.

Louis XVI would have overwhelmed us with the weight of his perfidy. That liberty of which we were the trustees was, perhaps, about to slip from our hands, had the throne of Louis XVI existed for an instant longer. We had an obligation to overthrow it, but there . . . our powers stopped. And if the welfare of the nation was, for a single instant, our supreme law, if that law, the first among all, gave us duties as well as rights, we ought to have stopped when we had taken such measures as were necessary to preserve the general safety and our liberty.

Our powers ceased when the king was king no longer. If Louis XVI committed perfidious crimes, he merited, a thousand times over, he merited the forfeit of his throne, which was the penalty set by the Constitution. That penalty should have been pronounced against him in a regular and legal manner. I repeat, our powers had ceased to exist. We had only one course of action: to call upon the people, to call together a National Convention. And we did so.

The National Convention was formed. It had been formed to pronounce upon that forfeiture, to write a new constitution, to make new laws of governance, and during that time, to conduct the government in the most advantageous possible way.

The National Convention therefore, was called to pass upon the deposition of Louis XVI; but convinced with reason that the existence of liberty and public prosperity is not compatible with the existence of a king, the Convention abolished the monarchy. From that moment, Louis had ceased to be king in law. From that moment, there were no more kings, and I fervently hope that they will never, never again defile the soil of the French Republic.

I recognize that the foundation of the Republic, and the suppression of monarchy are in no way a statutory judgment against Louis XVI, and are in no way a punishment directed against him as a man. A sovereign people can change the form of its government at will. It can dethrone its kings, even though they be guilty of no crime. But here, the National Convention, charged with the question whether Louis XVI had been deposed, has nothing more to decide since, by his de facto deposition, he has already undergone the only punishment determined for those crimes which he committed while he was yet king.

And if the National Convention did have the mission of making further judgment on Louis XVI, I maintain that that mission could not be fulfilled, since a judgment within the social order can consist only in the application of a preëxisting law. And as there is no further preëxisting law which might be applied to Louis XVI, there may now be no further sentence passed against him. I believe I have demonstrated these propositions. There is no law which can be applied to Louis XVI.

You will respond that the indefeasible laws of nature apply. Louis XVI is the avowed enemy of the nation; kings are the avowed enemy of the human race; they are savage beasts which must be destroyed at every chance in the interest of society, in the interest of all humanity.

Citizens, hear me out. I shall always respect the laws of nature. They are the sacred base of all our rights. In society, however, as these rights can only be exercised reciprocally, it was necessary to indicate limits, so as to avoid conflict, so that each individual might exercise his rights with the greatest possible latitude. These limits are determined by statute law and by that law alone.

'If a savage king', you say, 'had murdered my wife or my son, surely I would have the right to assassinate him in turn?'

Yes, at the moment of the crime, since at that moment you would be driven by a passion too violent to be resisted. But if the assassin of your wife or your son had been taken by officers of the law, if he was under the protection of the law, if several days had passed since your first rush of passion, do you think that you could assassinate him in turn? Certainly not. And if you did, you yourself would be a criminal.

Well then, this same truth may be applied to Louis XVI. If, on the tenth of August, I had found him, a dagger in his hand, covered with the blood of my brothers, if I had known on that day, known as a certainty, that it was he who had given the order to slaughter the citizens, I would have been the first to snatch him from this life and from his crimes. My right to such an act comes from nature, from my principles, from my heart. No one would have dared stop me.

But several months have passed since that horrible scene, since the last acts of treachery. Now he is entirely under our control; he is without arms, without means of defense. We are Frenchmen, that says enough. We should drive from us the furies of righteous vengeance and heed only the voice of reason. Reason will lead us, quite naturally, under the rule of law. And the law, as I have said before, and as I repeat with regret, the law says nothing about this guilty man, despite the enormity of his crimes.

Now Louis XVI can only fall under the sword of the law. The law says nothing concerning him. Consequently, we cannot judge him.

But is it really so much in the interest of the French Republic that he be judged?

Citizens, permit me to remind you at this moment of the love, the enthusiasm, of the Frenchman for liberty, the energy of a free people, the constantly replenished means of this rich and fertile land. Without doubt, whatever becomes of Louis XVI, he can never again enslave us.

At a time when Louis XVI was strong with our strength, when he held our strength enchained by his arbitrary will, when the despots of Europe were allied behind his cause, when our sense of community had made but little progress, Louis XVI saw the scepter of tyranny broken in his hands. And can you believe, Representatives, that he is still to be feared today, when he is no longer in a position as favorable to him as it was perilous for us, when the despots, his allies, flee before our brave soldiers, when the dawn of liberty heralds our victorious forces everywhere, when our neighbors will soon be our imitators and our friends? Yes, citizens, such fear would be cowardly; such fear would be an insult not only to Frenchmen, but to the entire human race.

And if the yoke of despotism were still to be feared, do you really believe that the death of Louis XVI could keep it from us? Does he not have a son, brothers, kinsmen who should succeed to his claims and who would inherit his means to threaten our liberty? In the place of one head cut off others will appear, and our position will be unchanged. England caused the head of the criminal Charles Stuart to fall upon the scaffold, and yet England is still subjected to a king. Rome, on the other hand, was more generous and merely exiled the Tarquins; and Rome for many years enjoyed the happiness of being a republic.[1]

It is in no way in our interest to judge Louis XVI. That was the second proposition I wished to prove to you, and I have fulfilled my purpose.

But do we not have the right to take, with respect to him, measures for the general safety? Louis XVI is certainly our enemy; we have surprised him in the midst of the blackest treason. He was armed against us, we attacked, and we conquered. We broke the spell of his strength, we took him captive; now he is in our hands and entirely in our power.

Citizens, this is the moment for consulting the code of nations, the rights of war, and we will find that we may unquestionably regard Louis XVI as the prize of victory, keep him forever prisoner, exile him, or ask for ransom if his partisans should wish to have him once again.

These are our rights, citizens. Now let us consider which is the path we should follow. We could keep him prisoner here, but we must consider the disadvantages of this measure. Louis XVI in captivity could continue to

---

[1] According to Livy, Lucius Tarquinius was formally deposed and his exile decreed at an assembly of the Roman people called by the tribune Brutus. The king himself was out of the city at the time and was never allowed to return: *History of Rome*, Book I, sections 59–60.

attract followers. There are men who, incapable of rising to the height of the Revolution, are sufficiently weak and ignorant to have a fondness for monarchy and kings. There are factious men who would profit from this weakness and ignorance to spread anarchy and disorder among us as a means of destroying our liberty. They would seek to raise themselves on our ruins, sacrificing their clay idol in the process. Such undertakings would meet with no success. The example of the past may speak here for the future. Factions, however, are a malady of society and especially of republics, and we should be prepared to forestall them.

It is true that if we were to take that course, we could extract a very considerable ransom. I have even heard, in the committee for surveillance, that we could get one hundred millions. But in dealing with a question which touches on general security, Frenchmen are too strong to be swayed by financial considerations.

Citizens, the measure most in harmony with our principles, with our interests, with our natural generosity, would be, in my opinion, to drive him from French soil, to leave him complete freedom to solicit aid against us among all the powers of Europe, whence he will bear his remorse or the impotent rage which his defeat occasions.

Thus he will teach the world a double lesson: that kings have power only by the ignorance of the people; and that the people are free as soon as they are resolved to be so.

In any event, our position will be unchanged, since all the despots will necessarily be our enemies, or at least those who have the courage or the power to declare themselves against us. I will go further: we would find a sure advantage in that Louis XVI would be a burden upon them.

It is in this course of action, Citizens, that we will avoid a monstrous and interminable trial, perhaps with untoward results. It is in this course of action that we can be sure of finding the general approbation which we will have earned by having fulfilled our obligations. Finally, it is in taking this course that we shall be truly great, truly worthy representatives of a people who desire always to be free and generous.

Consequently, I move that the resolution of the committee not be considered, and I propose the following substitute:

'Whereas Louis XVI has several times perjured himself; whereas he has committed acts of treason against the French nation; whereas he had a plan to enslave that nation under the yoke of despotism; whereas he had raised a part of Europe against that nation for the aforementioned purpose; whereas he caused the coin of France to be passed to her enemies who were armed and allied against her; whereas by precise orders he caused the slaughter of many thousands of citizens who had committed no other crime than that of loving liberty and their country;

'Whereas it would be strict justice to cause Louis XVI to expiate his crimes on the scaffold; but if the French nation wishes to show him mercy, it has the incontestable right to keep him imprisoned as an enemy conquered and taken while armed, and it could equally exile him from its territory, as a vicious and dangerous man, unworthy of partaking in the advantages of the social contract:

'Whereas a penalty, however just, should be applied only when it serves the interest of society, and as the death of Louis XVI can be of no public utility, as France is too strong, both in principle and in the infinite resources of its territory, ever to be enslaved by Louis XVI and all the despots of the world,

'Finally, whereas the nature of all Frenchmen is to be generous, even with their most cruel enemies, be it enacted by the National Convention:

'Art. I.   Louis XVI is forever banished from the soil of the French Republic.

'Art. II.   If, after his expulsion from France, Louis XVI should ever return, he will be punished by death. In this case, all citizens are enjoined to attack him as an enemy, and a reward of 500,000 pounds will be paid to anyone who can furnish proof of having taken and slain him on French soil.

'Art. III.   This present decree shall be sent to the divers powers of Europe with whom we have political or commercial relations.'

3. SAINT-JUST
13 November 1792

Louis-Antoine-Léon Saint-Just came to the podium immediately after Morisson. This was his maiden speech; he had not been a member of the Constituent or Legislative Assemblies; he was 25 years old. No doubt he had waited impatiently through the first months of the Convention for an occasion when he could utter such bold and striking propositions as he now put forward. His was the most brilliant speech of the debate and the first statement of what can be called the authentic Jacobin position. The way was open, for Robespierre had been silent on the subject of the king's trial, and at the Jacobin club the members had confined themselves to the strident demand that Louis (somehow) be brought to justice. Saint-

Just had already advanced himself as a theorist: in 1791 he published a small book, imitative of Montesquieu, *L'Esprit de la Révolution*, in which he defended the new Constitution and even the new monarchy. Now he left that work behind him; his new inspiration was Rousseau; he spoke less of *esprit* and more of *volonté*. He was to become the theorist of the Terror — its principles are already implicit in this speech — and the best and the cruelest of Jacobin orators. In the January voting, he was also one of the briefest: 'Because Louis XVI was the enemy of the people, of its liberty and its happiness, I conclude for death.' He was guillotined himself, with Robespierre, in July 1794.

I shall undertake, citizens, to prove that the king can be judged, that the opinion of Morisson which would respect inviolability and that of the committee which would have him judged as a citizen are equally false, and that the king ought to be judged according to principles foreign to both.

The legislative committee, which has given you sound counsel about the vain inviolability of the king and the maxims of eternal justice has by no means, it seems to me, developed all the consequences of these ideas. The draft proposed to you has no root in these principles and so cannot draw strength from them.

The single aim of the committee was to persuade you that the king should be judged as an ordinary citizen. And I say that the king should be judged as an enemy; that we must not so much judge him as combat him; that as he had no part in the contract which united the French people, the forms of judicial procedure here are not to be sought in positive law, but in the law of nations.

Failing to make these distinctions, the committee fell into forms without principles, forms which would lead to the king's impunity, which would make him too long our cynosure, or which would leave on his sentence a stain of unjust or excessive severity. I have often observed that mistaken measures of prudence, delays, and reflections were here truly imprudent; and after the measure which retards the time when we shall be given laws, the most baneful would be that which would cause us to temporize with the king. Some day, perhaps, men as far removed from our prejudices as we are from those of the Vandals, will be astounded at the barbarousness of an age in which to judge a tyrant might be thought impious, where the people, having a tyrant to judge, raised him to the rank of citizen before examining his crimes; and thought rather of what would be said about them than about the task in hand; and when they made of a guilty man, belonging to the lowest class of humanity, I mean the class of oppressors, a martyr to their pride.

Some day men will be astonished that in the eighteenth century humanity was less advanced than in the time of Caesar. Then, a tyrant was slain in the midst of the Senate, with no formality but thirty dagger blows, with no law but the liberty of Rome. And today, respectfully, we conduct a trial for a man who was the assassin of a people, taken *in flagrante*, his hand soaked with blood, his hand plunged in crime.

Those same men who are to judge Louis are charged with founding the Republic. Those who attach any importance to the just punishment of a king will never found a Republic. Among us, subtlety of spirit and of character is a great obstacle to liberty; we embellish all error and, more often than not, truth for us is only the seduction of taste.

In the report which has been read, your legislative committee has given you an example; Morisson has given you a more striking one. In his eyes, liberty and national sovereignty are matters of fact.[1] Principles have been advanced, and their most natural consequences have been ignored. A degree of uncertainty has become apparent since the report. Everyone sees the trial of the king from his own point of view. Some have not yet abandoned monarchy: they fear an example of virtue which would be a bond of public spirit and unity in the republic. Others seem to fear that later they will suffer for their courage: they lack all energy. The disputes, the perfidies, the malice, and the anger which show themselves in turn are meant to entrap that soaring vigor of which we have such need; else they are a mark of the impotence of the human spirit. We must courageously advance toward our goal and if we wish a Republic, strive toward it seriously. We judge ourselves with severity, even with zeal; we think only of tempering the energy of the people and of liberty whereas we hardly reproach our common enemy; and everyone, either from weakness or shared guilt, looks to the others before striking the first blow. We seek liberty, and we are becoming each others' slaves. We seek nature, and live armed like wild savages. We desire the republic, independence, and unity, and we are divided and treat gently with a tyrant.

Citizens, if the people of Rome, after six hundred years of virtue and of hatred for kings, if Great Britain, after the death of Cromwell, saw kings reborn despite their energy, what must not those good citizens among us fear, those who are friends of liberty, seeing the axe tremble in our hands, seeing a people, from the first day of its liberty, respect the memory of its chains! What sort of Republic can we create in the midst of private quarrels and common weakness?

---

[1] Saint-Just is elliptical here, but he presumably means that Morisson had spoken as if liberty and national sovereignty had already been achieved, whereas for Saint-Just they are principles still to be enforced.

Some men search for a law which would allow the punishment of the king. But in the form of government from which we come, he was indeed inviolable with respect to each citizen. Between the people as a whole and the king, I do not however recognize any natural bond. It may be that a nation, stipulating the clauses of the social contract, might cloak its magistrates with dignity so that rights would be respected and laws obeyed by everyone. But that dignity, being for the profit of the people, has no warrant against them; it is theirs to give and to take away and can shield no one from their judgment. The citizen are bound by the contract; the sovereign is not; else the prince would have no judge and would be a tyrant.[1] Thus Louis' inviolability did not extend beyond his crime and insurrection, for, if his inviolability were found to continue, if his inviolability were so much as considered, the result would be, Citizens, that he could not have been deposed and that the people would have been accountable for his power to oppress them.

The social contract is between citizen and citizen, not between citizen and government. A contract affects only those whom it binds. As a consequence, Louis, who was not bound, cannot be judged in civil law. The contract was so oppresive as to bind the people and not the king; such a contract was of necessity void, since nothing is legitimate which is not sanctioned by ethics and nature.

All these reasons should lead you to judge Louis, not as a citizen, but as a rebel. By what right, moreover, would he require us to judge him in civil law, on account of our obligation toward him, when it is clear that he himself betrayed the only obligation that he had undertaken towards us, that of our protection? Is this not the last act of a tyrant, to demand to be judged in conformity with the laws that he destroyed? And, Citizens, were we to grant him such a trial, that is, in conformity with the laws, that is, as a citizen, by that means he would try us, he would try the people itself.

For myself, I can see no mean: this man must reign or die. He will prove to you that all his acts were acts of state, to sustain an entrusted power; for in treating with him so, you cannot make him answer for his hidden malice: he will lose you in the vicious circle created of your very accusations.

Citizens, thus it is that the oppressed people, in the name of their will, secure themselves with indissoluble chains forged of their own pride, whereas ethics and utility should be the single rule of laws. Thus, pricing

---

[1] The word 'sovereign' here refers to the people as a whole. In the next paragraph, Saint-Just draws a further conclusion from the premise that only citizens are bound by the social contract: the prince is not bound either, for he is not a citizen. So sovereign and prince face one another as enemies.

our errors too high, we play at combatting them, rather than marching forward to truth.

What judicial procedure, what investigation, would you undertake into the enterprises and the pernicious designs of the king? Having first recognized that he was not inviolable for the sovereign people, and then, having seen his crimes writ large with the blood of the people, having seen the blood of your defenders flow, so to speak, to your feet, even to this image of Brutus, let us respect the king no longer. He oppressed a free nation; he declared himself its enemy; he abused its laws; he must die to assure the tranquillity of the people, since to assure his own, he intended that the people be crushed. Did he not review the troops before combat? Did he not take flight rather than halt their fire? What steps did he take to quell the fury of the soldiers? The suggestion is made that you judge him as a citizen, whereas you recognize that he was not a citizen, and that, far from protecting the people, he had them sacrificed to himself.

I will say more: a Constitution accepted by a king did not bind citizens; they had, even before his crime, the right to proscribe him and to send him into exile. To judge a king as a citizen, that will astound a dispassionate posterity. To judge is to apply the law; law supposes a common share in justice; and what justice can be common to humanity and kings? What has Louis in common with the French people that they should treat him well after he betrayed them?

A man of great spirit might say, in another age, that a king should be accused, not for the crimes of his administration, but for the crime of having been king, as that is an usurpation which nothing on earth can justify. With whatever illusions, whatever conventions, monarchy cloaks itself, it remains an eternal crime against which every man has the right to rise and to arm himself. Monarchy is an outrage which even the blindness of an entire people cannot justify; that people, by the example it gave, is guilty before nature, and all men hold from nature the secret mission to destroy such domination wherever it may be found.

No man can reign innocently.[1] The folly is all too evident. Every king is a rebel and an usurper. Do kings themselves treat otherwise those who seek to usurp their authority? Was not Cromwell's memory brought to trial? And certainly Cromwell was no more usurper than Charles I, for when a people is so weak as to yield to the tyrant's yoke, domination is the right of the first comer, and is no more sacred or legitimate for one than for any

[1] This is the most famous of Saint-Just's sentences. It should be compared with the following passage from his *Spirit of the Constitution*, written only a year earlier: 'The monarch [under the new Constitution] does not reign, whatever be the sense of that word, he governs...' (chapter VIII).

other. Those are the considerations which a great and republican people ought not to forget when judging a king.

We are told that the king should be judged by a tribunal, like other citizens ... But tribunals are established only for members of the polity, and I cannot conceive by what lapse of the principles of our social institutions a tribunal could be judge between king and sovereign. How could a tribunal have the power to give us a master and to absolve him, and how could the general will be cited before a tribunal?

We will be told that the verdict is to be ratified by the nation, but if that is possible, why can the nation itself not pass judgment? If we did not feel the weakness of such ideas, whatever form of government we might adopt would find us slaves. The sovereign would never be in its place, nor the magistrate in his, and the people would be unshielded from oppression.

Citizens, the tribunal which ought to judge Louis is not a judiciary tribunal: it is a council; it is the people; it is you. And the laws which ought to guide us are those of the law of nations. It is you who must judge Louis, but you cannot be a court of law, a jury, and a prosecutor; a formal trial would be unjust; and the king, regarded as a citizen, could not be judged by the same men who accused him. Louis is an alien among us; he was not a citizen before his crime; he had no suffrage, he could not bear arms. Since his crime, he is still less a citizen, and by what abuse of justice would you make him a citizen to condemn him? As soon as a man is guilty, he leaves the polity. Quite the contrary, Louis would gain entry by his crime. I would say more: if you declare the king a citizen, he will slip from your grasp. What obligation of his would you allege in the present state of things?

Citizens, if you are eager that Europe admire the justice of your verdict, these are the principles which ought to determine it. Those which the legislative committee proposes are a monument of injustice. In such a trial, forms are a mockery; you will be judged according to your principles. I shall always contend that the spirit in which the king is judged is also the spirit in which the Republic will be established. The theory behind your verdict will be that of your public offices, and the measure of your philosophy in the verdict, will be the measure of your liberty in the Constitution.

I repeat: a king cannot be judged according to the laws of the land, or rather, the laws of polity. The committee admitted as much, but for them the idea died before it could bear fruit. There was nothing in the laws of Numa by which to judge Tarquin; nothing in the laws of England by which to judge Charles I: they were judged according to the law of nations.

Force was used to repel force, to repel an alien, an enemy. That is what legitimized these expeditions, and not empty formalities which have no principle but the consent of the citizen by the contract.

I shall never place my personal will in opposition to the will of all. I shall desire what the people of France or the majority of its representatives may desire. But, as my personal will concerns a portion of the law which has not yet been written, I shall open my mind to you.

It is not sufficient to say that in the order of eternal justice, sovereignty is independent of the existing form of government and thence to infer that the king should be tried. Natural justice and the principle of sovereignty must be extended to the very spirit in which the trial is conducted. We will have no Republic without these distinctions which permit all the parts of the social order their natural movement, just as nature creates life from a union of elements.

All that I have said, then, is proof that Louis should be judged as an enemy alien. I might add that it is not necessary that the sentence of death be sanctioned by the people. The people can pass laws by its will, since these laws are vital to its happiness; but the people itself can not erase the laws against tyranny; the rights of men against tyranny are private; and there is no act of the sovereign which can truly oblige a single citizen to pardon such a crime.

Therefore, you must decide if Louis is the enemy of the French people, if he is an alien. If the majority of you decide to absolve him, then that verdict must be ratified by the people, for if no act of the sovereign can truly constrain a single citizen to pardon the king, how much the less can an act of the magistrature constrain the sovereign!

But make haste to judge the king, for there is no citizen who does not have the right that Brutus had over Caesar; and you could no more punish such an act committed against that alien than you could have found fault with the death of Leopold and Gustave.[1]

Louis was another Catiline: the murderer, like that Roman consul, would swear that he saved his country. Louis waged war against the people: he was conquered. He is a barbarian, an alien, a prisoner of war; you have seen his perfidious schemes; you have seen his army; the traitor was not king of the French, he was king of a band of conspirators. He raised secret troops, he had private magistrates, he regarded the citizens as

---

[1] This passage seems to justify in advance the assassination of Louis, though Leopold II, brother of Marie-Antoinette, died a natural death; Gustave III of Sweden was assassinated on 30 March 1792 as he was preparing to join the war against France.

his slaves. Secretly, he had proscribed all good men of courage. He is the murderer of the Bastille, of Nancy, of the Champ-de-Mars, of the Tournai, of the Tuileries; what enemy, what alien has done us more harm? Wisdom and discretion speak with one voice: let him be judged promptly. He is a kind of hostage, preserved by villains. They seek to move us to pity; soon they will buy our tears; they will do anything to touch us, to corrupt us. People! If the king is ever absolved, remember that we are no longer worthy of your confidence and that you may accuse us of perfidy.

4. PAINE

2 1 November 1 7 9 2

Thomas Paine sat in the Convention as the deputy for Pas-de-Calais, Robes-pierre's home district, where he had been the candidate of the Incorruptible's local associates (Robespierre himself accepted the call of the Parisian electors). They knew him as an international revolutionary, a hero of the American struggle, an out-law in his native England. He was all that, and it is as an internationalist that he speaks here, less against Louis than against the other kings of Europe, still firmly on their thrones. But the *Robespierristes* had misjudged their man: Paine was a friend of Brissot and Condorcet; his political principles were those of the Gironde. Equally important, perhaps, his moral principles were those of his Quaker parents. He was absolutely opposed to the death penalty, and that opposition was at the root of his future conduct during the trial of Louis.

Paine had joined the French Revolution, but he spoke French hardly at all. His speech, written in English, was translated by Condorcet and read to the Conven-tion by Maihle, then serving as secretary. The call for a full exposure of the king's conspiracies' probably stems from the dramatic news of the previous day, when the discovery of Louis' *armoire de fer*, a secret cabinet full of incriminating documents, had been announced to the Convention. It was now clear that Louis had in fact plotted with the agents of foreign monarchs at war with France: he too was an internationalist.

I think it necessary that Louis XVI should be tried; not that this advice is suggested by a spirit of vengeance, but because this measure appears to me just, lawful, and conformable to sound policy. If Louis is innocent, let us put him to prove his innocence; if he is guilty, let the national will deter-mine whether he shall be pardoned or punished.

But besides the motives personal to Louis XVI, there are others which make his trial necessary. I am about to develop these motives, in the language which I think expresses them, and no other. I forbid myself the use of equivocal expression or of mere ceremony. There was formed among the crowned brigands of Europe a conspiracy which threatened not only French liberty, but likewise that of all nations. Every thing tends to the belief that Louis XVI was the partner of this horde of conspirators. You have this man in your power, and he is at present the only one of the band of whom you can make sure. I consider Louis XVI in the same point of view as the two first robbers taken up in the affair of the Store Room; their trial led to discovery of the gang to which they belonged. We have seen the unhappy soldiers of Austria, of Prussia, and the other powers which declared themselves our enemies, torn from their firesides, and drawn to butchery like wretched animals, to sustain, at the cost of their blood, the common cause of these crowned brigands. They loaded the inhabitants of those regions with taxes to support the expenses of the war. All this was not done solely for Louis XVI. Some of the conspirators have acted openly: but there is reason to presume that this conspiracy is composed of two classes of brigands; those who have taken up arms and those who have lent to their cause secret encouragement and clandestine assistance. Now it is indispensable to let France and the whole world know all these accomplices.

A little time after the National Convention was constituted, the Minister for Foreign Affairs presented the picture of all the governments of Europe — those whose hostilities were public and those that acted with a mysterious circumspection. This picture supplied grounds for just suspicions of the part the latter were disposed to take, and since then various circumstances have occurred to confirm those suspicions. We have already penetrated into some part of the conduct of Mr Guelph, Elector of Hanover, and strong presumptions involve the same man, his court and ministers, in quality of king of England. M. Calonne has constantly been favoured with a friendly reception at that court.[1] The arrival of Mr Smith, secretary to Mr Pitt, at Coblentz, when the emigrants were assembling there; the recall of the English ambassador; the extravagant joy manifested by the court of St James' at the false report of the defeat of Dumouriez, when it was communicated by Lord Elgin, then Minister of Great Britain at Brussels — all these circumstances render him [George III] extremely suspicious; the trial of Louis XVI will probably furnish more decisive proofs.

[1]Calonne had been Controller-General from 1783–7; he was now a chief advisor to the king's younger brother, Artois, seeking to organize the counter-revolution.

The long subsisting fear of a revolution in England, would alone, I believe, prevent that court from manifesting as much publicity in its operations as Austria and Prussia. Another reason could be added to this: the inevitable decrease of credit, by means of which alone all the old governments could obtain fresh loans, in proportion as the probability of revolutions increased. Whoever invests in the new loans of such governments must expect to lose his stock.

Everybody knows that the Landgrave of Hesse fights only as far as he is paid. He has been for many years in the pay of the court of London. If the trial of Louis XVI could bring it to light, that this detestable dealer in human flesh has been paid with the produce of the taxes imposed on the English people, it would be justice to that nation to disclose that fact. It would at the same time give to France an exact knowledge of the character of that court, which has not ceased to be the most intriguing in Europe, ever since its connection with Germany.

Louis XVI, considered as an individual, is an object beneath the notice of the Republic; but when he is looked upon as a part of that band of conspirators, as an accused man whose trial may lead all nations in the world to know and detest the disastrous system of monarchy and the plots and intrigues of their own courts, he ought to be tried.

If the crimes for which Louis XVI is arraigned were absolutely personal to him, without reference to general conspiracies and confined to the affairs of France, the plea of inviolability, that folly of the moment, might have been urged in his behalf with some appearance of reason; but he is arraigned not only for treasons against France, but for having conspired against all Europe, and if France is to be just to all Europe we ought to use every means in our power to discover the whole extent of that conspiracy. France is now a republic; she has completed her revolution; but she cannot earn all its advantages so long as she is surrounded with despotic governments. Their armies and their marine oblige her also to keep troops and ships in readiness. It is therefore her immediate interest that all nations shall be as free as herself; that revolutions shall be universal; and since the trial of Louis XVI can serve to prove to the world the flagitiousness of governments in general, and the necessity of revolutions, she ought not to let slip so precious an opportunity.

The despots of Europe have formed alliances to preserve their respective authority and to perpetuate the oppression of peoples. This is the end they proposed to themselves in their invasion of French territory. They dread the effect of the French revolution in the bosom of their own countries; and in hopes of preventing it, they are come to attempt the destruction of this revolution before it should attain its perfect maturity. Their attempt has not been attended with success. France has already vanquished their armies; but it remains for her to sound the particulars of the conspiracy, to discover, to expose to the eyes of the world, those despots who had the infamy to take part in it; and the world expects from her that act of justice.

These are my motives for demanding that Louis XVI be judged; and it is in this sole point of view that his trial appears to me of sufficient importance to receive the attention of the Republic.

As to 'inviolability', I would not have such a word mentioned. If, seeing in Louis XVI only a weak and narrow-minded man, badly reared, like all his kind, given, as it is said, to frequent excesses of drunkenness — a man whom the National Assembly imprudently raised again on a throne for which he was not made — he is shown hereafter some compassion, it shall be the result of the national magnanimity, and not the burlesque notion of a pretended 'inviolability'.

5. ROBESPIERRE
3 December 1792

Maximilien Robespierre, deputy for Paris, first among the Montagnards, here repeats the argument of Saint-Just and lends it the authority of an established political leader. Probably the two had consulted earlier, for in mid-November Robespierre was already advising his constituents that it was the law of nations and not the criminal code of France that applied to kings. But he had said nothing at the Jacobin club or before the Convention until this date. Perhaps he felt inhibited by the strong stand he had taken in the Constituent Assembly against the death penalty. In any case, from now on he took a more active part. On 4 December, he proposed again that Louis be condemned to death immediately, without a trial of any sort. What was necessary, he argued, was that Louis be judged, not that he have '*un procès en forme*'. But the Convention refused to take this course, and two days later it adopted a decree, drafted by the deputy Quinnet and consistent with the Maihle report, establishing a procedure which at least partially followed that of a normal courtroom.

But though he did not carry the Convention, one senses in this speech Robespierre's peculiar power. 'He will go far', Mirabeau had said of him, 'because he believes everything he says.' His speeches have something of the tone of sermons;

they are exhortations to republican virtue, denunciations of monarchic vice. When he voted for death in January, Robespierre repeated his central theme. 'I know only one way to conquer [tyranny]: it is to raise the French character to the heights of republican principles. . .'. What is sadly unclear, however, is that he had any more faith in ordinary Frenchmen than a Calvinist preacher in fallen humanity.

Citizens, the Assembly has unwittingly been brought far from the true question. There is not trial to be conducted here. Louis is not an accused man. You are not judges. You are, and you can only be, statesmen and representatives of the nation. You do not have a verdict to give for or against a man, but a measure to take for the public safety, a precautionary act to execute for the nation. A deposed king in a Republic is good only for two things: either to trouble the tranquillity of the state and to undermine liberty, or to strengthen both. And I maintain that the character of the deliberations hitherto goes directly against this latter aim. In fact, what course of action is wanted to unite the new-born Republic? Is it not to engrave on the hearts of all eternal contempt for royalty, and to strike dumb all the partisans of the king? Thus, presenting his crime to the world as a problem, his case as the subject of the most serious discussion, the most religious and the most difficult which might occupy the representatives of the French people, placing an immeasurable distance between even the memory of what he was and the dignity of a citizen — therein lies the secret of making him once more dangerous to liberty.

Louis was king, and the Republic is founded. The great question with which you are occupied is settled by this argument: Louis has been deposed by his crimes. Louis denounced the French people as rebels; to punish them he called upon the arms of his fellow tyrants. Victory and the people have decided that he alone was a rebel. Therefore, Louis cannot be judged; he has already been condemned, else the Republic is not cleared of guilt. To propose a trial for Louis XVI of any sort whatever is to step backward toward royal and constitutional despotism. Such a proposal is counter-revolutionary since it would bring the revolution itself before the court. In fact, if Louis could yet be tried, he might be found innocent. Do I say 'found'? he is presumed innocent until the verdict. If Louis is acquitted, where then is the revolution? If Louis is innocent, all defenders of liberty are slanderers. Rebels were friends of truth and defenders of oppressed innocence. All the proclamations of foreign powers were but legitimate responses to a faction which sought to rule. Even the imprisonment that Louis has suffered until now is an unjust vexation. The members of the Federation, the people of Paris, all the patriots of the French empire, are guilty, and this great trial pending before the tribunal of nature between crime and virtue, between liberty and tyranny, is at last decided in favor of crime and tyranny.

Citizens, take care! You are deceived here by false notions. You confuse the rules of positive and civil law with those of the law of nations; you confuse the relations between citizens with those between nations and an enemy conspiring against them. You also confuse the condition of a people in the midst of a revolution with a people whose government is firmly established. You confuse a nation which punishes a public official while keeping its form of government with one which destroys the government itself. We apply ideas with which we are familiar to an extraordinary case dependent upon principles which we have never put into practice. Thus, since we have become accustomed to see the crimes which we witness judged by uniform rules, we quite naturally have come to believe that under no circumstances can nations with equity proceed summarily against someone who has violated their rights. And where we do not see a jury, a court, a trial, we can find no justice. These terms, applied to ideas they do not commonly express, finish the deception. Such is the natural force of habit that it causes us to regard the most arbitrary conventions, even the most defective institutions, as an absolute rule of true or false, of just or unjust. We do not once imagine that for the most part they must necessarily still spring from prejudices which despotism fostered within us. So bent were we beneath its yoke that we rise with difficulty to the eternal principles of reason; so that everything that aspires to the sacred source of all laws seems, in our eyes, to be tainted with illegality, and the very order of nature seems to us disorder. The majestic movements of a great people, the sublime force of virtue often seem to our eyes like the eruptions of a volcano or the end of civilized society. Certainly the contradiction between the weakness of our customs, the debasement of our spirits, and the purity of principles and energy of character presumed by the free government to which we dare aspire, is not the least cause of the troubles which agitate us.

When a nation has been forced to resort to its right of insurrection, it returns to the state of nature insofar as the tyrant is concerned. How could the tyrant invoke the social contract? he abolished it. The nation, if it deems proper, may preserve the contract still, as it concerns the relations between citizens; but the effect of tyranny and of insurrection is to break completely all bonds with the tyrant and to reëstablish the state of war between tyrant and people. Tribunals and judiciary procedure are constituted only for the members of the polity.

It is too great a contradiction to suppose that the Constitution might preside over this new order of things. That would be to suppose that it could outlive itself. What laws replace it? those of nature, which is the basis of society itself. The salvation of the people, the right to punish the tyrant, and the right to depose him are all the same thing. The methods of procedure are the same. The trial of a tyrant is the insurrection; his sentence is the end of his power; his punishment, whatever the liberty of the people demands.

A people does not judge as does a court of law. It does not hand down sentences, it hurls down thunderbolts; it does not condemn kings, it plunges them into the abyss; such justice is as compelling as the justice of courts. If the people armed themselves against their oppressors for their own safety, how could they be forced to imperil themselves once more in punishing those same oppressors?

We have permitted ourselves to be led into error by examples from foreign lands which have nothing in common with us. To judge Charles I, Cromwell availed himself of a judicial commission; Elizabeth had Mary of Scotland condemned in the same way. It is natural that tyrants who sacrifice their equals, not to the people, but to ambition, should seek to deceive common folk by illusory forms. Here the question is not one of principles or of liberty, but of schemes and of intrigue. As for the people, however, what other law can they follow than justice and reason supported by their unlimited power?

In what republic was the need to punish the tyrant a subject for the courts? Was Tarquin called before the bar? What could have been the reply in Rome, if a group of Romans had dared declare themselves his defenders? What do we do? We invite lawyers everywhere to plead the case of Louis XVI. We consecrate as legitimate, acts which among a free people would have been regarded as the greatest of crimes. We ourselves invite the citizens to meanness and corruption. One day we may well be able to award the defenders of Louis civic crowns, for if they defend his cause, they may hope to be victorious; else you would offer to the world but a ridiculous comedy. And we dare speak of a Republic! We invoke forms because we lack principles; we pride ourselves on our delicacy because we lack energy; we flaunt a false humanity because the sentiment of true humanity is alien to us; we revere the shadow of a king because we do not know how to respect the people; we are kind to oppressors because we lack feeling for the oppressed.

The trial of Louis XVI! but what is this trial if not an appeal from the insurrection to some tribunal or some assembly? When a king has been destroyed by the people, who has the right to revive him so as to create a new pretext for riot and rebellion – and what other effects could such a system produce? By opening an arena to the champions of Louis XVI, you renew the dispute between despotism and liberty; you consecrate the right to blaspheme against the Republic and against the people. For the right to defend the former despot carries with it the right to say all that pertains to his cause. You reawaken all the factions; you animate and enliven a slumbering royalism. One could freely take a position for or against. What is more legitimate or more natural than to repeat everywhere the maxims which his defenders would be able to profess openly at the bar, and from your very rostrum? What manner of Republic is it, whose founders solicit everywhere its adversaries to attack it in its cradle? You see what rapid progress such a system has already made.

In the month of August last, all the partisans of the king were in hiding; whosoever had dared to undertake an apology for Louis XVI would have been punished as a traitor. Today, they raise their audacious heads without fear of punishment. Today, the most disparaged writers of the aristocracy once again confidently take up their envenomed pens or find successors who surpass them in shamelessness. Today, pamphlets which are the precursors of all crimes inundate the city in which you reside, the eighty-three departments, and make their way even to the portals of this sanctuary of liberty. Today, armed men who have come unbeknownst to you and in violation of the laws, have made the streets of this city echo with seditious cries demanding impunity for Louis XVI. Today, Paris encloses in its heart men gathered, you have been told, to snatch him from the justice of the nation. Now you need only open the walls to the athletes who eagerly court the honor of breaking their lances in the royalist cause. What do I say! Today, Louis has a share of the representatives of the people. Some speak for him, some against him. Two months past, who could have conceived that there would be a question whether he was inviolable or not? But from the time when a member of the National Convention presented this idea as a serious question, preliminary to all other debate, inviolability, with which the conspirators in the Constituent Assembly covered their first broken oaths, has been invoked to protect their final outrages.[1] O Crime, O Shame! The tribunal of the French nation has echoed with the panegyric of Louis XVI. We have heard boasts of the virtues and the good deeds of the tyrant. We were barely able to snatch from the injustice of a precipitous decision the honor or the liberty of our best citizens. Worse yet,

---

[1] On 13 November, the Girondin leader Pétion, formerly mayor of Paris, had insisted that the first question before the Convention was still: *can* the king be judged?

we have seen the most atrocious slanders against those representatives of the people known for their zeal for liberty received with a joy scandalous to behold.[1] We have seen one part of this Assembly proscribed by the other almost as soon as it was denounced by folly and perversity combined. The cause of the tyrant alone is so sacred that it cannot be discussed long enough or freely enough. And why should this astonish us? The two parts of this phenomenon stem from the same cause. Those who are interested in Louis or his like must thirst for the blood of partiotic deputies who ask for the second time that he be punished. They can forgive only those who have softened in his favor. Was the plan to enslave the people while slaughtering their defenders at any moment abandoned? And all those who proscribe them today, calling them anarchists and agitators, are they not themselves bound to foment the disorder which their perfidious system promises? If we are to believe them, the trial will last for several months at least, continuing until the coming spring when we can expect a general attack from the despots. And what a chance for the conspirators! what food for intrigue and the aristocracy! Thus all the partisans of tyranny can still hope for aid from their allies; foreign armies can encourage the audacity of counter-revolutionaries while foreign gold tempts the fidelity of the tribunal which is to pronounce on the fate of Louis. What! All the savage hordes of despotism prepare themselves once again to tear at the entrails of France in the name of Louis XVI! Louis still wars against us from the depths of his prison cell; and some doubt if he is guilty and can be treated as an enemy! I should like to believe that the Republic is not a vain word employed to amuse us; yet what other means might they use to reëstablish monarchy?

The Constitution is invoked in his favor. I have no intention of repeating here all the unanswerable arguments brought forth by those who have deigned to combat that sort of objection.

On that subject I shall say but a word for those yet unconvinced. The Constitution forbade all that you have done. If the king could be punished only by deposition, you cannot sentence him to that without a formal judicial proceeding. You have no right to keep him imprisoned. He has the right to seek his release and an award of damages. The Constitution condemns you. Go, throw yourself at the feet of Louis XVI and plead for clemency.

As for me, I should blush to discuss such constitutional logic-chopping

---

[1]At the first meetings of the Convention, Girondin deputies had launched a sharp attack against Marat, whom they accused of inciting violence and seeking a dictatorship: they undoubtedly hoped to catch Robespierre also.

more seriously. I relegate it to the schools, or the law courts, or better yet, to the closets of London, Vienna, and Berlin. I cannot treat further of a subject whose very deliberation, I am convinced, is scandalous.

It is a great case, they say, and must be judged circumspectly, slowly and wisely. It is you who make a great case of it, nay, it is you who make it a case. What do you find great in it? Is it the difficulty? No. Is it the person? In the eyes of liberty there is no one baser; in the eyes of humanity, there is no one more guilty. He can now deceive only those who are viler than he. Is it the utility of the result? That is but another reason for haste. A great case is a bill for the people, a great case is that of an unhappy man, oppressed by despotism. What is the motive of the endless details which you recommend to our attention? Do you fear to cross the opinion of the people? as though the people itself feared anything but the weakness or the ambition of its representatives; as if the people were a herd of slaves, stupidly attached to a stupid tyrant whom it had proscribed, wishing, whatever the price, to wallow in baseness and servitude. You speak of opinion. Is it not yours to direct, to fortify? If opinion errs, if it becomes depraved, whom shall we blame if not you yourselves? Do you not fear the foreign kings leagued against you? O without a doubt, the way to defeat them is to appear to fear them. The way to confound the despots of Europe is to respect their accomplice. Do you fear other peoples? Then you believe in an innate love of tyranny. Why then do you aspire to the glory of freeing the human race? By what contradiction can you suppose that the nations which were unsurprised by the proclamation of the Rights of Man will be struck with panic at the punishment of one of its most cruel oppressors? Finally, you fear, they say, the views of posterity. Yes, posterity will indeed be astonished, by our inconsequence and our weakness; and our descendants will laugh as much at the presumption as at the prejudices of their fathers.

Some say that it would require genius to plumb the depths of this question. I maintain that it requires good faith alone. It is less a matter of self-enlightenment than of avoiding self-deception. Why should what once seemed so clear now seem obscure? Why should that which the good sense of the people can easily decide be altered for the deputies into an almost insoluble problem? Do we have the right to have a will contrary to the general will and a wisdom which differs from universal reason?

I have heard the defenders of inviolability advance a bold principle, one which I myself should have hesitated to bring forward. They said that those who, on the tenth of August, would have sacrificed Louis XVI would have done a virtuous deed; but the only basis for this opinion is to be found in the crimes of Louis XVI and in the rights of the people.[1] Now has the space of three months changed the crimes or the rights of the people? If then he was saved from an indignant people surely it was only so that his punishment, solemnly ordered by the National Convention in the name of the nation, might impress itself the more on the enemies of humanity. But to reopen the question whether he is guilty or susceptible of punishment is to betray the faith given the French nation. There are perhaps people who, either to prevent the Assembly from achieving a character worthy of it, or to take from the nations of the world an example which would raise spirits to the level of republican principles, or from even more shameful motives – there are people who would not be sorry to see a private hand usurp the functions of national justice. Citizens, beware of this trap. Whoever would dare give such counsel serves only the enemies of the people. Whatever may happen, the punishment of Louis XVI is good only in so far as it bears the solemn character of public vengeance.[2] Of what importance to the people is the contemptible person of him who was the last king?

Representatives, what is important to the people, what is important to you, is that you fulfill the duties with which the people have entrusted you. The Republic has been proclaimed, but have you given it to us? You have not yet passed a single law which justifies that name. You have not yet reformed a single abuse of despotism. Remove but the name and we have tyranny still; and moreover, viler factions, more immoral charlatans, new stirrings of disorder and civil war. The Republic! And Louis still lives! And you still place the person of the king between us and liberty! Let us beware turning criminal by force of scruple; let us beware that in showing too much indulgence for the guilty man we join him in his guilt.

A new difficulty: what shall the punishment of Louis be? Death is too cruel. No, says another, life is crueler yet; I ask that he live. Attorneys of the king, is it pity or cruelty which determines your attempts to preserve him from the punishment of his crimes? As for me, I abhor the death penalty dealt freely by your laws; I have neither love nor hate for Louis; I hate only his crimes. I asked for the abolition of the death penalty from the Assembly which you still call Constituent.[3] And it is not my doing if the first principles of reason seemed to them moral and political heresy. But you, who would never invoke those principles in favor of so many

---

[1] The reference is to Morisson's speech, above, p. 117.
[2] Robespierre is repudiating Saint-Just's hint about assassination, above, p. 126.
[3] Robespierre had made a major speech against capital punishment on 30 May 1791 before the Constituent Assembly.

unhappy men whose misdeeds are less their own than those of the government, by what fatal chance do you remember them only now when you plead the case of the greatest of all criminals? You ask for an exception to the death penalty for the only man who could make that penalty legitimate. True, the death penalty in general is a crime since, following the unchanging principles of nature, it can be justified only in those cases where it is vital to the safety of private citizens or of the public. Public safety never calls for the death penalty against ordinary crimes because society can always prevent them by other means and render the guilty man incapable of doing further harm. But a deposed king, in the midst of a revolution as yet unsupported by just laws; a king whose very name draws the scourge of war on the restless nation: neither prison or exile can render his existence indifferent to the public welfare. And that cruel exception to the laws ordinarily accepted by justice can be imputed to the nature of his crimes alone.

Regretfully I speak this fatal truth – Louis must die because the nation must live. Among a peaceful people free and respected both within and without their country, it would be possible to listen to the counsel of generosity which you are given. But a people which is still struggling for its liberty after so much sacrifice and so many battles; a people among whom the laws are not yet inexorable save for the unfortunate; a people among whom the crimes of tyranny are a subject of dispute, such a people must wish to be avenged; and the generosity with which you are flattered would resemble more closely that of a troop of brigands dividing their spoils.

I propose to you an immediate legal action on the fate of Louis XVI. As for his wife, you will send her back to the tribunals, along with all the other people accused of the same crimes. His son will be kept in the Temple until peace and public liberty have a firmer hold among us. As for Louis, I ask that the National Convention declare him, from this moment on, a traitor to the French nation, a criminal toward humanity. I ask that for these reasons, he give an example to the world in the very place where, on the tenth of August, the martyrs of liberty gave their lives; and that this memorable event be consecrated by a monument destined to nourish in the hearts of all people a sense of their own rights and a horror of tyrants; and to nourish in the spirit of tyrants, a salutary terror of the justice of the people.

6. CONDORCET
3 December 1792

The Marquis de Condorcet, mathematician and *philosophe*, friend of D'Alembert and Turgot, provides one of the first examples of the intellectual in politics. But he was not a successful politician, partly because of that dangerous sense of superiority that haunts his successors still, partly because he was no orator; he had no flair for the decisive phrase. In revolutionary politics, more than in any other kind, a gift for public speech is absolutely necessary to the man who hopes to wield power. The text that follows – it will be all too apparent to the reader – was never spoken: it was circulated as a pamphlet in late November and then inserted in the records of the Convention, along with other similar documents, as an 'addition' to the debates of 3 December. It is, nevertheless, the finest Girondin statement and so requires publication here. Condorcet makes the case against inviolability with a great deal more care than was politically necessary; the legal arguments are dense and often hard to follow; but the whole effort suggests the intensity of his commitment to what Saint-Just called 'forms without principles' – that is, to procedural justice.

Like Paine, Condorcet was opposed to capital punishment. On the crucial roll-call of 7 January, he acknowledged that the legally prescribed penalty for treason was death and that to punish the king differently would be 'a crime against equality'. But the death penalty was against his principles. 'I will never vote for it.' He then urged 'the gravest penalty in the Penal Code short of death'. His enemies during the Terror did not have similar compunctions. In the summer of 1793 he was proscribed and forced into hiding (where he wrote his extraordinary *Sketch for a Historical Picture of the Progress of the Human Mind*). Hunted down in March of 1794, he would certainly have been brought to the guillotine, but he died, probably by his own hand, in his prison cell.

In a case where an entire nation has been wronged and is at once prosecutor and judge, it is the opinion of mankind, the opinion of posterity, to which that nation is accountable. It must be able to declare: all the general principles of jurisprudence recognized by enlightened men in all lands have been respected. It must be able to defy the blindest partiality to cite a violation of the slightest rule of equity; and when that nation judges a king, then kings themselves, in their inmost hearts, must feel moved to approve the judgment.

It is important to the happiness of mankind that the conduct of France towards the man it too long called its king should be the final step in curing other nations of whatever superstition in favor of monarchy may remain among them. Above all, we should beware lest we increase that superstition among those still ruled by it. All nations do not recognize the eternal truths, the unshakable foundation of the French Republic; and whereas our philosophers and our soldiers spread them to foreign nations; whereas tyranny trembles as much before our maxims as before our armies, we would be imprudent to surprise, to frighten perhaps, byt the boldness of our actions, those whom we may cause to respect severe but impartial equity. Thus, it is to the laws of universal justice, common to all constitutions, unalterable in the midst of clashing opinions and the revolutions of empires, that we must submit our decisions.

Can the former king be judged?

An action can be grounds for legitimate punishment only if a previous law defined that action expressly as a crime; and it can be punished only with a penalty which likewise was prescribed by a previous law. This is an axiom of humanity and justice.

If, however, the law failed to distinguish in the list of crimes those which circumstances made more heinous, one ought not to conclude that the law wished to exempt them from punishment, but only that the aggravating circumstances did not seem to require the prescription of a specific penalty. The laws of Solon include none against parricide. Shall we conclude that the monster who was guilty of this crime was intended to remain unpunished? No, surely he was to be punished as for a murder.

If then, the laws of France say nothing specifically about a king who conspired against the people, although he be much more guilty than a citizen, it does not follow that he should be spared, but only that those who wrote the laws did not wish to distinguish him from other conspirators. He should be judged then by the usual law, if another law did not specifically exclude him.

Was such an exclusion expressed by the Constitution? Citizens, if such an impunity had been made law, if the Constituent Assembly had committed such a crime against humanity, if the nation had been weak enough to accept that dishonorable law by its silence, by the election of representatives, by the oaths which were demanded of them, then, as a friend of justice, as a friend of liberty, I would say: 'the king cannot be judged and punished'.

But that scandalous impunity was never enacted.

Two articles make this clear. In one, the person of the king is declared inviolable and sacred. The other declared that for all crimes committed after his legal abdication, he would be judged like other citizens.

It is necessary then, to discuss the sense of these two articles; and however minute this discussion may seem, I hope that you will forgive my entering into it, if you but conceive that there is no liberty in a country where verdicts are not decided by positive law alone. Does not the social contract consist essentially in the agreement to submit to previous and common rules those moral relations with other men which are founded on, and whose legitimate principles are determined by, natural law?

In a well-governed state, positive law should be nothing other than a consequence or an application of natural law adopted, approved, or at least already known by the people subject to the law. Thus, the question would not be whether one ought to pronounce sentence according to natural or arbitrary law, but whether actions should be judged according to what was regarded as just when they were committed rather than according to what was regarded as just at some later time.

The person of the king was declared sacred. Either 'sacred' has no meaning, or it has the sense which it is given in the religious principles of the various sects. In the case of unjust acts of violence, there is a crime against religion in addition to the crime against society. In legal convictions, the guilty man is stripped of his rights before the sentence is passed, so as to inspire a greater respect for a personage in a sense supernatural. By this expression, the constitutional king was likened to a bishop, a priest, whose persons were sacred, without, for all that, being exempt from the power of the laws.

The authors of the Constitution who, in instituting monarchy created a power outside of nature, believed it necessary to add superstitious terrors for the security of kings. But the result of that expression is merely that, if monarchy had not been abolished, the deposition would have had to be decreed in a separate judgment.

The word 'inviolable', is not defined by the Constitution as it is applied to the king; but it is defined elsewhere, as it applies to the representatives of the people.[1]

Their inviolability entails two conditions, quite distinct, and both applicable to the king. The first is that they might not be made to suffer for what they did or said as representatives, and as soon as there was a king established by the Constitution he must necessarily have shared in this kind of inviolability.

This prerogative, extended to all the king's executive acts, posed dangers which that of the deputies did not. Thus the king was required to have these acts validated by the signature of a minister responsible for their legitimacy. The nation was not without checks, and if it had not all those

---

[1] For the relevant passages from the Constitution, see the Appendix.

which might be demanded by the principles of justice rigorously applied, at least it had all those compatible with the existence of so bizarre an institution as monarchy.

Thus, all that the king did as the repository of national power cannot be imputed to him. But he is accused by common report of crimes foreign to his royal duties. It was not as king that he paid for libels to ruin the credit of the nation, that he sent subsidies to the enemies of France, that, in concert with his brothers, he formed a league with the enemies of the nation; it was not as king that, in despite of the laws which he himself had approved, he armed foreign troops against the citizens of France.

The other condition of the inviolability of the deputies was that they could not be prosecuted except by decree of the legislature. Thus when the Constituent Assembly discussed the question of the inviolability of the king, this point was mentioned, and with reason, for by the very nature and importance of his functions, he could not be answerable before a tribunal on the summons of those public officials whose conduct he was to oversee. It was shown that the man who had the authority to suspend the formation of laws, the head of the executive, the head of the army and the navy, should not be exposed to the risk of being stopped from these great tasks by the will of a particular tribunal. With the same success, the arguments used to exempt the deputies from the common order of judicial prosecutions were used in his favor.

It is true that the course of justice, should a deputy be prosecuted, was described and that no one dared do the same for the king. But the base maxim, that a king who was an incendiary, an assassin, a parricide, should remain unpunished, never stained the laws of a France already more than half free. Do you believe that if such a servile principle had been inserted into the text of the Constitution, the nation would have consented to adopt, or at least to try the Constitution, and to regard it as a binding law? Would we have dared show it to the world as a Constitution less disfigured by gross violations of natural law than those of the greater part of the nations of the earth?

Some will reply that the inviolability of a king should be complete, since he could have no impartial judge. This is to argue that the magnitude of the crime should become a title to impunity; that crimes against the safety of an entire people should have been placed beyond the reach of the law. Thus, the leader of any conspiracy which had imperiled nation and liberty could say to the people: 'You cannot judge me, for I have wronged you all; there is no one among you whom I have not caused to fear for his rights, for his property, for his life.' And since each man regains his individual right to see to his safety as soon as the law ceases to protect it, this refinement of justice would become the signal for disorder and arbitrary vengeance.

Some will mention, as a proof of that absolute impunity, the article by which the king, in the case of legal abdication, is to be judged for his subsequent crimes like any other citizen. But for crimes subsequent to the period of their duties, the *inviolable* deputies are also judged like other citizens.

The inviolability of the king and of the deputies, expressed by the same word, should be understood in the same way; with this difference alone, that the Constitution prescribed for the latter the way in which they were to be judged, whereas in reference to the king it remains silent. This silence alone was doubtless enough to awaken the indignation of men who cherished in their hearts the sentiment of liberty and equality.

Thus, the impunity of the king was not decreed by the Constitution. Yet that document did not set forth the way in which he was to be judged. It enacted that if he ceased to be king, he would, for his subsequent crimes, be prosecuted and judged like any other citizen; but it decided nothing as to how he might be judged or prosecuted for his prior crimes.

Here I could end my examination of the articles of the Constitution. Indeed, if one is to keep strictly to the letter of the law to decide if a man must be prosecuted or punished, if he cannot be prosecuted or judged when the words of the law do not formally mention him, is it not equally equitable to refuse him privileges beyond those granted explicitly by the letter of the law, especially when exceptions are to be made, and above all, exceptions counter to the usual course of justice, exceptions founded on political considerations? Suppose that we take in the most favorable sense those exceptions which apply to men in general and affect only a few by the laws of chance which are the same for all. Yet shall we do the same for those which might be established in favor of a special class? Does not the imperious law of equality prescribe then that those same exceptions be restricted to what is to be found in the letter of the law?[1]

I shall reply, however, to an indirect consequence of the Constitution, by which some have been struck. The Constitution provides that upon certain offenses committed by the king, his abdication is presumed. For

---

[1] This is a difficult passage. Condorcet's meaning seems to be this: we may interpret the law generously when privileges are being extended or exceptions made which everyone might enjoy (though, by pure chance, only some men do, in fact, enjoy them), but the principle of equality forbids us to do this when what is at issue is the prerogative of a special class – or a single man.

the crimes subsequent to his abdication, it treats him as a citizen. There fore, its intention was, in the case of those other offenses, to subject him only to the loss of his throne, which from that point became the only punishment he might suffer.

An examination of the actions which would provoke the loss of the throne suffices to make us feel the weakness of such an argument.

Indeed, they are all necessarily public actions for which a judicial inquiry would be useless if the general safety permitted the least exception to the principle of submitting all accusations to the same rules of judgment. Moreover, among those very acts, some could be considered not to be true crimes except by the later conduct of the king; others could be prosecuted only in an illusory manner.

Thus, for example, if revoking his oath, if obstinately remaining outside the territorial limits of France, he became guilty by the sole assertion that he retained his right to the throne, one might suppose that that guilt would cease were he to submit to the legal abdication decreed by the Constitution. One might almost consider from the same point of view, his failure to oppose by an official decree any enterprises undertaken in his name.[1]

Finally, in the event that the king might be at the head of an enemy army, the law treating him for his crimes after abdication like any other citizen, could not without absurdity be viewed as an amnesty for all that might have preceded that act of overt rebellion — for the crime, that is of having incited civil war. Why then were the legislators silent? Doubtless they felt that the king was then in a state of open war, and that he could be prosecuted only after having been vanquished while persisting in his rebellion, only after having added new crimes to those which had called for his abdication.

It is impossible to understand these laws any other way. Indeed, how could the same men who would have punished a willful absence by abdication, have wished to see plots for proscription and assassination go unpunished? How would they have punished the retraction of an oath more severely than the violation of that same oath by acts of treason or tyranny? How could failure to resist by a formal decree have seemed more criminal than an ostentatious resistance, belied by perfid-

---

[1] Condorcet is here suggesting that for certain acts of the king, listed in the Constitution, deposition is the appropriate legal response: the king has (implicitly) abdicated; the legislature can do no more than recognize and proclaim this fact. In the next paragraphs, he goes on to suggest that punishment is justified when the king continues to act in a way hostile to the nation after his (implicit) abdication: he can then be judged like any citizen. The whole passage is a tortured effort to defend the constitution-makers of the Constituent Assembly.

ious connivance with those same enemies against whom he pretended hostility?

Is it not more natural to think that the writers of the Constitution were content to mark a legal proceeding for cases so plain as to render useless a judicial investigation, and that they left, to be determined by circumstances, those which would have demanded such an investigation? Doubtless they believed that it would be difficult to plan in advance a form proper to such unforeseen and extraordinary events as must necessarily precede the trial of a king. Is it not enough to be obliged to accuse the majority of the Assembly of timidity and reticence, that Assembly whose wisdom and courage have so just a claim to the gratitude of the nation? How, on the face of it, could we consider that body guilty of having so openly contradicted the same Declaration of Rights that it regarded as its first title to fame? Why, given two ways of regarding the question, should we choose that which assumes in the work of these same men, proclaimed by them on the same day, so shocking a contradiction?

Finally, a man cannot demand favorable conditions for a contract which he did not carry out, or which he openly breached. For example, a debtor whose creditor promised to take no action against him on condition that the debtor give him a house, fully furnished, could legitimately be prosecuted if, following that agreement, he had removed a portion of the furnishing. Why then, might the members of the Constituent Assembly not have believed that the king, in violating the conditions of the Constitution, lost the right to counter judicial prosecutions with that inviolability which he held from the Constitution alone? that he might be judged for the crime of violation of the Constitution by virtue of the principles of common law, and that an explicit statement was not required?

How, moreover, could the Constituent Assembly have set down in the Constitution the method by which the king was to be judged? The legislature, in accord with the spirit of the Constitution, could not have the power to accuse him. To whom could that power belong? To the nation alone, and thence to the representatives which it named to the Convention. It would therefore have been necessary that the Constitution indicate to the National Assemblies precisely the same plan of conduct that the Assembly of 1792 followed on the tenth of August. And if one recalls with what timid circumspection the Constituent Assembly spoke of the inalienable right of the people to change its constitutional laws, one will be less astonished to see that the Assembly has not dared facilitate the exercise of this power by placing in the Constitution a means by which, in the case of serious accusations brought against the king by the citizens, the legislature might call a National Convention.

It has been said that Louis XVI ought not to be judged, for, if he had not counted on an absolute inviolability, he would perhaps have refused the crown. What! he would have refused the crown if he had not been told: You may commit any crime with impunity, you may even betray, for the second time, that people which has given you the throne in recompense for the first betrayal? Yet did Louis XVI, already declared inviolable, and in the same terms, before the first violation of his oath, believe that he was beyond judgment when he was brought back from Varennes? And did Louis XVI not know that his base servants, despite all their vileness and all their power, could not bring about the adoption of this article, so clear and so simple, nay, they could not even cause it to be proposed: 'the king, whatever crime he may commit, shall never be punished therefore, other than by deposition'? How then could he have believed that such was the sense of the articles of the Constitution, since the framers of that document would not even suffer this sense to be brought directly before them? How could he find an assurance of absolute impunity in the distressing silence which met his greatest efforts?

It is time to teach kings that the silence of the laws about their crimes is the ill consequence of their power, and not the will of reason or equity.

The question, then, has been reduced to an examination whether the rule of justice which demands that a prior law determine the offense and the punishment does not also demand that the law which establishes the procedure of judgment be prior.

Now I do not believe that justice demands this. Indeed, the only argument which might cause that priority to be regarded as necessary is this: That the people have a right to the assurance that they cannot be arbitrarily subjected to unjust proceedings, to a proceeding which, created for a single defendant, could be contrived according to personal passions or prejudice. Yet there can be no question here of creating arbitrarily a singular manner of judgment; quite simply, here we must apply the manner of judgment established for others to a single man who is in extraordinary circumstances.

Here, moreover, let us once again appeal to positive law. What is the charge? A crime against the general safety of the state. Who should be the accuser? The assembly of the representatives of the people. Who should be judge? The high court of the nation. Some will say that since this court has been abolished, all acts of treason prior to its abolition cannot be prosecuted, and if the National Convention established a tribunal for these same crimes, it could judge only those which occurred after its creation.

This is the argument which he would have to advance who wished to claim that the king cannot be judged or that the National Convention cannot establish the manner of his judgment.

Some will say that a tribunal ought not to be formed for a particular man. This argument has no consequence but that the king has the right to ask to be judged by an ordinary tribunal. It would follow, moreover, from this maxim, that any difficulty of form which might arrest a judgment, would assure the impunity of the accused whose prosecution had caused the difficulty. Furthermore, that which justice truly demands is that in all forms of judgment, in the choice of judges, in the rules of judicial procedure, the general principles of jurisprudence in favor of the accused should be preserved or even extended.

The crimes imputed to Louis XVI, outside his exercise of royal duties, can therefore be judged and punished like crimes of the same sort committed by any other man.

I would add, that even if we were to accept the impunity of these crimes as legally established, Louis XVI could still be judged.

Indeed, we must not fail to distinguish the right to prosecute and the right to punish. They are not only different in theory, they are so in fact in those lands where the execution of a verdict requires the consent of a power other than the tribunal which passed sentence and where, nonetheless, this power has no authority to suspend criminal investigations. Such, for example, is the law of England, where the king may suspend or remit the sentence; yet he cannot stop prosecutions. Crime is punished to strike fear into those who meditate it. Crime is punished so that those who are guilty cannot do society further harm by new transgressions. Before it can rightfully be punished, a crime must be prosecuted and verified. But is this the only motive which may determine the prosecution and judgment of an offense? Is it not also useful that society know the authors of a crime, though they go unpunished? And if the offense itself is in doubt, is it not useful to know if it is real or imagined? Has not society the right to know exactly how far it has been injured? And how much greater this right is when the safety of an entire people might have been threatened.

France has been betrayed, and it has the right to discover how far and by whom. May such knowledge not be necessary to its safety and influence the precautions which it must take for its defense? Therefore, France has the right to prosecute and judge Louis XVI, even if he enjoys absolute inviolability.

The monarchy is abolished in France; the will of the National Convention is that of the people; this required only the use of an inalienable and indefeasible right. The idea of a nation bound to one of its public officials by ties it might not lawfully break so long as he remained loyal to the conditions of the contract, is a chimera which only the enemies of liberty and equality among men still dare support. Such is the opinion of all members of this Assembly and, doubtless, of all Frenchmen.

Yet other nations may not be of our mind. And if there should be one where a contrary opinion prevails, which considers that the guilt alone of Louis XVI could justify his deposition, how useful then does it become to establish the crimes of the former king, even if his inviolability prevent his punishment. This alone might dissuade those who governed such a country from being hired into the cause of our enemies. Might it not be that the French received the decree abolishing monarchy with such joy because they were convinced of the crimes of Louis XVI? And do you not owe it to them to leave no doubt of the reality of those crimes? Would you be at liberty to deliver the citizens to a plague of uncertainty concerning the most indubitable facts by failing to order that the guilty man be judged?

Thus, even if one gives constitutional inviolability a force most contrary to reason and to justice, it remains true that the French nation can have a real interest in establishing the crimes of the former king; and, as a consequence, that the nation has the right to judge him.

Finally, let us suppose that the National Convention regards that constitutional inviolability as a source of absolute impunity. It remains to be known whether Louis XVI has a right to such a prerogative. In accepting the monarchy in its new form, he was obliged to submit to the Constitution; he was obliged to consider it as a law binding upon him. If he did nothing but receive the crown as the degraded remains of the one to which he believed himself entitled by the absurd right of birth, if the new conditions affixed to the exercise of his office were to him but usurpations to which he feigned adherence, intending to resume his former prerogatives, if there is proof of this perfidy, is it not evident that Louis XVI was never legitimately a constitutional monarch, and that he has no right to any of the prerogatives of inviolability attached to that position by the Constitution alone?

The expression, 'the king accepted the Constitution', was doubtless a political absurdity. The Constitution was not a convenant between the king and the people in the sense that the king could have failed to submit to it without renouncing his throne or that the people could have abdicated their right to change it. Yet it is no less true that, in another sense, any citizen who accepts a position of public trust enters into a contract with the entire nation: one engages himself to serve; the other to procure certain advantages; the contract is reciprocally binding as long as the law remains by which the position was established. The nation retains the right to change the law, but it cannot have the right to violate that law.

Any man who, before signing a contract, protested against those conditions he thought burdensome, cannot legitimately lay claim to those conditions that are favorable to him. Thus let us grant for the moment that Louis XVI, after having broken his engagements, retained his right to impunity, which was one of the advantages accorded with the engagement. Nevertheless, although one may claim that the Constitution reserved such rights for him even after the violation of his promise, it is evident at the least that this same document does not reserve any of these advantages for him in the case of a protestation made in advance or in the case of prior engagements contrary to those contracted for with the nation — above all if he persisted in them after having accepted the crown.

Thus, Louis XVI can be judged, since this protestation and these prior engagements maintained afterward are among the crimes of which he is accused; and it is evident that for such offenses he cannot claim any manner of inviolability.

There is, then, no hypothesis which one might defend to prove that the former king cannot be judged, except that of his hereditary right to the crown, a hypothesis which no Frenchman can admit without guilt, which no man can maintain without madness, vile and stupid.

I would propose, therefore, that since constitutional inviolability cannot be extended to the personal offenses of Louis XVI, it be decreed that he may be judged and punished.

Should the contrary proposition be adopted, I will make the following proposal: (1) that Louis XVI can be judged and punished for the offense of having beforehand protested his acceptance of the crown and of having made prior engagements, maintained since, contrary to those which his acceptance entailed; (2) that for other offenses he may be judged, although, by the decision here assumed to have been adopted, he cannot be punished.

How should Louis XVI be judged?

I shall first try to prove that he cannot be judged by the National Convention. Next I shall indicate what form of judgment seems to me the most proper to demonstrate the justice of the nation, assuring the impartiality of the tribunal and investing in it the necessary authority, derived from public opinion, to pronounce a condemnation or an acquittal without risk of reproach for having yielded to bribery or fear.

Actions which directly threaten the rights or the safety of the nation seem to call for a tribunal which appertains equally to all parts of the Republic. The treasonous acts of a public official whose functions touch the state as a whole cannot, it would seem, be judged by a tribunal limited to any one portion of the country. Thus, the National Convention, a tribunal chosen by it, a tribunal elected by the departments – these are the only possible choices.

Can the National Convention judge the former king? Without a doubt, no. First, he can be judged only in a manner not yet established. The Convention would be at once legislator, accuser, and judge; this accumulation of powers or functions would violate the first principles of jurisprudence. Judges who themselves have declared that they wished to be judges; judges who are subject only to self-given rules, to forms they chose to impose upon themselves; judges who can, in the course of an investigation, change or modify those forms – such judges embody an abuse of power that any society wishing to remain free should not permit. The principle, no less sacred, which demands that the impartiality of judges be beyond suspicion, would be no less violated. Indeed, can those among us who had seats in the Constituent Assembly when Louis XVI gathered an army and threatened at once Paris and the representatives of the people, be judges of a tyrant who plotted against them? Can those among us who were here on the tenth of August, who, if the army had conquered were destined for death, now be judges of the man who proscribed them? Louis is accused of guilty collusion with foreign enemies, and among the crimes imputed to him can be counted the perfidious accord between the plans of the émigré princes and those of the men at the Tuileries. Now, as men who were marked by these infamous plots as victims of the tribunals of the new despotism, can the members of the two Assemblies be judges of him who had consigned them to his hangmen? Some will say that all citizens, all friends of liberty, were equally threatened, and that in consequence of this reasoning, it would be impossible to find any judges. But a brigand who, in spreading terror over the land, menaces all the inhabitants, doubtless is their enemy, and it is in the interests of all that he not go unpunished. However, one will not admit to the number of judges those to whose land he laid waste, those whose persons he threatened; yet one would not suggest the exclusion of the remaining citizens. The impartiality demanded of judges is a personal impartiality, the absence of all interest, of all private passions. Those generous and universal passions by which the entire mass of a people may be moved are not to be feared since, in enlightened men with cool heads, these passions are inseparable from love of justice.

Another principle should place the duties of judge still further from us. He may legitimately be challenged who has, in advance, voiced an opinion on the innocence or guilt of the accused. Because such a man can be moved by that false shame which holds us to our own opinions, he cannot be considered exempt from bias.

And that false shame is quite natural, since fickleness, interest, weakness, and passion are more often the cause of changed opinions than a longer meditation or a deeper study; and public censure rarely forgives such changes. Would it be just to give an accused man judges who, in order to declare him innocent, would be forced to renounce an officially expressed opinion? men sure therefore to be accused of perfidy or corruption, and unable to answer but by admitting to an inexcusable fickleness.

Not only the Legislature, but the Convention itself declared its opinion of the crimes of the former king. The Legislature proclaimed that opinion in several declarations which it adopted and made public in its name. The Convention proclaimed it in a solemn declaration addressed to the Swiss nation.

Finally, let us realize that we are charged to prepare the Constitution which is to be proposed to the people, to clear the road of true equality by discarding a great number of civil laws, to enfranchize several large classes of citizens, to organize public instruction and aid for the poor, and finally, to watch over the defense and the tranquillity of the state at a time when we have at once a powerful league to combat, the scattered remains of one or several conspiracies to stifle, and a social system to regulate from its very foundations.

Can we, in the midst of so much business, give over a portion of our time to the procedure which would be necessary if all the formalities are to be observed rigorously? How would we be able to avoid reproach, either for having spoken too lightly and hastily, or for having lost, in judging the case of one man, time to which the entire nation has a just claim?

Even if at this moment the people would gladly see us take up that duty, should we not fear that the consequent neglect of their other interests, incidents which would make them perceive the disadvantage of such an accumulation of powers, orations, chance words, a display of disapprobation or of ill humor which would cast a cloud over our impartiality, would soon change that first approval to reproach?

The attitude of a tribunal should be more austere than that of a deliberative assembly. In changing our functions from one day to the next, will we be certain of changing our habit as well?

From the frontiers of France (and soon in the far corners of Europe), the voice of calumny can already be heard: 'it is not the people which seeks the judgment of Louis but a handful of factious and splenetic men who have led astray or subjugated the more timid or uncertain spirits'. In vain did the Legislative Assembly, irritated by long combat against the plots of the court, limit itself strictly to the bounds set for it by the Constitution. In vain, disdaining to imitate the usurping ambition of the Long Parliament of England, did the Assembly eagerly move to return to the people powers which were no longer enough to save them. In vain was the Convention formed of men cloaked in the trust of the nation, after the events which cast Louis from the constitutional throne. The enemies of the French Republic dared, nonetheless, to represent to all people, as the enemies of a dethroned king, those who exercised the powers of which he had been stripped. Well then, let us impose silence on these cries of disquieted tyranny, of servitude frightened by the fall of one of its idols. Let the entire nation name the judges, and let its will no longer be misunderstood.

The greater part of the reasons which ought to keep us from acting as judges also forbids our choosing them. The nation alone has that choice; it alone can be regarded as absolutely exempt from any interest other than the common interest, from any special bias.

I will propose, therefore, that Louis be judged by a tribunal whose judges and whose jurors be named by the electoral bodies of the departments. This tribunal, following the principles I have set forth, should approximate, as much as is possible, ordinary tribunals and differ from them only in the great solemnity demanded by the very nature of the accusation and by dispositions more favorable to the accused, since justice demands that in revoking his right to be judged by a common tribunal, his situation not seem the worse.

The electoral bodies of each department would elect a commissioner and a certain number of jurors. This distinction is necessary because the commissioners' duties would presuppose a knowledge of the law and an acquaintance with legal forms, and men should be chosen whom the electors believe meet these conditions.

The jurors will designate those commissioners who will be charged with the prosecution, those who will perform the duties of judge, those who are to defend the accused in the event that he reply but by protestations, in the event that he not find voluntary defenders, or in the event that the partisans of monarchy think it good for their cause that he appear unable to find any.

These official adversaries will help keep us from ceding too readily in the examination of the facts to that interior conviction produced by the entire system of conduct of Louis XVI. That conviction could make the proof of particular facts too easy, and it is important that we convince the nations whose leaders fight us or conspire against us. The secret partisans of the throne await but the moment when they may shroud the crimes of the monarchy in the hasty trial of a king. The individual is nothing for them, and they would willingly sacrifice him if they were able, by reproaching the Republic for an irregular verdict, to acquire a few more friends for the cause of the crown.

The law would grant the accused the right to challenge a certain number of judges. The challenges of the jurors would be allowed in greater number than they are in the usual case. And it would be necessary that after these challenges enough men remained to form a jury, the opinion of which by the very number of its members would have an imposing authority, worthily representing in the eyes of foreign peoples the majesty of a great nation, and banishing all ideas of seduction, of secret practices, of fear, or of bias.

The law demands that a guilty verdict be brought by a plurality of the jurors to two, that is, of eight votes or four-sixths of the total. Although according to abstract theory, a plurality of eight votes, whatever the number of jurors, gives the verdict an equal probability, divers considerations weaken this as the number increases.

It is therefore necessary to demand a greater plurality. On the other hand, the plurality of four-sixths becomes much too large as the number of jurors is increased. Even if the verdict about the truth of a fact can be influenced by differences of opinion foreign to the fact itself, to demand so proportionally great a plurality as does the usual law (given here the very large number of jurors) would not be to assure the truth of the verdict, but to denature it to the point where it was nothing but a duel between the two opinions which would divide the jurors.

It is therefore between these two extremes that we must choose, and the choice should not be made until after the number of jurors has been established.

It has been proposed that what is not public in ordinary trials should be so in this one, but such a change is contrary to the very nature of decisions by jurors. Charged with pronouncing a verdict according to their consciences alone, the jury should retain the most absolute independence; not only the power of the nation, but the opinion of the people should not be able to exercise any authority over it; it should remain free as thought itself. A man who makes such a decision, therefore, would be wrong if he so much as considered public opinion, nay its very existence, though it were the universal verdict of mankind. Knowing this, could you submit the decision, once made, to public opinion?[1]

---

[1] This argument applies also against the proposal for an appeal to the people, a national referendum on the Convention's verdict. Condorcet voted against the appeal in the January balloting.

Such a change would suffice to destroy all the precautions taken to place the impartiality of the nation beyond question in the eyes of Europe. Moreover, it would furnish a dangerous example: no interest, no consideration can permit us to weaken a principle, a sacred guarantee of liberty and of the private safety of citizens.

If it is violated with respect to a man who has been king, who can answer that a proposal will not be made to violate it equally for the head of a party who might be a threat to the state, for a citizen whose case, its importance swollen by his reputation or his talents, divided opinions in the whole nation? Who can answer that soon this same distinction will not be applied to a man who, neither dangerous nor well-known, has made only an empty claim to such qualities, a man whose enemies were eager to endow him with such fatal advantages, the more surely to ensnare him.

Therefore, the judgment of the king should be entrusted to a special jury. The jury should be chosen by all the departments, not because the accused was once a king, but because the crime directly concerns the whole nation. It should be appointed by the electoral bodies, since we are treating of election for a specific body and not of appointing successively citizens for an ordinary duty, as in the naming of common jurors.

I shall pass now to a third question. Where should the king be judged? This question seems to me to have an importance more imagined than real. If there are dangers to the tranquillity which ought to accompany all the acts of this solemn judgment, they are everywhere the same. Everywhere you will find yourselves confronted by either the movements of a great mass of citizens or of an armed force, idle and numerous. Everywhere you will have the same intrigues to outwit, everywhere conspirators will find means of action, differing according to circumstances, but equally dangerous.

As for the importance of opinion, it is weakened by this consideration alone, that objections will always be directed against the course which has been chosen, whatever it may be: there will always be motives to suspect and plans to denounce.

I shall limit myself, then, to two observations: one, that if the judgment is made, according to the natural order, in the place where the crime was committed, where the accused resided, you must give the tribunal the means to surround itself with an independent force to assure the liberty of the deliberations.

If, on the contrary, you decide that it must be done elsewhere, then you must leave the jurors the right to choose the place of their sessions and, in order to assure them complete independence, decide on a city other than Paris for their first meeting, with the condition that this city alone will be excepted from their choice. Since no city other than Paris has been indicated by prior consideration, that exclusion cannot be regarded as a true limit to freedom of choice and by this means that part of the people in the midst of whom the decision will be made will be entirely disinterested.

Should Louis XVI be judged? Should the verdict which will be pronounced against him be executed, whatever it might be? These two questions are essentially distinct, and it is necessary that they be examined separately. Louis must be judged because the precautions which the nation would have a right to take with reference to him, for the general safety, are not the same if he is declared innocent by the tribunal or if, being found guilty, the penalty alone is remitted.

Louis XVI should be judged because the revolution which has led us to the establishment of a Republic had, as its principal cause, the treason of him to whom the Constitution had entrusted all our means of defense.

It is important to prove to Europe, by a juridical discussion which allows cross-examination, that these motives were not chimerical, that they were not a pretext ably seized upon by a small group of men who wished to change the form of the Constitution.

The rights of the nation, doubtless, would not be changed. Abolition of the monarchy, equally, would be legitimate; but it is important for the cause of liberty that its defenders cannot be accused of having misled the people in order to incite them to reassert their legitimate rights. It is important that the nation know if it was led to the moment when the convocation of a Convention became necessary by those who sought to enlighten or by those whose end was to deceive.

The accusers of Louis XVI have the right to demand that a solemn judgment be pronounced between them and him, and that national justice decide if they were rash in their accusations; if they were slanderers or worthy citizens; if they dreamed, imagined, or discovered a great conspiracy.

Finally, if you weigh all the opinions by which France is divided, its relations with other lands, its internal situation, does not all this indicate that the juridical examination of these deeds is necessary, not for public safety, but for the prompt and peaceful consolidation of France?

Are not these oft multiplied proofs of treason already assailed? Has not the neglect of some formalities already been adduced to sap the authenticity or the authority of documents upon which these proofs are founded? Only a formal investigation, permitting cross-examination, before judges who had no part in the discussions raised between Louis XVI and the defenders of the rights of the people, can destroy such objections, scorned today, yet objections which supported by the gold of kings could by accrediting slanders against the French Revolution delay among other peoples the progress of liberty.

In a word, you owe to yourselves, you owe to mankind, the first example of the impartial trial of a king.

Should the verdict, whatever it may be, be executed without consulting the national will, either directly or by means of the representatives of the people? The question here, without doubt, is whether society has the right to sentence a man to death; whether such a penalty may be so necessary as ever to render it just. But the nature of this general question is such that, once it has been raised, there is an obligation to express an opinion. I believe a capital sentence to be unjust whenever it is applied to a guilty man who can be imprisoned without danger to society; and this truth is subject to rigorous demonstration.[1] I believe that, with the exception of this case alone, which should not occur under a truly free constitution once it is well established, the absolute suppression of the capital penalty is one of the most efficacious means for the perfection of the human species, by destroying that penchant to ferocity which has too long been a dishonor to man. I believe that the example of murders ordered in the name of the law becomes all the more dangerous to public conduct as the constitution of a country leaves all men therein a greater portion of their natural independence. Penalties which permit reform and contrition are the only penalties suitable to a regenerate human race.

Let me return to the subject of this discussion. Is the existence of Louis XVI favorable or adverse to sincere or pretended partisans, foreign or French, of constitutional or hereditary monarchy? Does it benefit their plans or not, that the throne which they wish to reinstate may be occupied by a child or must necessarily be occupied by a man made vile by his conduct, odious by his crimes? Is it in the interest of the French Republic to diminish the interval which separates from the throne persons living in foreign lands where they will long be the active and docile instruments of all our enemies?

In a word, as the existence of these hereditary pretenders is a necessary

---

[1]Condorcet may be thinking here of the argument of Beccaria, *On Crimes and Punishments*, chapter XVI. But Beccaria suggests an exception: 'when it is evident that even if deprived of liberty. [the criminal] still has connections and power such as endanger the security of the nation ... The death of a citizen thus becomes necessary when a nation is recovering or losing its liberty ...' — trans. Henry Paolucci (Indianapolis, 1963), p. 46. Condorcet may have the same 'case' in mind in his next sentence.

evil, can the conservation of our liberty be influenced by changes in the order of the claims, in the interest, in the hopes, in the means of the persons called to take part in this absurd substitution?

Will our severity frighten or irritate the enemy kings and the devotees of monarchy? Will the still swaying sentiments of several nations be alienated or encouraged? These are questions to which it is difficult to reply without having been able to observe the effects of our first resolution on France and on Europe. Such questions seem to demand that the National Convention reserve the right to modify the judgment of the tribunal, or to submit it to the people, indicating to them the means of executing it.

If the judgment were favorable, would the nation have lost all rights over the man who had been king? Let us suppose that in the exercise of his usurped authority, a hereditary absolute monarch had committed no injustice, no violence; let us suppose that, blinded by his education, he believed in good faith that his authority was legitimate; let us admit these two hypotheses which no king, perhaps, has ever realized. Can it not be said then, that the involuntary nature of the error remits the penalty? But the right to caution against the effects of this error remains nonetheless. One does not punish a madman, but one takes those measures necessary to assure that he cause no injury. And if the liberty of Louis XVI, innocent, were dangerous for the safety of the nation, doubtless it would retain the right to deprive him of that liberty.

Yet how could we, without injustice, reserve the right to take precautions for our safety in the case of acquittal, without at the same time reserving for ourselves the right to modify the penalty in the case of conviction?

Thus, by giving political considerations all the weight which they might be expected to have, we see that they are foreign to the question of judgment, but that they may influence the commutation of the penalty or the precautions which might be demanded by the interest of the nation. To judge an accused king is a duty; to pardon him can be an act of prudence; to retain the possibility of such a course is an act of wisdom in those to whom the political destiny of a nation has been confided.

I would therefore propose a postponement of the question whether and by whom the judgment may be modified, until the other questions have been decided, and just before the tribunal is seated.

Such are my reflections on a subject which belongs to the order of human things, which philosophy may treat for once according to principles of justice and with a sense of cool impartiality.

Long since kings have been mere men in the eyes of reason; and the time approaches when they will be so in the eyes of government as well. Yet only now when the prejudices which surround a throne have disappeared at last, while yet the influence of kings on the destiny of nations remains, can it be possible, and yet still useful, to put into practice the rights of peoples over these beings beset by error and vileness, phantoms of all manner of superstition.

When Europe has but one king to judge, then his trial, having become an ordinary case, will no longer merit the attention of the world.

7. MARAT
3 December 1792

It was as a journalist that Jean-Paul Marat had his greatest influence. In the Convention, he was often a center of controversy, but he was never an influential deputy. Nor, though he was surely radical enough, did he play an active part at the Jacobin club. He was by temperament unsympathetic to the cold rationality and the republican *hauteur* of Robespierre and Saint-Just. His was a populist and demogogic radicalism, more closely connected than theirs to the mood of the Parisian streets. He was also a republican of the last minute, having long supported monarchy, despite his contempt for King Louis and his passionate hatred for aristocrats. With regard to the trial, he never endorsed the Jacobin position. Though he had, only a few months before, urged the people to 'rise and let the blood of traitors flow again', though he was famous and infamous throughout France for his calls to proscription and massacre, he favored a trial for Louis Capet. That is the position he takes here, in a speech written for the Convention, but never delivered, and published both in that body's official record and in his own *Journal de la Républic français* (successor to the better known *L'Ami du peuple*). A few days later, he intervened in the debate to condemn the demand that the king's death be voted immediately and 'by acclamation'. He sensed the political importance of a trial, its value as an educational spectacle. But he had, of course, no doubt as to what its outcome should be. In January, he voted for 'death within 24 hours'.

The crimes of Louis XVI are unhappily all too real; they are patent; they are notorious. Need we ask if a nation has the right to judge, and to punish by death, a public official raised to the highest rank, when he has concealed himself behind a mask of hypocrisy the more securely to plot against the nation? when he oppressed his countrymen with the authority confided to him for their protection? when he made of the laws an instrument of vio-

lence to crush the partisans of the Revolution? when he robbed the citizens
of their gold as a subsidy for their foes, robbed them of their subsistence
to feed the barbarian hordes who came to slaughter them? when he caused
his hirelings to hoard, to create famine, to dry up the sources of abundance
that the people might die from misery and hunger? when he declared himself the leader of traitors and conspirators? when he turned against the
nation those arms he had been delivered for its defense? when he wove the
plot to have the defenders of liberty slaughtered, to enchain the people
once again? It is an insult to reason, an outrage to justice, a perversion of
nature. Need we ask if a despot, stained with all possible crimes, if a monster still covered with the blood of those friends of France whose slaughter
he had commanded, can be brought to judgment and condemned to death?
To ask such a question would be to mock humanity and to renounce all
shame.

No, Gentlemen, I will not do you the injury of believing that a single
man could be found among you who would question this truth, unless interest led him to do so. If you have made it the basis of the public discussion of the great trial which will soon begin, it is less to illumine a point
under question than to furnish patriotic orators a unique occasion to display
the absurdity of the sophisms used in the defense of the ex-monarch by his
creatures, the partisans of monarchy and the tools of despotism.

Your committee on legislation has made clear by a series of arguments
drawn from natural law, from the law of nations, from civil law, that
Louis Capet should be brought to judgment. That step was necessary for
the instruction of the people; for it is important that all members of the
Republic be brought to this conviction by different routes suitable to their
different spirits. The representatives of the sovereign people can see the
question only in its political aspects.

Among the speakers who preceded me at this rostrum, those who saw
the question from this point of view, harking back to a supposed initial
contract and arguing for the reciprocity of the conditions stipulated between people and prince, have thence inferred that Louis Capet, having
broken his contract by his crimes, has fallen from the throne and can be
considered only as a simple citizen: an erroneous conclusion, laboriously
deduced from a vain sophism. There was never a contract between the
people and their agents, although there was a binding one between the
sovereign and its members. A nation which delegates its powers to agents
does not contract with them; it assigns them some function in the general
interest. They may very well on occasion refuse these functions; yet the
agents remain always accountable to the nation, and it can at any time

withdraw these functions without their consent. Thus, with whatever luster these duties may be surrounded, they should never be considered as anything but an honorable burden. Such are, Gentlemen, the true bonds which exist between the sovereign and its agents. The original contract which has been cited as the basis for these bonds is completely imaginary. If such a contract exists, it is only among conquering nations; and even then, it can have no effect save when the head of the army, become the chief of state, has found the means to inspire fear or rather, when he is in open war with a nation which he has forced to surrender. What! Shall we take the crimes of a usurper as a starting place to establish his prerogatives, and shall we take as legitimate and sacred rights the usurpation of sovereignty by the first agent of the people? Such, nonetheless, is the odious contract which existed between the French and their princes: an iniquitous contract which the representatives of the French people renewed with Louis Capet, heir to the usurped power of his ancestors, after the excess of his speculations had forced him to assemble the Estates General to fill the abyss which he had dug, and after his last attempt, which caused the nation to rise against the tyranny, forced him to lower himself and ask for mercy. Such a contract is null and void, not only because it offends the dearest interests and the most sacred rights of the people, but because the people have not ratified it. All the many loyal addresses their faithless deputies spread out before their eyes, with such complaisance, as unequivocal proofs of their approbation, had been vilely purchased. Rather, I might say, they had almost all been perfidiously presented by counter-revolutionary administrative bodies.

Let us examine the facts: after thirteen centuries of servitude and tyranny, despotism would have been forever struck down had the nation, too long bent under the yoke, been able to stand strong and erect and to keep vigorously its magnanimous resolution to reclaim its rights. Despotism would have been forever struck down if the representatives of the people had had the courage to profit from the consternation of the despot and his henchmen, to cast him from the throne and to reëstablish liberty. But, to our grief, those weak representatives who at first, to remain in their position, gave evidence of resistance to the orders of the tyrant, no sooner saw themselves supported by armed citizens than they compounded with the court and used no more energy than was needed to collect their bribes. Nor did they delay long before setting up a shameful trade in the inalienable rights of the people. Some were even so criminally bold as to confer upon the despot the horrible privilege of disposing of provinces and selling the inhabitants thereof like so many sheep. I shall pass in silence over the long list of injurious, unjust, vexatious, oppressive, and tyrannic decrees passed by a base and corrupt majority, which seemed to have no other end but to shore up despotism under the pretext of regenerating the Empire. Surprised from time to time by a timid minority, these were the fatal decrees which did dishonor to the Constituent Assembly and stained the Constitution; atrocious decrees against which I have so often spoken with bitterness inspired by a holy indignation.

Who does not know the guile with which the faithless delegates of the people piled sophism upon sophism to render the prince sacred and inviolable, to invest in him the supreme executive power, to confer upon him the right to make the principal appointments, to render him the arbiter of the legislature, to raise him above the law, to place in his hands the keys to the national treasury, the care of the public wealth, the disposition of the armed forces, on land and at sea, and the destiny of the state – until the moment when these senators bereft of shame, throwing off their mask and recognizing no further control, undertook with the aid of an organized massacre to turn the public force which they had misled and enchained against the people, designing to have them slaughtered or to forge them new chains. That was the moment when the sham representatives of the sovereign people, on their knees before a simple functionary, substituted for his title of first public official, that of born representative of the nation, invested in him the highest authority, placed all power once again in his hands, and provided a thousand means by which he might, with impunity, effect the ruin of the people and the destruction of liberty by force. And should it be necessary, they provided that he might flee to put himself at the head of enemy armies, suffering no penalty but presumed abdication, to which he might always reply by a simple denial. And that is the monstrous Constitution which, ready to pass like a dream, will nonetheless be forever a source of shame to its authors and which would appear to wise eyes a monument of folly and madness, were it not a monument of venality and villainy. This is the monstrous Constitution which has been made a bulwark for Louis Capet against that nation which he betrayed and whose downfall he so often plotted after having so long been the cause of its distress.

All the same, let us admit for the moment these so called constitutional laws, and let us consider such provisions as must be claimed that the tyrant may elude his bloody deserts. The Constitution declares the person of the king to be inviolable and sacred. But that inviolability, which the legislators were careful to avoid defining clearly, and which is invoked today in favor of Louis the traitor as a certificate of impunity, applied only to the legal acts of the monarch. It was therefore merely the privilege not to be called to account for the choice of means by which the laws were executed. As such, inviolability could have no end but to smooth the course of the political process by preventing constant hindrance to him who was supposed to give it movement and life.

Ridiculous sophists, you have undertaken to cover with the aegis of inviolability the former monarch become traitor, perjurer, and assassin. But your blindness, whatever its nature, cannot be so profound as to lead you to maintain that in rendering Louis Capet inviolable, the legislators conferred upon him the privilege of pillaging the public treasury with impunity; of corrupting those in whom authority had been vested, ministers of the law, representatives of the people; the privilege of supporting legions of spies, of brigands, of assassins; of aiding the enemies of the state with the gold, the munitions, and the arms destined for the defenders of liberty; of conspiring for the ruin of the country and of enjoying afterward the fruits of his crimes. But should the legislators have designed this, was it within their rights? For such is the right which you unthinkingly demand, to benefit the dethroned despot, when you invoke his inviolability to shield him from judgment.

Let us have no illusions. It is only too evident by the ambiguity of the laws in several cases, and by their silence in others, that the Constituent Assembly, especially during revision, had applied itself to arranging all possible means by which the king could conspire with impunity against public liberty.[1] But, thanks to their base natures, the legislators who had prostituted themselves to the court dared not openly consummate these outrages. Thus the Constitution, monstrous as it is, contains nonetheless clauses which are quite precise, so that we may try the tyrant and condemn him.

Those who wish to make a bulwark of the Constitution cite an article of the Declaration of Rights: 'That no man can be accused, arrested, or detained, except in cases determined by the law, and according to the forms which the law hath prescribed',[2] whence they assert that no one shall be punished save by virtue of a law prior to his crime. Let us accord them that.

They go further to cite several articles of the Constitution when they conclude that Louis XVI ought not to be punished, or ought to suffer no punishment but forced abdication. Let us look at the texts: 'The king, on

---

[1] After the king's flight to Varennes, the Constitution was revised by the Constituent Assembly in ways which tended to make it more acceptable to Louis, but the sections on inviolability and 'express or legal abdication' were not changed at that time.
[2] Article VII.

his accession to the throne, or at the period of his majority, shall take to the nation in the presence of the legislative body, the oath — "to be faithful to the nation and the law", to employ all the power delegated to him to maintain the Constitution decreed by the constituting national assembly, in the years 1789, 1790 and 1791, and to cause the laws to be executed.

'If, a month after the invitation of the legislative body, the king has not taken the oath; or if, after taking it, he retracts, he shall then be held to have abdicated the royalty.

'If the king put himself at the head of an army, and direct the forces of it against the nation, or if he do not oppose, by a formal act, any such enterprise undertaken in his name, he shall be held to have abdicated.

'After abdication, express or legal, the king shall be in the class of citizens, and may be accused and tried like them, for acts posterior to his abdication.'

Yet all these cases consider nothing but the refusal of the king to take the oath of fidelity to the laws, his retraction of that oath, his flight at the head of an army whose forces he would direct against the nation. Nowhere are mentioned plots woven in the very bosom of the state to extinguish liberty, to enchain the people once again, or cause their slaughter; nowhere the seizure of coin and grain; nowhere the plots to lay the way for national bankruptcy and bring famine to the land; nowhere the undermining of the courts of law, and the devices used to corrupt public officials; nowhere the vexations, the crimes, and the murders perpetrated on a multitude of citizens, friends of liberty. Now, in all these cases, about which the Constitution maintained the deepest silence, the monarch could be considered only as an ordinary citizen; since the article which follows immediately on that concerning inviolability cited by the defenders of Louis the traitor, says: 'There is no authority in France superior to that of the law. The king reigns only by it; and it is only in the name of the law that he can require obedience.' Whence it follows that he was himself subject to the rule of law, like any other citizen.

Article three of the Declaration of Rights says: 'That the same crimes shall be subject to the same punishment without any distinction of persons.'[1] Laws brought to bear against ordinary citizens must then have their entire execution with respect to Louis Capet, whence it follows that he should suffer the penalties meted to traitors and conspirators.

Finally, if it were true that Louis Capet was above the Constitution in

---

[1]This is actually the third article of Part I of the Constitution, which lists the 'guaranteed' rights of French citizens.

those cases stipulated as royal prerogatives, and that in this respect he had the 'exclusive privilege to violate with impunity all laws', it is no less beyond doubt that the articles on which his defense is supposed to be based suffice to cause his condemnation.

The Constitution declares that after his abdication, the king might be accused and judged for his posterior acts. Now, there is an article which clearly states that 'He shall be held to have abdicated by the retraction of his oath of fidelity to the nation, and the law; of his oath to use for the maintainance of the Constitution, the authority confided in him.'[1] His abdication, therefore, dates from the moment when he conspired the ruin of the nation and began to subvert the Constitution after having accepted it. He can, then, be judged for the treason he has plotted since.

Another article says that 'if he do not oppose, by a formal act, any armed force undertaken against the nation in his name, he shall be held to have abdicated'. His abdication may also be dated from the moment the Prussians, the Austrians, and the émigré rebels invaded France. And as the Tuileries massacre occurred after their invasion, he must be judged as a traitor to the country and the assassin of several thousand Frenchmen. What will be the result if it is proven, and there is little room for doubt, that he himself raised those hordes of enemy brigands who ravaged France?

There is more here than is needed to silence the officious defenders of Louis Capet who will come, the Constitution in hand, to demand impunity for his atrocious crimes. They will claim that he purchased the exclusive privilege to conspire freely against the state from the faithless representatives of the people. But those infamous law-mongers dared not stipulate that impunity with either enough clarity or with enough breadth to shield him from the sword of justice.

As for you, Gentlemen, whom the nation has commissioned not only to wreak vengeance on traitors, but to replace by wise laws the Constitution so long the cause of its unhappiness and nearly, at last, of its ruin. Neither concerted omissions, nor the appalling defects of this shameful monument of servitude will restrain you from leading to judgment a despot cast from the throne, nor keep you from making the tyrant expiate, by an ignominious penalty, the long chain of his misdeeds. On the inalienable law of nations and on the positive laws of states, you will found the judgment of Louis Capet. There is no doubt that a people has the right to punish its agents if they are guilty. And in what free State do the laws not punish with death princes who conspired for the ruin of the nation? I repeat, it would be

[1] Marat here combines and paraphrases several constitutional articles: see the Appendix.

an outrage at once to all law to invoke the law in defense of the former monarch. They all condemn him as a peculator, a prevaricator, a traitor, a conspirator; as a tyrant stained with all crimes, as a monster still covered with the blood of his fellow citizens whose slaughter he commanded.

He is already more than punished, his partisans will cry, by the cruel sentence to a life lived among a free nation whose head he was and whose shame he has become. Let him live then, and let him feel every instant the weight of shame and of remorse.

If the Constitution were written and liberty were consolidated, if the wounds of the state were healed, if peace reigned among us, if abundance flowing through its various channels had begun once again to bring life to the Empire, if the nation could rest at last in the shadow of wise laws and look forward to happy days, perhaps then we might be able to remember the scourge of monarchy but as a painful dream; perhaps we might be able to abandon the tyrant to his regret, to the long punishment of life in recompense for the ills he has done us, or rather, for the liberty which followed his attempted crimes. But, Gentlemen, if you were ever able to lend an ear to the sophisms of those who wish to spare his life, while yet subjecting him to the rule of law, concern for the public safety alone should cause you to reject any penalty which is not capital. As long as the former monarch draws breath and an unforeseen event may set him once again at liberty, he will be the center of the conspiracies of all the enemies of France; and if his prison does not become the home of their endless plots, it will become their rallying point. Thus, there will be no liberty, no security, no peace, no rest, no happiness for the French, no hope for other peoples of breaking this yoke, unless the tyrant's head is struck off.

Must I speak to you of the bloody scenes, the disasters, the dissolution of the state, the slaughter of all the friends of liberty, of your own suffering, which would be the result of his dreadful vengeance if he were ever to escape and place himself at the head of enemy armies who even now ready themselves to turn on us? What pen could describe them, what heart so hard that it could bear the thought?

Louis Capet, Gentlemen, did not plot alone for the ruin of the nation; once placed before the bar he will denounce his accomplices, his ministers, his agents, the disloyal deputies, the administrators, the judges, the generals, who conspired with him against public safety. The investigation connected with his trial is therefore the surest means to deliver at last the nation from its most redoubtable enemies, to strike fear into traitors, to cut off their plots at the root, and finally, to assure liberty, tranquillity, and public felicity. Without these, your efforts to reëstablish order and prepare for the reign of law will be in vain.

'The former monarch must be judged; that is beyond doubt; but by whom shall he be judged?' I would reply, by an ordinary tribunal of the state, composed of the direct delegates of the people – if one could confide so important a case to an ordinary tribunal and if a prompt decision were not so important for the public safety. Let there be no more doubt: Louis Capet is still the rallying point for the enemies of liberty as he is the subject of their hopes. He can therefore be judged only by the National Convention which represents the nation itself. Do not answer that there will be incompetence of jurisdiction, so as to invoke for the accused the title of born-representative of the people; a false and lying title conferred upon him by baseness, perfidy, and craft, to raise him above the law. The monarch was only the foremost public official; for that title he could claim no prerogative.

A final question remains to be examined. How should the former monarch be judged? With pomp and with severity. Far from us those false ideas of clemency and generosity by which the national vanity is flattered! How could we listen to them without calling down upon our heads the blame of the nation and all the ills which would befall the land if we left the former monarch the possibility ever again to plot? Thus, to grant a pardon would be not merely weakness, but treason, wickedness, and perfidy.

On the course you choose, Gentlemen, depends the safety of France, the establishment of the Republic. I conclude from this that the tyrant be judged by the Convention and that his punishment be capital.

8. SAINT-JUST
27 December 1792

On 10 December, Robert Lindet presented the formal indictment required by Quinnet's decree of the 6th. It was based to a large extent on the documents discovered in the king's secret cabinet. The next day, Louis stood at the bar of the Convention (where 'a profound silence reigned') and was interrogated by Barère, then its presiding officer and a leading figure of the Plain. Responding to the accusation that he had deployed troops against the citizens of Paris, Louis gave the answer that Saint-Just made the keynote of his second speech: 'I was the master . . . then, and I sought to do what was right.' But the young tribune did not speak for a second time to answer Louis. His purpose was to reproach the deputies for what he and Robespierre regarded as their lethargy, their intolerable patience with legal formality, their unpatriotic concern for the fate of a king. From 15 to 26 December, debate had been suspended in order to allow Louis' lawyers time to prepare their brief; the 26th was largely given over to the king's defense. When he and his lawyers withdrew, the Jacobin Duhem (who had opposed allowing Louis any legal counsel at all) moved to begin the roll-call immediately. But the Convention, after a confused debate, adopted instead the compromise motion of Couthon that 'discussion is open on the judgment of Louis Capet and that it will continue, all business ceasing, until the verdict is pronounced.' The next day, Saint-Just was the first to speak.

Citizens, when the people was oppressed, its defenders were proscribed, O you who defend that man whom an entire people accuses, you need fear no such injustice. Shadowed in darkness, kings persecuted virtue; but we judge kings before the eyes of all. Our deliberations are public, so none can accuse us of proceeding without caution. O you who defend Louis, you defend the French nation against the opinion of the world. The people, generous to the last, would not themselves pass judgment on their enemy; they entertained all doubts while yet they saw so many families in mourning for their children and while the best of citizens, through treason and tyranny, were buried in Argonne, throughout the Empire, and in Paris here about you.

Nevertheless, an ill-starred people who broke its chains and punished the abuse of power must justify its courage and its virtue. O you who seem the most severe judges of anarchy, surely you would not have it said of you that your rigor was for the people and that your sympathy was reserved for kings. No longer can we be permitted weakness, we who demanded the exile of the Bourbons; if we exile the innocent, how unbending then must we be toward the guilty!

If there were a friend of tyranny who could hear me, a man secretly steeped in plots to oppress us, he would still, perhaps, find ways to touch our pity. Perhaps he would find the means to paint the enemies of kings as savages without humanity. Posterity will not be forgot in the effort to move the pride of the representatives of people. . . . Posterity, you will bless your fathers, you will know then what it will have cost them to be free; their blood flows today over the dust which future generations of free men will bring to life.

Any man of feeling on this earth will respect our courage; what people ever made greater sacrifices for liberty! What people was more betrayed! What people less avenged! Let the king himself look into his heart: how, in the time of his strength, did he treat this people which today is no more than just, no less than great?

When first you deliberated the question of this trial, Citizens, I told you that a king was outside the state, and that whatever covenant may have been agreed upon between the people and the king (if we set aside the fact that any such covenant was illegitimate), nothing bound the sovereign, who by nature was above the law. Nonetheless, you formed a tribunal, and the sovereign stands at the bar with the king who pleads his case and defends himself before you. You permitted that insult to the majesty of the people. Louis has cast the blame for his crimes on the ministers whom he oppressed and deceived. 'Sire', wrote de Morgue to the king, 16 June 1792, 'I resign: Your Majesty has annulled in private what I have done to execute the laws.'[1] On another occasion, de Morgue vindicates his counsel, that the king approve the writ against fanatic priests. What sort of prince was this, before whom a minister need defend his probity? And that man should be inviolable! Such is the circle in which you are placed: you are the judges, Louis the prosecutor, and the people the accused

I do not know where this travesty of the plainest ideas of justice will lead you. The trap would have been less finely sprung had Louis taken exception to your jurisdiction. That denial of the sovereignty of the people would have been the final proof of his tyranny. But there has been occasion to note that since the Revolution the behavior of the king has not tended to open resistance: tractable, with an air of rude simplicity, he knew well the art of dividing men. His constant policy was to stand unmoving, or to move with all parties, just as today he seems to aid his judges in order to make the insurrection appear but the rising of a lawless mob.

The temper of a large assembly may easily be altered if their passions be touched. Can any fail to see that the same spirit which earlier guided the plain and winding course of tyranny now guides its defense? Formerly the people were not to be defied. Neither will you be defied. You were oppressed modestly; that is how the oppressors will defend themselves. Such conduct seeks less to persuade you than to constrain and corrupt your energy. What then is the art, what then the means of dazzling men's eyes by which great culprits gain your respect?

---

[1] Jacques-Augustin de Morque (Mourges) replaced Roland as Minister of the Interior on 13 June 1792, when the Girondin ministry was dismissed by the king; he resigned five days later.

Yet these questions should be examined from the beginning lest we be accused of having acted lightly in so serious a matter. I will not follow the defense in its details, but rather in its spirit.

No one, I think, will assert that the Estates were caused to assemble in 1789 from a desire to lighten the burden of the people and to restore liberty. The necessity of countering parliaments whose claims vexed the pride of the throne; the troubled state of the economy and of the exchequer; specious means to squeeze the people by their own hand; the unyielding spirit of provincial estates; the dominance of the court which the dark humor of the king sought to humiliate; add to these the ambition of a proud and plebeian minister[1] – there are the motives which caused the Estates to be called.

In its first days, the National Assembly took power only from the nobility. By the hand of the people, isolated monarchy crushed rank and station. The king had not conceived that the end of rank should hasten the end of tyranny. After the National Assembly had struck these first blows, the king used all his authority to oppress the Assembly itself. Imagine the tyranny of a single man, in a great state where rank has been abolished and where legislative power is dominated by the prince. The crimes of tyranny are sometimes so finely wrought that only long afterwards do their workings become penetrable.

The king strove to paralyse a power he called forth only so that it might serve his own. You know with what energy he at first enjoined his will upon the representatives of the communes. Even in that, did he follow the fundamental laws of monarchy? Consider those laws and you will find that no prince before him brought to the Estates schemes so profound, so tyrannic, so dissimulated. You will recall with what artifice he rejected the laws which ended feudal and ecclesiastical rule. But when the courage of the people had swept all away, Louis armed himself with moderation. All that could be done to seduce the people without compromising his power, he did. He was not niggardly with sweet words to soothe the wounds of the people and lead them to weakness and to affection for those who had been their lords. He did all the ill he could, undiscerned by the people; and he did it pretending to respect the new laws which he sought to make detested.

Then the king appeared black and fierce among his courtiers whose weakness and impotence in bold enterprises he understood; then the king appeared among the people, celebrating their victories. Poor people!

[1] Jacques Necker, Genevan banker, Controller-General in 1789, had urged the calling of the Estates.

You, who gave cries of joy on the great road to Versailles, and who formed a triumphal procession for him who prepared to greet your defenders with a scaffold and you with chains and misery, you did not know how dear your weakness and your blindness would cost you some day.

Louis answered, when your president asked him about the violence which he loosed against the people: 'I was master then; I did what seemed right to me.'

I do not wish to discuss the means which Louis used to oppress the people and produce that which he calls right. No more do I contest the title, 'master', although in our system of monarchy and by the admission of his own ancestor, kings ruled only by law. But we should recall that after the failure of his plots, which he admits having formed because he was then, as he says, the master, he was hypocrite enough to mark with joy the advantages of the people; that he said to the people against whom he had sent armies and against whom he spent all the force of tyranny, that he sought only his liberty; that he rejoiced at the flight of the soldiers and at the death of those who did no more than execute his orders, because he was the master; that he affected disinterest and love of the people while privately he held quite different views, and while he was taking deadly measures that his rule might continue. What then must we think of the apparent simplicity with which he replies: 'I was master then, and I sought to do what was right'?

At least, Louis, you were not exempt from sincerity. And what law of the realm, what noble sentiment, led you to treachery when you were the weaker?

It is true that such conduct was then immune from judgment if a prince cared little for the scruples of men of good will. You were above the people, as you used to say, yet you were not above justice and your birth did not put you out of the reach of courageous men who join together for public safety. Then you could not be judged; yet were you the less guilty and despite your birth, did you not have to give account as soon as your treachery was laid bare?

I could excuse the dissimulation employed to preserve those hideous rights still dear to a heart without pity, attributing all to the habit of ruling, to uncertainty, to fear of these first storms. But later, when the National Assembly had made useful reforms, when it had presented the Rights of Man for the approval of the king, what unjustified defiance, or rather, what motive if not thirst for power and horror at public happiness, led him to thwart the representatives of the people?

The man who said, 'my people, my children', the man who said he drew breath only for the happiness of the nation, who said his only happiness was their happiness, his only regret their sorrows, that man refused those people their most sacred rights, hesitated between the nation and his pride, and desired public prosperity without desiring that which constitutes it.

Louis wept; was it from pity or rage? We know of spirits softened by fear and cruelty, such as that of Louis XI, who invoked heaven before his murders; but history records no system of tyranny like that of this king, built on kindness and the appearance of goodness. Everywhere he cloaked himself in the robes of France and sought to seduce the affections which were due to France alone, a trap the more cunning as Louis, through hidden violence and intrigue, undermined the laws and drew advantage from the strength and guile of his conduct, from hearts softened for unhappy virtue.

Those tears still run in the hearts of all Frenchmen; they cannot comprehend such disloyalty; long have they loved Louis, the designer of their enslavement. The unhappy man has since put to death those who loved him most then.

How many crimes were required to disabuse them! Neither the flight of the king, nor the protestation by which he sacrificed liberty, nor his refusal to appear before the altar of the federation, when the nation called him that he might take the federation to his heart: none of this sufficed to open the eyes of a people obstinate in its love.

The scepter was left in his hands. What was his gratitude? What his benefactions? How did he reign? The people knew liberty only by the red flag.[1] The government, which sought to stifle the spirit of liberty, did not lay down its arms in that monarchy; and while the people were slaughtered at Nancy, while Bouille was congratulated, in Paris sentimental scenes were played: scenes whose author was cold-blooded crime.[2] The people were deceived and bribed with a few coins, and they were told, 'I should like to have more.' Nonetheless, you have learned of the treasure remitted to Septeuil and of the drafts on foreign credit — and Louis played the indigent.[3]

Louis tainted virtue; to whom henceforth will it appear innocent? Thus all will shun you, men of feeling, if you love the people, if you are

---

[1] The red flag was a sign of battle before it became an emblem of revolution.

[2] François Claude Amour Bouille, French general, was made commander of the army of the Meuse, Saar, and Moselle by the king in 1790, then forced to flee France for his part in the attempted escape of Louis the following year.

[3] Septeuil was the king's treasurer, whose accounts became available after the discovery of the secret cabinet.

moved by their fate: a false king who travestied such sentiments has made you suspect; a show of feeling will be cause for shame.

Yet with what cares was Louis occupied, when after having crossed Paris thus, he returned to the palace? Let us examine his papers. Brigands were paid to fashion public opinion; betrayal poisoned everything, even to the applause of the representatives, even to the ears of the citizens in the assemblies of the people. Spies were hired, and you know with what art the mesh of corruption was knotted.

Among the papers of the king were found no wise maxims for princes, nothing of the rights of man, nothing indeed which might give the boldest of sophists grounds to argue that Louis had ever loved liberty. Plans to abuse the Constitution, plans to destroy it, that is what we found. Those were the subjects to which the king devoted his private thoughts. For any man capable of reflection, Louis' conduct is in accord with his principles, as these are now laid open to public view.

The people, good and credulous, without ambition and without intrigue, would never have hated the prince, if the prince had respected its laws and had governed with probity. Sedition was created the better to arm the law, the better to accuse the people, the better to authorize cruelty.

All this is shown us in the best possible light. Louis justifies his crime on the pretext that it is but human nature. His supporters do not scruple to use equivocations: the 600,000 *livres* were remitted, not by the orders of the king, but by the orders of Monsieur, his brother. But where then did Louis hear of it, and what constitutional connection is there between Monsieur and him?

They grasp at any straw. They have even tried to stain the insurrection with rumors of seditious parties. The people would no sooner rise if the prince be just, then would the sea if the air be calm. Can the people be happy and tranquil while its rights are contested, while the course of public order is undermined? The court was filled with cunning and devious men; there were no decent men to be seen at court. Men of wit were in favor there; men of merit were feared.

The people, on the twentieth of June last, asked for the approval of a law on which its peace depended.[1] In what free government does the abuse of law render crime inviolable and tyranny sacred? or make of the law a snare that guards the mighty from the people and grants the strong impunity from the weak?

[1] On 20 June 1792, third anniversary of the Tennis Court Oath, a mass demonstration in Paris demanded the abolition of the king's veto power.

How could the people have been calm in the midst of perils which threatened it from every side? It is easy to disguise the secret dealings of Louis with the Emperor and the king of Prussia in the treaty of Pilnitz; justice has no hold on great crimes. It is easy to hide the unrest in Avignon, the revolt in Jalès, with the veil of necessity which a great revolution brings with it. But let us judge by the heart and habits of the king, by the views entrusted to his papers, by his taste for counter-revolutionary projects, which were 'audaciously shown him'.[1] The crime is not seen, yet we are dazzled by it. It is easy to hide all their crimes, but the enemy did lie at our borders, terror struck the state, the army was in disorder, the generals were in collusion with the court and with the enemy. Insolence was writ on the faces of the enemies of the commonweal; the guards before the Tuileries menaced the citizens, menaced the legislators, menaced liberty. The king did not govern. As a ruler he was inviolable; was he so when he refused to rule? There were no political connections between him and the officials; executive power was exploited only to further conspiracy: he exploited the law; he exploited liberty; he exploited the people against the people. And now his supporters complain of sedition, they feign astonishment at the legitimate revolt of an entire people, and this revolt they attribute to factious parties! When every man in the state is outraged, when the bonds of confidence which bind the citizens to the prince are broken and the secret resentment of every man acts to swell the storm, to provoke universal upheaval, the prince has already ceased to exist: the sovereign has resumed the reins. Plainly, Louis observed too late that the destruction of old ideas had shaken the foundations of tyranny. By what motion of his conscience could he withhold his approval, whereby he imperiled the state? What conscience and what religion is it that deprives a man of all human feeling for his country and causes him to forget that he reigns for it and not for himself?

And was it really love of religion, that is, probity, which suggested to the king that letter written to the bishop of Clermont, in which he seemed to nurture a plan to seize once more the tyrant's scepter, having sworn an oath to uphold liberty? At least, no one can deny that his ambition overcame his faith, if the law was indeed repugnant to his heart. Sooner than forswear himself, he should have ceased to be king. There is no god who asks that his adherents disquiet the world, and that he be honored by treachery. Thus, no matter how such conduct is regarded,

---

[1] Saint-Just is quoting from the speech of de Sèze, attorney for the king, delivered on the previous day.

Louis deceived heaven, he deceived men: Louis is, in the eyes of all, a guilty man.

How could the people be tranquil, the people too pure, too simple not to discern, not to sense the disorder? You know now the schemes which the king himself contrived against them; time has justified only too well their mistrust. You have been told that, during the sack of the Tuileries, the law did not protect the papers which Louis might have used to counter these now brought against him. But why had he preserved these so carefully? Why are they covered with his notes? Ought he not to have spurned them with horror? Yet let us not take cruel pleasure, striking the accused at his weakest points; let us pass to the tenth of August.

The palace was filled with assassins and soldiers; you know only too well what occurred; the defenders of the king have painted the events in garish colors, offending truth. Louis says that he spilt no blood on the tenth of August, yet what did he do to prevent bloodshed? What tale of courage or of generosity can be told of him on that memorable day? In such a place, he said, he wished to prevent a great crime. But what greater crime could he have prevented than the slaughter of citizens? He appeared among you; he cleared his way by force. There, in that spot, the soldiers who accompanied him threatened the representatives of the people. He appeared in the legislative chambers; his soldiers violated that sanctuary. He made space for himself, so to speak, by blows of the sword aimed at the entrails of the country, in which he sought to hide. Once there, did he, for an instant, surrounded by tumult, seem to be troubled by the blood which was being shed? Devoid of gratitude to either party, he was troubled no more by the danger of his henchmen than by that of the people. I shudder with rage to think that a word, one single word from his mouth, would have stopped the soldiers in all their fury, a single word, perhaps a mere motion of the hand, would have calmed the people; but he did not have such confidence in those whom he had betrayed. The defenders of the king ask us, by way of justification for the garrison at the Tuileries before the tenth of August, what we would have done if the milling crowd had poured toward this Assembly.[1] What did the legislature do to assure its safety against the threats of the royal guards, the Swiss guards, and the courtiers? What did it do on the tenth of August? What did it do surrounded by 60,000 strangers in Paris? What did the Estates do in the Tennis Court? And have we not ourselves, until the present day, rejected armed force?

[1] The reference is to be speech of de Sèze.

Defenders of the king, what would you require of us? If he is innocent, the nation is guilty. We must respond in full, for the form of the question accuses the people.

I have heard talk of an appeal to the people of the verdict which the people itself will pronounce through our mouth.

Citizens, if you permit an appeal to the people, you will be saying to them, 'the guilt of your murderer is in doubt'. Do you not see that such an appeal would tend to divide the people and the legislature, would tend to weaken representation, to restore monarchy, to destroy liberty? And if, through intrigue, your verdict should be altered, I ask you, gentlemen, if you would be left with any course but to renounce the Republic and to lead the tyrant back to his palace, for there is but a small step from indulgence to the triumph of the king and thence to the triumph of monarchy. Yet should the accusing people, the ravaged people, the oppressed people, be the judge? Did it not decline that office after the tenth of August? Nobler, more scrupulous, less cruel than those who would send the accused before them, the people desired that a council might pronounce his fate. That tribunal has already shown too much weakness, and that weakness has already softened public opinion. If the tyrant appeals to the people who accuse him, he does that which Charles I never dared. In a flourishing monarchy, it is not you who judge the king, for you are nothing by yourselves, but the people judges and speaks through you.

Citizens, winged crime will fly through the Empire and captivate the ear of the people. O you who are entrusted with public morality, do not abandon liberty. When a people has escaped from oppression the tyrant is judged. Tyrants will stop at nothing in their attempts to weaken the people by raising the spectre of excess. Humanity, in their mouths, is cruelty to the people; pardon, which they urge on you, is the death knell of liberty. Must the people itself pardon the tyrant? Does not the sovereign, like the supreme Being, find laws to govern its conduct in ethics and in eternal justice? And by what law has nature sanctioned these great crimes? Louis' supporters ask that the verdict be sent before the people; what else would one propose, wishing to save the king and knowing that votes can be bought with foreign gold? No more should you forget that a single vote, in the case of a tyrant, suffices to prevent his pardon.

That day will decide the fate of the Republic; its doom is fixed if the tyrant goes unpunished. The enemies of the commonweal reappear, they meet, they grow in hope; the forces of tyranny gather the fragments as a reptile renews a lost limb. All evil men are of the king's party. Who here then can join him? False pity is on the lips of some, anger on the lips of others; nothing is omitted which might frighten or corrupt our hearts. Be steadfast in your severity and assure yourself of the gratitude of the people in time to come. Do not heed the empty consideration and empty clamor by which the schemers seek to play upon the respect you have for the rights of the people, the better to destroy them and deceive you. You called for war on all the tyrants of the world, and you would have respect for your own! Are bloody laws enforced only against the oppressed, and is the oppressor to be spared?

There has been talk too, among the people and even among you, of challenging those whose opinion is known. Those who, unmoved by interest, seek nothing but good on this earth will never be led by the spirit of vengeance to prosecute the king; but after the perils that the people and liberty have endured for two years past, love of their country should make them just and inflexible. And the ears that proud truth would wound, how pure are they? All that has been said to save this guilty man, we know; for we, in the spirit of rectitude and probity, have said it all within our breasts.

And if France has not rejected us in our weakness, by what right would the guilty man reject our justice? As soon as you have deliberated your verdict, the opinion of each of you has become a part of the law by which the decision is to be made. It is said that by giving an opinion against the king, we become his prosecutors. Not at all. We have simply arrived at a verdict, and Louis cannot challenge the judges sent by the people without challenging the people itself.

There have been strange misunderstandings over the principles and the character of this question. Louis wishes to be king; he wishes to speak as king even while he denies it. But a man unjustly placed above the law can present his judge only with his innocence or his guilt. Let Louis prove that he is innocent; that is his only title to challenge our actions. Innocence has no need to challenge its judges; it has nothing to fear. Let Louis explain how the papers you have seen may favor liberty, let him show his wounds, and let us judge the people.

Some will say that the Revolution is over, that we have nothing more to fear from the tyrant, and that henceforth the law would decree the death of a usurper. But, citizens, tyranny is like a reed which bends with the wind and which rises again. What do you call a Revolution? The fall of a throne, a few blows levied at a few abuses? The moral order is like the physical; abuses disappear for an instant, as the dew dries in the morning, and as it falls again with the night, so the abuses will reappear. The Revolution begins when the tyrant ends.

I have attempted to examine the conduct of the king; it is now for you to be just. You ought to ban all considerations but those of justice and of the commonweal. Above all, you must not compromise your liberty, so dearly bought. You must pronounce a verdict as the sovereign. If you do not, the greatest of criminals, and a king, will have been the first to enjoy from us a right refused to citizens, and the tyrant will once again be above the law, even after his trial. Nor should you permit any challenges, for the decision called forth the wishes and the opinions of all; if those who spoke of the king are challenged, we will challenge, in the name of France, those who said nothing for our country or those who deceived it.

France is in the midst of us; let each man choose between it and the king, between the exercise of justice by the people and the exercise of his own weakness.

Weigh, if you will, the example which you owe the world, the support you owe liberty, the unchanging justice you owe the people, against criminal pity for one who never felt such a sentiment. Say to watching Europe: *serve your kings against us; we rebelled against kings.* Have the courage to speak the truth, for it seems to me that there are those here who fear sincerity. Truth burns silently in all hearts, like a lamp burning over a tomb. Yet if there be someone among you unconcerned by the fate of the Republic, let him fall at the feet of the tyrant, let him return the knife with which he slaughtered your fellow citizens, let him forget all crimes of the king and tell the people that we have been corrupted, and that we have been less sensible of their interest than of the fate of an assassin.

To temper your judgment, you will hear of seditious factions. Thus the monarchy still dominates us, and the principles of the Republic count for naught – for it is to the genius of a Republic and to its legislators that factions will submit. To fear them now is to make the tyrant, by a pact between crime and the people, the guarantor of our liberty. The destiny of the nation would depend on his impunity. Such weakness is unworthy of you! Liberty is not earned without toil; yet in our present position, we need fear nothing, we need only be victorious and we will be raised in triumph. No considerations can stop the course of justice, the companion of wisdom and victory.

I ask that each member of the Convention appear in turn before the rostrum and speak these words: 'Louis is, or is not, convicted.' Afterward, punishment or acquittal will in like manner be decided by a call of the roll. Finally, the president will draft and read the verdict.

9. ROBESPIERRE
28 December 1792

The speeches of Robespierre and Vergniaud are the most important of the debate which took place after Louis' defense. They are not concerned with the arguments of the defense attorneys; both men thought Louis guilty as charged. What was immediately at issue was the appeal to the people, proposed on the 27th by the Girondin Salle. The appeal was an alternative to Condorcet's high court: if the people could not elect the judges, let them at least confirm (or not confirm) the Convention's verdict. But it was hardly a satisfactory alternative, for it would have ended a judicial or semi-judicial proceeding with a national referendum. Condorcet himself opposed it. Salle's proposal is usually and rightly described as a maneuver to save the king's life, and the arguments adduced for the maneuver, as I have suggested in my introduction, are not theoretically interesting. But the speeches of Robspierre and Vergniaud have deeper implications. They reveal the underlying convictions, even more, the sensibility, of the two factions – and of the two men. Robespierre is especially self-revealing. His sense of persecuted virtue, his ambivalent relation to the 'people', his fear of plots and conspiracies, are all expressed with more poignancy here than in the frightening denunciations of his everpresent enemies which follow upon his rise to power.

Citizens, by what mischance has the question which might most readily have united all our votes and all our interest as representatives of the people become only the signal for rage and dissension? Why are the founders of the Republic divided over the punishment of the tyrant? I am unshaken in my belief that we all feel the same deep abhorrence for despotism, that we are all warmed by the same zeal for the holy cause of equality, and I conclude that we should rally with no difficulty to the principles of public interest and eternal justice.

I shall not repeat that there are forms of procedure which, though not of the bar, yet remain sacred; that there are indestructible principles, superior to the categories created by habit and by prejudice; that the true judgment of the king is the spontaneous and universal movement of a people weary of the tyranny which oppresses it. That is the surest, the most equitable of all judgments.

I shall not repeat here that Louis was already condemned before the decrees in which you declared that you yourselves would judge him. I wish to discuss only that system which prevailed; I might even add that I share with the weakest among us all the particular affections which might interest a man in the fate of the accused. Inexorable, when I calculate abstractly the severity which the justice of the law should employ against the enemies of mankind, I have yet felt the republican virtues weaken in my heart in the presence of the guilty man humiliated before the power of the sovereign people. Hate for tyrants and love of humanity have a common source in the heart of a just man who loves his country. But, Citizens, the final proof of devotion which representatives of the people owe to their country is to sacrifice those first natural movements of sensibility to the safety of a great people and to oppressed humanity.[1] Citizens, sensibility which sacrifices innocence to crime is a cruel sensibility; clemency which compounds with tyranny is barbarous.

Citizens, let me call you back to the supreme interest of the nation: its safety. What is it that demands your attention to Louis? It is not thirst for a vengeance unworthy of the nation; it is the need to strengthen public liberty and tranquillity through the punishment of a tyrant. Any manner of judgment, any system of delays which compromises public tranquility is in direct opposition to your aims. And it were better had you simply neglected to punish him than that his trial lay fuel upon our troubles and kindle civil war.

Each instant of delay brings us a new danger; all delays awaken guilty hopes and further embolden the enemies of liberty. They encourage dark defiance and cruel suspicions in the midst of this assembly. Citizens, the voice of the alarmed nation urges you to hasten the decision which is to reassure it. What scruple yet fetters your zeal? I can find a motive neither in the principles of the friends of humanity, nor in those of philosophers, nor in those of statesmen, nor even in those of the most subtle and profound casuist. The procedure has reached its final stage. The day before yesterday the accused declared to you that he had nothing further to say in his defense. He recognized that all the procedures he had desired had been carried out. He declared that he would ask no others. The moment when his justification is still fresh in our ears is the most favorable to his cause. There is no tribunal on earth which would not adopt such a system with a clear conscience. An unhappy man, taken *in flagrante* or simply accused of an ordinary crime, with proof a thousand times less striking, would have been condemned within twenty-four hours.

Founders of the Republic, according to these principles you have long

---

[1]That natural feelings must be repressed by republican citizens and magistrates is a common theme of Rousseau's writings: 'if the voice of nature is the best counsellor to which a father can listen in the discharge of his duty, for the Magistrate it is a false guide . . . and leads sooner or later to the ruin of himself and of the State'. *A Discourse of Political Economy*, in *The Social Contract and Discourses*, trans. G. D. H. Cole (New York, 1950), p. 288.

since been able, in your hearts and in your conscience, to judge the tyrant of the French people. What was the reason for a new delay? Would you seek new evidence against the accused? Would you hear witnesses? Such an idea has never entered any of our heads. Did you doubt the crime? No, for you would have doubted the legitimacy or the necessity of an insurrection; you would doubt what the nation firmly believes; you would be a stranger to our Revolution; and far from punishing the tyrant, you would have put the nation on trial.

The day before yesterday, the only motive which was alleged to postpone the conclusion of this business was the necessity of soothing the conscience of some members who were supposed not yet to be convinced of the crimes of Louis. That unwarranted, insulting, and absurd assumption was denied by the discussion itself.

Citizens, it is important here for you to consider the past, to recall for yourselves your own principles and even your own commitments. Already struck by the great questions which I have just mentioned, you had on two occasions by solemn decree decided the time when the judgment was to be made irrevocably. The day before yesterday was the second time.[1] When you delivered each of these two decrees, you promised yourselves that it would be the last delay, and far from thinking that you were violating justice and wisdom by such an act, you were rather inclined to reproach yourselves with being too easy. Were you deceived then? No, Citizens, your views were sounder in their first moments and your principles surer. The more you lose your vigor and your wisdom by permitting delay, the more the will of the representatives of the people, gone astray perhaps without their knowledge, departs from the general will which should be their supreme regulator. Such is the natural course of things, such is the unfortunate bias of the human heart. I cannot dispense with recalling for you here a striking example, analogous to our own circumstances, which should be instructive. When Louis, coming back from Varennes, was brought for judgment to the first representatives of the people, a general cry of indignation against him rose up in the Constituent Assembly. They were of one voice in condemning him. Shortly thereafter, there were other ideas; sophisms and intrigues overcame liberty and justice. It became criminal to demand before the National Assembly that the full severity of the law be used against Louis.

[1] The Quinnet decree of 6 December had called for a vote on the day after the king's formal defense; the motion adopted on 26 December had simply stated that all business would cease until there was a vote. 'If some among us still have doubts', Couthon had argued, 'discussion is necessary . . .'

Those who ask today for the second time that he be punished for his crimes were then proscribed, persecuted, calumniated throughout France, precisely because they had remained, in too small a number, faithful to the public cause and to the severe principles of liberty. Louis alone was sacred; the representatives of the people who accused him were but factious fellows, seekers after disorder and, worse yet, republicans. Nay, the blood of the best citizens, the blood of women and children, flowed for him on the altar of France. Citizens, we too are men, let us profit from the experience of those who have come before us.

I did not believe, however, in the necessity of an uninterrupted proceeding as the decree put to you proposed. Nor am I influenced by the motives of those who believed that this measure would indict the justice or the principles of the National Convention. No, there was a reason, grounded in ethics, which could easily justify all, even the proposal that you be considered only as judges:[1] that reason was to remove all trace of foreign influence, to guarantee impartiality and incorruptibility by leaving the judges alone with their conscience and the evidence, until the moment when they would have passed sentence. Such is the motive of the English law which imposes upon their jurors the restraint which has also been suggested for you; such was the law adopted by a people famous for their wisdom. A law of this sort would have dishonored you no more than it dishonors England and the other nations which have followed the same maxims. But I considered it, and I consider it still, superfluous, since I am convinced that the conclusion of this affair will not be delayed beyond the time when you are sufficiently enlightened, while your zeal for the public welfare is a law for you more imperious than any decree which you might proclaim.

It was difficult, moreover, to reply to the reasons which I have just elaborated. To delay your judgment, you have heard about the honor of the nation and the dignity of the Assembly. The honor of nations consists in being free and virtuous, in striking down tyrants and avenging reviled humanity. The glory of the National Convention consists in displaying a great character and sacrificing servile prejudices to the sublime principles of reason and philosophy. It consists in saving the nation and strengthening liberty by offering a great example before all the world. I can see its dignity reduced as we forget the vigor of republican maxims, as we are lost in a maze of useless and ridiculous chicanery, and as the speakers before

---

[1] That is, *not* as legislators — until the king had been judged: the reference again is to the Couthon decree.

this Assembly cause the nation to embark once again on the course of monarchy.

Posterity will admire or despise you according to the degree of vigor you show on this occasion; and that vigor will be the measure as well of the boldness or the pliancy with which the foreign despots treat you. It will be the wages of our servitude or of our liberty, of our prosperity or of our misery. Citizens, victory will decide if you are rebels or bene-factors of humanity, and the greatness of your character will decide the victory.

Citizens, to betray the cause of the people and our own conscience, to deliver the nation to all the disorder which delay in such a trial must awaken, that is the only danger we have to fear. It is time to leap over the fatal obstacle which has so long barred our course. Then doubtless we will march together toward our common aim of public felicity; then the hateful passions which mutter too often in the sanctuary of liberty will yield to love of public welfare and to the holy emulation of the friends of the land; and all the plots of enemies of public order will be confounded. But how far we still are from this goal if that strange opinion which at first we could hardly have dared imagine, which then we suspected, was, finally, in fact proposed openly. As for me, from that moment, I saw the confirmation of all my suspicions and all my fears.

At first we seemed to be troubled by the consequences which delays in the progress of this affair might bring. Now we risk rendering it inter-minable. We feared the unrest which each moment of delay might bring, and here we are guaranteed the overthrow of the Republic. Why, of what matter is it that a fatal plot be hidden beneath a veil of prudence or even beneath the pretext of respect for the sovereignty of the people? Such was the art of all tyrants under the mask of patriotism, who have until now assassinated liberty and been the cause of all our ills. These are not sophistical declamations, but results which you must weigh.

Yes, I say openly that I no longer see the trial of the tyrant as anything but a means to bring us back to despotism by way of anarchy. Citizens, I call you to witness. The first time there was any discussion of the trial of Louis the Last in the National Convention called expressly to judge him, when you left your departments enflamed with the love of liberty, filled with that generous enthusiasm which the recent proofs of the con-fidence of a magnanimous people inspired in you, which no foreign influence had changed, nay, at first when the question of opening this affair arose, suppose someone had said to you: 'You think that you will have done with the trial of the tyrant in a week, in two weeks, in three months; you are mistaken. It will not be you who will pronounce his sentence, who will judge him in the end. I hereby propose that you send this affair to the twenty or thirty thousand sections into which France is divided, so that they may all pronounce on this point; and you will adopt this proposal.' You would have laughed at the assurance of a man making such a motion. You would have rejected such a motion as incendiary, designed to kindle civil war. What is there to say! We are assured that tempers have changed. Such is the influence of a plague-ridden atmosphere among many of our number, that the simplest and most natural ideas are often stifled by the most dangerous sophisms.

Let us impose silence on all our prejudices, on all suggestions, and let us coolly examine this question. You are about to convoke the primary assemblies, so as to cause them to concern themselves, each one separately, with the fate of the former king: that is, you will change all the assemblies of the cantons, all the sections of the cities, into so many stormy arenas where the combat will be carried on for or against the person of Louis, for or against the monarchy – there are many people in whose eyes there is little distance between the despot and despotism. You guarantee that these discussions will be perfectly peaceful and exempt from any dangerous influences. But guarantee then that bad citizens, that moderates, that *feuillants*[1], that aristocrats will find no access; that no wily and long-winded lawyer will take men of good faith by surprise and create pity for the tyrant in the hearts of simple men who cannot see the political consequences of so fateful an indulgence or so unconsidered a decision. What! Would not the weakness of the Assembly itself, not to use a stronger word, be the surest means of rallying all royalists, all enemies of liberty, of whatever persuasion? The surest means of calling them back to the assemblies of the people which they fled the moment you were named, in that happy time at the height of the Revolution which gave some little vigor to expiring liberty?

Why would they not come to the defense of their leader, since the law itself calls upon all citizens to discuss this great question freely and fully? And who is more eloquent, more adroit, more rich in resources than the intriguers, the *honnêtes gens*[2], that is, than the scoundrels of the old and even of the new regime? With what art will they declaim at first against the king, only to conclude finally in his favor! With what eloquence will

---

[1] In July 1791 the conservative wing of the Jacobins had seceded and formed a new political group which met in the convent of the *Feuillants*. The group broke up after the insurrection of 10 August, and many of its members went into exile.

[2] 'The respectable people' – Robespierre uses this conventional phrase ironically.

they proclaim the sovereignty of the people, the rights of humanity, only to bring back monarchy and aristocracy! But citizens, will those who are found in the primary assemblies really be the people? Will the farmer leave his plow? Will the artizan leave the work upon which his daily bread depends, to come page through the penal code and deliberate in a tumultuous assembly the nature of the penalty Louis Capet has incurred, and many other questions, perhaps, which will be no less foreign to his thoughts? I have already heard a distinction made between the people and the nation on the occasion of this very motion. I myself believed these words to be synonyms, yet I observed that the old distinction which I heard made by part of the Constituent Assembly was being revived, and I know that we must understand by the people, the nation without those men formerly privileged and the *honnêtes gens*.[1] I know that these *honnêtes gens*, that all the intriguers of the Republic, could easily gather in force in the primary assemblies, permanent and unending, abandoned by the greater part of the nation, ignobly called 'the people', and there lead good men astray, even perhaps, treat faithful friends of liberty as cannibals, as anarchists, as factious men. For myself, I can see in this 'call to the people' nothing but a call away from that which the people wished, away from that which the people did at the moment when their force was exerted, at a time when they truly expressed their will, that is, at the time of the insurrection of the tenth of August; a call to all the enemies of equality whose corruption and baseness were the cause of the insurrection itself. For those who most feared the salutory disorder which attends the birth of liberty are the very same men who desire to cause the disorder which can bring back despotism or aristocracy. What an idea! To seek to judge the case of a man, nay, half his case, by a tribunal composed of twenty or forty thousand individual tribunals! If our aim were to persuade the world that a king was a creature above humanity, if our aim were to render the shameful malady monarchy incurable, what better means could we find than to convoke a nation of twenty-five million men to judge him, to pass the sentence which he may have incurred? And the idea that the powers of the sovereign people should be reduced to deciding the penalty is doubtless not the least subtle part of this system.

This was doubtless suggested so as to elude some of the objections which might be raised. Because it was thought too ridiculous that a trial would have a preliminary investigation conducted by all the primary

---

[1] Salle did not in fact make any such distinction when he moved the appeal to the people, though he did distinguish between 'le peuple français tout entier' and 'le peuple parisien'.

assemblies of the French Empire, it was proposed that only the question of what degree of severity the crime of Louis might provoke should be submitted to the assemblies. This did nothing but multiply the absurdities without diminishing the drawbacks. If indeed a part of Louis' case is brought before the sovereign people, who can stop them from examining the whole? Who can contest their right to review the trial, to accept written accounts, to hear the justification of the accused, to admit the accused to plead for a free pardon from the nation assembled, and thence to present his entire case. Do you believe that the hypocritical partisans of a system contrary to equality will neglect a chance to make the weight of such pretexts felt, and to lay claim to the full exercise of the rights of the sovereign? And from then on, there will be a trial begun in each primary assembly. But even if it were restricted to the question of the penalty, that would have to be discussed. And who will not feel the right to carry on the discussion eternally, when the Conventional Assembly itself dared not come to a decision? Who can say when the great question might be decided? The speed of the conclusion will depend on many things: on the intrigues which will agitate each of the diverse sections of France; then on the speed or the delay which accompanies balloting in the primary assemblies; next on the negligence or the zeal, on the fidelity or partiality, with which the votes themselves will be recorded by the directing bodies and transmitted to the National Convention which will collect them.

However, the foreign wars are not yet ended. The season is approaching when despots, allied and accomplice to Louis XVI, will spend all their strength against the emerging Republic; and they will find the nation deliberating over Louis XVI; they will find it occupied by the question whether he deserved death; they will find it consulting the penal code or weighing the reasons for treating him with indulgence or with severity; they will surprise it agitated, exhausted, wearied by these scandalous discussions. Then, if the intrepid friends of liberty today so furiously persecuted are not already sacrificed, they will have something better to do than dispute over a point of procedure. They will have to fly to the defence of the nation; they will have to leave the platform and the stage of assemblies turned into quibblers' arenas by the rich, natural allies of monarchy, by the egoists, by the base and the weak, by all the champions of *feuillantisme* and of aristocracy. What! The citizens who today fight for liberty, all our brothers who have abandoned their wives and children to fly to its aid, will they be able to deliberate in your cities and in your assemblies when they are in our camps or on the battlefield? And who more than they has the right to vote in the cause of tyranny or liberty? Will the men who stayed quietly at home have the right to decide in their absence? What! Is the cause not particularly theirs? Are these not the courageous soldiers of our lines, who since the start of the Revolution scorned the bloody orders of Louis when he commanded the massacre of their fellow citizens? Are these not the men who, since that time, have been persecuted by the court, by Lafayette, by all the enemies of the people? Are they not the brave volunteers who, not long ago, saved their country by their sublime devotion, repelling the satellites of the despots whom Louis has leagued against us? Such brave men would be condemned were we to absolve the tyrant or his like. They would be made to suffer the vengeance of despotism and aristocracy, which has never ceased pursuing them, for through all time there has been a struggle to the death between true patriots and the oppressors of humanity.

Thus, while the most courageous citizens spent the last drops of their blood for France, the dregs of the nation, the basest and most corrupt men, all the reptiles of chicanery, all the proud bourgeois and aristocrats, all the former privileged classes hidden behind the mask of civic virtue, all men born to grovel before a king and join him in oppression, masters of the assemblies deserted by simple and indigent virtue, would, with impunity, destroy the work of the heroes of liberty, would deliver their wives and children to servitude, and alone, insolently, would decide the destiny of the state. There is the horrid end that the most profound hypocrisy, to speak plainly, that the most shameless roguery, dares to hide beneath the name of the sovereignty of the people whom it seeks to destroy. Do you not see that this plan threatens the destruction of the Convention itself, that once the primary assemblies are convoked, intrigue and *feuillantisme* will cause the consideration of propositions which could only serve their perfidious purposes. They will reëxamine everything, even to the proclamation of the Republic, the cause of which is quite naturally tied to questions concerning the dethroned king. Do you not see that the insidious turn given to the judgment of Louis only reproduces in another guise, the proposal made to you by Guadet, that the primary assemblies should be convoked to review the choice of deputies; a proposal which, at the time, you rejected with horror.[1] Do you not see that it is not possible for such a multitude of assemblies to be in complete agreement? Do you not see that this dissension alone, at a time when our enemies approach, is the greatest calamity of all? This civil war will

[1] Guadet's motion was made on 9 December as part of a maneuver aimed at Marat.

join its fury to the scourge of foreign war; and the ambitious intriguers will compound with the enemies of the people over the ruins of France and the bloody corpses of its defenders.

In the name of public tranquility, under the pretext of avoiding civil war, this senseless scheme was proposed! Civil war, the return of the monarchy, is to be feared if you do not act promptly to punish the king who conspired against liberty. The way to destroy tyranny is to preserve the tyrant; the way to prevent civil war is to kindle it without delay. Cruel sophists! Thus they argued to deceive us. Is it not in the name of peace and liberty that Louis and Lafayette and all his accomplices in the Constituent Assembly and elsewhere disturbed the order of the state, slandered and assassinated patriotism?

To bring you to accept this strange system, you were presented with a dilemma no less strange, at least to me: 'Either the people desire the death of the tyrant or they do not; if they do, what harm can there be in consulting them? If they do not, by what right can you command it?'

Here is my reply. First, I do not doubt that the people desire it, if by the people you mean the majority of the nation, without excluding the most numerous, most unfortunate, and the purest portion of society, that portion on which all the crimes of egoism and tyranny weigh heaviest. That majority expressed its wishes at the moment when it threw off the yoke of your former king; it began, and it upheld the Revolution. That majority has rectitude; it has courage; but it has neither finesse nor eloquence; it strikes down tyrants, but it is often the dupe of rogues. The majority should not be wearied by repeated or long assemblies where an intriguing minority too often dominates. It cannot be in political gatherings when it is in workshops; it cannot judge Louis XVI while it nourishes, by the sweat of its brow, the robust citizens which it gives to the nation. I have faith in the general will, especially when it is awakened by the pressing interest of public safety. I fear intrigue, and especially the disorder which it brings, in the midst of snares laid long since. I fear intrigue when the emboldened aristocrats raise a haughty head, when the émigrés return in despite of the law, when public opinion is played upon by pamphlets with which a dominant faction inundates all France and which never say a word of the Republic, which never illuminate the trial of Louis the Last, which encourage only opinions favorable to its cause, which slander all those who seek his condemnation with the most zeal. I see in your system nothing but a plot to destroy the work of the people and to rally the enemies which they vanquished. If you have so scrupulous a respect for the sovereign will of the people, know how to respect it; fulfill the mission with which you have been entrusted. To return to the people a question which they charged you to decide with dispatch is to toy with the majesty of their sovereignty. If the people had the time to gather in order to judge these proceedings, or to decide questions of state, they would not have entrusted the care of their interests to you. The only means to bear witness to your fidelity is to make just laws and not to give them civil war. And by what right do you insult the people by doubting their love of liberty? To affect such a doubt is nothing but to cause and encourage the impudence of all the partisans of monarchy.

Can you reply to this dilemma: either you believe that intrigue will dominate the deliberations which you will bring about, or you think that the deliberations will be dominated by love of liberty and of reason. In the first instance, I admit that your measures are perfectly conceived to provoke the overthrow of the Republic and the return of tyranny. In the second case, the Frenchmen gathered will receive with indignation the step which you propose to them. They will despise the representatives who did not dare fulfill the sacred duty which was entrusted to them. They will detest the base politics of those who remember the sovereignty of the people only when they wish to use it to treat circumspectly with the shadow of monarchy. They will be indignant to see that their representatives pretend to ignore their mandate; they will say to you: 'Why do you consult us about the punishment of the greatest of criminals when guilty men most worthy of indulgence fall beneath the sword of the law without our intervention? Why should the representatives of the nation pronounce on the crime, and the nation itself pronounce on the penalty? If you are competent to deal with one of these questions, are you not all the more so for the other? If you are bold enough to dare the resolution of one question, why are you too timid to approach the other?

'Do you know the laws less well than the citizens who chose you to make their laws? Is the penal code closed to you? Cannot you read there the penalty given to conspirators? And, when you have decided that Louis conspired against liberty or against the welfare of the state, what difficulty do you find in declaring that he has incurred this penalty? Is this inference so obscure that thousands of assemblies are needed to draw it?'

From what shameful motive was an attempt made to lead you to such an excess of absurdity? To frighten you, you were presented with the image of the people calling you to account for the blood of the tyrant. Frenchmen, listen: you are thought ready to call your representatives to account for the blood of your assassin, to spare them from having to call

him to account for your own blood, and you, the representatives, are
sufficiently despised so that it is claimed you may be terrified into for-
getting virtue. If those who despise you are those who persuade you, I
have no more to say: fear knows no reason. And in that case, it is not the
question of Louis XVI which must be sent to the people, but the entire
Revolution, for, in order to found liberty, to wage a continuing war against
all despots and all vices, our courage must be proven by more than barren
cant.

Citizens, I know the zeal which animates you for the public good.
You were the last hope of the nation; you may still save it. Why must
we believe that we have begun an ill-omened course? By terror and slander,
intrigue misled the Constituent Assembly, the majority of which was well-
intentioned and which had at first done such great things. I am alarmed
by the similarity I perceive between two periods of our Revolution which
the same king has rendered all too memorable.[1]

When the fugitive Louis was brought back to Paris, the Constituent
Assembly also feared public opinion. It feared all that which surrounded
it. It did not fear monarchy, it did not fear the court and the nobles; it
feared the people. Then it believed that no armed force would ever be
large enough to defend it against them. Then the people dared show their
long-pent desire to see Louis punished. The partisans of Louis showered
endless accusations upon the people; the blood of the people was spilled.

Today, I admit, no one would have us absolve Louis. We are still too
close to the tenth of August and the day when monarchy was abolished.
But we are asked to adjourn the end of his trial at a time when foreign
powers are about to descend upon us, and to allow him the resource of
civil war. Today, no one would seek to declare him inviolable, but only
to assure that he remains unpunished; they seek not to reëstablish him
on the throne, but merely to await events. Today, Louis still has this
advantage over the defenders of liberty, that they are pursued with more
vigor than is he. No one can doubt that they are now slandered with more
care and at more cost than in July of 1791. And, certainly, the Jacobins
were not more disparaged in the Constituent Assembly then than they now
are in this body. Then, we were the factious men; today, we are the
agitators and the anarchists. Then, Lafayette and his accomplices neglected
to have us murdered; we must hope for the same clemency from his successors. Those great friends of peace, those famous defenders of the law,

[1]The earlier period was the month after Varennes, when Robespierre (virtually alone) advocated
putting the king on trial.

have since been declared traitors. But we gain nothing from that, while their old friends, several members of the then majority, are here to avenge them by persecuting us. But there is a fact which no one has mentioned and which is nonetheless worthy of provoking your curiosity: after a preparatory pamphlet distributed according to the custom of all members, the speaker who proposed and elaborated with such art and feeling the system of taking the question of Louis to the primary assemblies, sprinkling his discourse with the usual declamations against patriotism, is precisely the same man who, in the Constituent Assembly, gave his voice to the dominant cabal to define the doctrine of absolute inviolability, and who vowed our proscription for having dared defend the principles of liberty[1] ... in a word, it is the same man who, and this must be said, two days after the massacre on the Champ-de-Mars, dared propose a decree which would have established a commission to judge, without appeal, as quickly as possible, the patriots who had escaped the assassins' swords. I do not know if, since then, the ardent friends of liberty who still today press for the condemnation of Louis have become monarchists, but I heartily doubt that the men of whom I speak have changed their principles. It has been demonstrated to my satisfaction that under only slightly different circumstances, the same passions and the same vices tend irresistibly toward the same end. Then, intrigue gave us an ephemeral and vicious constitution; today, intrigue prevents us from writing a new one and leads us toward the dissolution of the State.

If there were a way to prevent this misfortune, it would be to tell the entire truth, it would be to expose to you the disastrous plan of the enemies of public welfare. But what means have we to execute even this duty sucessfully? What sane man, having some experience of our Revolution, could hope to destroy in a single moment the monstrous work of calumny? How could austere truth dissipate the marvels by which base hypocrisy seduced credulity, and perhaps civic spirit itself?

I have observed what is going on around us; I have observed the true causes of the dissension among us; I see clearly that the system the perils of which I have depicted will doom the nation, and some unhappy premonition warns me that this system will prevail. I could predict, with considerable certainty, the events which will follow this resolution, according to my knowledge of the persons who direct it.

[1] At this point, Salle interrupted, demanding the floor on a point of personal privilege. He was allowed to speak immediately after Robespierre and argued (rightly) that it was he who had proposed to the Constituent Assembly those sections on abdication which established that royal inviolability was *not* 'absolute'.

What is sure is that whatever the result of this fatal measure, it must be to the advantage of their views. To provoke civil war the resolution need not even be executed completely. They trust to the unrest which is created within us by this stormy and endless deliberation. Those who do not wish to see Louis fall beneath the sword of law will not be sorry to see him sacrificed by a popular disturbance: they will neglect nothing in their attempts to provoke one.

Unhappy people! Your very virtues are used to lead you to your ruin. The masterpiece of tyranny is to provoke your just indignation, and later, make a crime not only of the indiscreet steps to which it brought you, but of the very signs of discontent which escape you. Thus, a perfidious court, with the aid of Lafayette, will draw you to the altar of the nation as to a snare where it will murder you. Yet, alas, if the many strangers who crowd within your walls, unknown to the authorities, or if the very emissaries of our foes attempt the life of the fatal subject of our deliberations, even that act would be imputed to you. Then they would raise the citizens of the other parts of the Republic against you, they would arm all France against you if possible, in recompense for having saved France.

Generous people! You served the cause of humanity too well to be held innocent in the eyes of tyranny. They would soon snatch us from your view to consummate their detestable plans in peace. In farewell, we leave you decay, misery and war, and the destruction of the Republic. Do you question this plan? Then you have never reflected on the system of defamation worked out in your midst and before your legislature. You do not know the history of our sad and stormy sessions.

The man who told you yesterday that we were progressing toward the dissolution of the National Convention by calumny, spoke the truth. Do you need proof other than that discussion itself? What other object does it now seem to have, but to strengthen all the sinister fears which slander implanted to poison weak spirits by perfidious insinuations, to fan the fires of hate and discord?

Is it not evident that this is less the trial of Louis XVI than that of the staunchest defenders of liberty? Is it against the tyranny of Louis XVI that we revolt? No, it is against the tyranny of a small number of oppressed patriots. Are the plots of the nobility feared? No, it is the ambition of I know not which deputies of the people who stand ready to take the place of the aristocrats. The tyrant is to be preserved to furnish opposition to a few impotent patriots. Perfidious men control all public power and the state treasury, and they accuse us of despotism. There is no hamlet in the Republic where we have not been slandered with an unheard of impudence.

The treasury is emptied to corrupt the public with a storm of pamphlets. They dare, in spite of public faith and the most holy laws, to violate the privacy of the mails to stop all patriotic dispatches, to stifle the voice of liberty, of truth, of outraged innocence. And they complain of slander! They despoil us of all, even to our suffrage, and they denounce us as tyrants! They represent as acts of revolt, the mournful cries of oppressed patriotism overwhelmed by perfidy, and they fill this sanctuary with cries of vengeance and fury!

Yes, doubtless there is a plot to degrade the Convention and perhaps to cause its dissolution as a result of this interminable question. This plot is not found among those who seek energetically the principles of liberty, not among the people who have sacrificed everything to it, not in the majority of the National Convention which seeks the good and the true, not even among those who are the dupes of intrigue and the blind instruments of foreign passions. This plot thrives among a score of rascals who hold the reins, among those who are silent about the greatest concerns of the nation, who abstain above all from announcing an opinion on the question of the last king, but whose silent and pernicious activity causes all the ills which trouble us and prepares all those who await us.

How can we escape this abyss if not by returning to our principles and to the source of our ills? What peace can exist between oppressed and oppressor? What concord can reign where even the freedom of the vote is not respected? Any violation of such freedom is an attempt on the nation; a representative of the people does not permit himself to be stripped of the right to defend the interests of the people; no power can take this right from him without taking his life as well.

Already those who sought to assure continued discord, to control the deliberations, conceived the idea of dividing the assembly into majority and minority, a new means to insult and silence those who were designated as the latter. I do not recognize majority and minority here. The majority is composed of the good citizens. It is permanent since it belongs to no party; at each free deliberation it is renewed, since it belongs to the public cause and to eternal reason. And when the Assembly recognizes an error, the fruit of surprise, of haste, or of intrigue (which sometimes happens), then the minority becomes the majority. The general will is not formed in secret conventicles or around the tables of ministers. The minority retains an inalienable right to make heard the voice of truth, or what it regards as such. Virtue is always in the minority on this earth.[1]

[1] Hearing this last sentence, Marat shouted, 'All this is nothing but charlatanism!' The secretary put the interpolation into the record.

Without this, would not the earth be peopled by tyrants and slaves? Hampden and Sidney were of the minority, for they died on the scaffold. Critias, Anitus, Caesar, Clodius, were all of the majority; but Socrates belonged to the minority, for he swallowed the hemlock.[1] Cato was of the minority, for he tore out his bowels. I know many men here who will, if need be, serve liberty in the manner of Sidney; and were there only fifty. . . This thought alone must send a shiver through the base intriguers who wish to corrupt or to mislead the majority. Until that time, I ask at least that priority be given to the tyrant. Let us unite to save the nation and let the deliberation assume at last a character more worthy of us and of the cause which we defend. Let us at least banish the deplorable incidents which do us dishonor. Let us not spend more time in self persecution than would be needed to judge Louis, and let us know how to gauge the subject which disquiets us. Everything seems to conspire against the public welfare. The nature of our debates agitates and embitters public opinion, and unhappily, that opinion reacts against us. The mistrust of the representatives seems to grow with the citizens' alarms. A proposal which we ought to hear calmly, irritates us; malevolence daily exaggerates, imagines, or creates tales whose aim is to strengthen prejudice; and the smallest causes can lead us to the most terrible effects. The mere expression, sometimes too animated, of the feeling of the public, which should be easy to control, becomes the pretext for the most dangerous measures and for propositions which most threaten our principles.

People, spare us at least this disgrace; keep your applause for the day when we have passed one law that is of use to humanity. Do you not see that you give them pretexts to slander the sacred cause which we defend? Rather than violate these firm rules, turn your backs on the spectacle of our debates. Remember the ribbon which your hand but lately held as an insurmountable barrier around the fatal dwelling of our tyrant, then still on the throne.[2] Remember that order has been maintained thus far without bayonets, by the virtue of the people alone. Far from your eyes we will

[1] John Hampden, a parliamentary leader in the English Revolution, in fact died a natural death; Algernon Sidney, also a member of the Long Parliament and an opposition leader in the last years of Charles II, was executed for high treason in 1683. The next four names hardly make an obvious series, except that all of them were political leaders in periods of republican decadence: Critias was one of the Thirty Tyrants who ruled in Athens after the Peloponnesian War; Anitus, a democratic leader of the same period, was one of the accusers of Socrates; Caesar overthrew the Roman republic; Clodius, an associate of Caesar's, contrived the exile of Cicero in 58 B.C.

[2] In July 1791 a tri-colored ribbon had been stretched across the Tuileries Gardens and the guards that the king had put there to safeguard his privacy and his person were dismissed. No-one, it is said, broke through the ribbon. Robespierre, like Saint-Just in the previous speech, opposes the establishment of an armed guard for the Convention.

not struggle the less for liberty. We alone must now defend your cause. When the last of your defenders has perished, then avenge them if you wish, and take on the charge of making liberty triumph.

Citizens, whoever you are, set up a watch around the Temple;[1] arrest, if it is necessary, perfidious malevolence, even deceived patriotism, and confound the plots of our enemies. Fateful place! was it not enough that the despotism of the tyrant weighed so long on this immortal city? Must his very safekeeping be a new calamity for it? Is the trial to be eternal, so as to perpetuate the means of slandering the people who took him from the throne?

I have proven that the proposal to submit the question of Louis to the primary assemblies would lead to civil war. If I cannot contribute to the salvation of my country, I wish at least to be recorded, at this moment, for the attempts I have made to warn you of the calamities which threaten it. I ask that the National Convention declare Louis guilty and worthy of death.

10. VERGNIAUD
31 December 1792

Pierre-Victurnien Vergniaud, a prominent lawyer from Bordeaux, was the first deputy chosen by the electors of the Gironde in September, 1792, and in the Convention he was one of the leaders of the Girondins and certainly their finest orator. This speech has been called (in the 11th edition of the *Encyclopædia Brittannica*) 'one of the greatest combinations of sound reasoning, sagacity, and eloquence which has ever been displayed in the annals of French politics'. A pardonable exaggeration, for it is a noble effort in a lost cause. But reason and sagacity might have dictated another course, if the goal was to save the king's life. Only 287 deputies voted for the appeal to the people which Vergniaud here defends, while 334 voted against the sentence of death. Since 26 more voted the Maihle proviso – including Vergniaud himself – the number of deputies opposed to *immediate* death was only one vote short of a majority. Reprieve was well within reach, if someone like Vergniaud had taken the lead in that battle.

In the Legislative Assembly and the Convention, Vergniaud presided over the fall of kingship in France: he was in the chair on 10 August, and it was he who,

[1]The king's prison, since 13 August 1792.

stepping down, formally moved the suspension of the king; he was in the chair again on 17 January, and it was he who read the tally of the crucial roll-call and formally declared, 'in the name of the National Convention, that the penalty it has pronounced against Louis Capet is death'. Like many other of the Girondins, he was almost certainly a convinced republican. But he was unable to shape or control the new Republic. Only ten months after king and kingship died in France, Vergniaud himself was tried before a revolutionary tribunal and condemned to death. He was guillotined on 31 October 1793.

Citizens, in a matter so closely touching the public tranquillity and the nation's reputation, we should distinguish carefully between our passions and our principles, between the promptings of the soul and measures for the general safety. The better to arrive at a result worthy of you, permit me to put to you some ideas concerning the sovereignty of the people. I believe in their truth. Let me be shown, not by threats or slanders, which are suited only to confirm a free man in his opinion, but by solid arguments, that these ideas are false, and I shall abandon them.

What is the sovereignty of the people of which we hear so much, and to which I should like to think our homage is not mere words, to which I am sure the National Convention, at least, renders sincere homage?

It is the power to make laws, rules, in a word, all the acts concerning the happiness of society. The people exercise this power either themselves or through their representatives. In the latter case, and it is the one in which we find ourselves, the decisions of the representatives are executed as laws. But why? Because they are presumed to be the expression of the general will. Their validity comes from this assumption alone. This assumption alone causes them to be respected.

As a result, the people retain the right, inherent in their sovereignty, to approve or improve. As a result, if their presumed will does not coincide with the general will, the people retain the right to manifest their wishes. As soon as such a wish is made known, it should supersede the presumed will, that is, the decision of the national representatives. To take this right from the people would be to take sovereignty from them, to transfer it, by a usurpation nothing short of criminal, to the hands of the representatives chosen by the people, to transform their representatives into kings or tyrants.

Your conduct has been in accord with these principles. But you have distinguished between the Constitution and purely legislative acts, whether statutory or for the protection of the general safety. Since the Constitution formed the basis of civil society, the contract which united the citizens, you thought, and quite rightly, that it should be presented for the formal acceptance of all the members of society.[1] As for purely legislative acts, as they are necessarily very numerous, they vary according to time, place, and circumstances. It would be contrary to the nature of representative government to submit them for deliberation to the people who elected representatives precisely because the extent of their territory or other causes kept them from the direct exercise of their sovereignty. You thought also, and quite rightly, that a tacit ratification would suffice for such acts, that is, it would suffice to enforce them that there be no challenge from the people who retain at all times the right to manifest their wishes. Let me reduce these diverse propositions to a single one: any act emanating from the representatives of the people is an act of tyranny, a usurpation of sovereignty, if it is not submitted to the people for either formal or tacit ratification. Therefore, the judgment which you will pass on Louis should undergo one of these two processes of ratification.

To reply that even after its execution your judgment will be subjected to tacit ratification is to insult the people with the greatest impudence. There is no silent ratification; silence can be regarded as approbation only when he who is silent has the means to make himself heard with effect. Now it is evident that if your judgment were executed, the people would be able to present only sterile and empty challenges.

You were compared to ordinary tribunals in that their judgments are executed without any sanction from the people. From this it was concluded that the principles which guide us did not demand sanction for your decisions.

What dissembling! Could such an objection have been put forth in good faith? The judges in the tribunals have, it is true, a mandate from the people; but their mandate does not imply representation. They have no private will to express; they have only the instrument of the general will already expressed in the law. They merely apply that law through which the people have, in advance, sanctioned their judgments.

You, Citizens, you are at once bearers of a mandate from the people and their representatives. Your private will is always assumed to be the expression of the general will not yet manifested. And it is precisely this assumption from which legislative acts draw their strength that creates the need to submit them for formal or tacit ratification. It is as representatives of the

---

[1] In fact, the Constitution of 1791 was never voted on by the people; it was presented to them only in the sense that Vergniaud specifies below, when he refers to the oath of allegiance to which citizens were asked to subscribe. Hence the obvious weakness of the argument Vergniaud goes on to make: that only the people can revoke the king's inviolability.

people that you have united the functions of grand jury, of trial jury, of legislators to determine the form of judgment, and of judges to apply the sentence. Such an accumulation of powers was considered legitimate because the powers you received from the people were limitless. I might observe, in this respect, that however broad your powers may be, they cease by their very nature where despotism begins. Let us accept that such an accumulation of powers was legitimate. Nevertheless, it is so terrifying, it is such a monstrosity in the political process: were it ever to recur (and with the maxim that your powers are limitless, what would keep it from being repeated?) – were it to recur, it would lead us to tyranny with such speed that I am not afraid to say, there can be no act you might pass which has so great a need of the ratification of the people to be legitimate.

If further reasons were needed to assure the triumph of such evident truths, there is a powerful one I can invoke. When Louis accepted the Constitution, the people said to him: 'Ministers will be answerable for your actions; you yourself will be inviolable.' I do not intend to insult my reason by making myself an apologist for the absurd dogma of royal inviolability. Inviolability such as must be supposed to assure impunity to Louis, full and total inviolability which would cover all crimes of kings, would be a withdrawal of the individual called king from the national sovereignty and, on the part of the people, a renunciation of their sovereignty in favor of that same individual. Now no law could make legitimate that withdrawal, that renunciation rejected by nature. This principle, long stifled beneath the mass of our prejudice, is today universally recognized. To contest it would be to deny the light of reason.

However, if it is true that Louis cannot avail himself of the promised inviolability against the people whom he betrayed, it is equally true that the people alone can punish Louis without respect to this inviolability with which they themselves invested him. Let me clarify this point. It was not merely the assembly of the people's representatives which promised inviolability to Louis; it was the people themselves, all the individual citizens, by the oath they all took to preserve the Constitution. Today you may declare that as a principle of eternal truth, the promise of inviolability made to Louis by the people was not binding on them. But the people alone can declare that they do not wish to keep their promise. You may declare as a principle of eternal truth that the people could never validly renounce their right to punish an oppressor; but the people alone can declare that they wish to make use of the dreadful right which they renounced. This is no ordinary assumption. The desire of the general will has been made manifest; it has declared for inviolability. Express a contrary desire if public safety seems to demand it; but do not undertake to substitute that private desire for the general will already known, unless it has given its assent. Otherwise you will usurp sovereignty; you will become guilty of those crimes for which you wish to punish Louis.

It has been claimed that there will be insurmountable difficulties in convoking the primary assemblies; that it would mean taking the plowman from his plow, the workman from his work, wearying the citizens, wearing out their strength in dissertations on legal formalities, on subtle chicaneries. Furthermore, it has been added, foreign powers would profit from this reduction of our forces and, while we were busied in these wretched discussions, would invade our territory for a second time. And if the true friends of liberty joined together to repulse them, they would have the sorrow, while fighting for their country, of fearing the resurrection of tyranny within it.

I will admit that in this very moving speech I found great appeal to our feelings; I still seek in it a reason which might persuade me.[1] Where, in fact, are these great difficulties? Is the proposal to send to the primary assemblies Louis' written statement, all the evidence produced against him, and the judgment of the Convention, and to submit all to their examination in the same way that the judgment of a *sénéchal* was submitted to a *parlement*? This would be truly a political absurdity. Let us clarify our ideas and be still so as to listen to ourselves. We have two obligations to fulfill. The first, to give the people a means of expressing its desires concerning an important act by the national representatives; the second, to show them a simple means without disadvantages. Here then is the question. Either we discuss this following the hypothesis of Salle or as a verdict rendered, which you should send for ratification.[2]

In the first case you would have pronounced on a question of fact, that is, whether or not Louis was guilty. The business of the primary assemblies would be the application of the punishment. Assuming that a verdict has already been rendered, the verdict supposes that the question of fact has also been decided. Again, what would be the business of the primary assemblies? the confirmation or the alteration of the penalty pronounced in the judgment. In either case, the question submitted to the primary assemblies will be the choice of penalty to be meted out to Louis. And how will they

---

[1] The reference is to Robespierre's speech of 28 December.
[2] Salle proposed that the primary assemblies determine the penalty *ab initio*; the alternative possibility is that they confirm or repudiate the Convention's decision.

make this choice? Nothing is simpler. You will indicate a day when they will meet; you will indicate a means of polling; each citizen will express his desire on a ballot; these will be collected by each primary assembly.

Perhaps it well be objected that if the citizens vote by ballot and without discussion, it will be impossible for them to choose the kind of penalty which policy might indicate as the most useful in the present circumstances. To this I respond that considerations which are drawn from the political order, for or against Louis, have strength only by the doubts which they raise concerning the general will. Uncertainty over whether the wishes of the people are those of the Convention could only aid the plots of agitators or furnish foreign powers with the means to attack the Convention, and to accompany the destruction of national representation with the destruction of liberty. Let such uncertainty disappear; let the will of the entire nation, whatever it may be, be clearly expressed, and fear will vanish along with pretexts for disturbance.

It has been said that we do not have the right to restrict the exercise of sovereignty in the primary assemblies. Once convoked to deliberate on the penalty of Louis, they may, if they wish, enter into the examination of all the details of the trial. But if such were the will of the people, what need would they have to await your decree? Your powers are dependent upon them; their sovereignty is independent of you. The primary assemblies will deliberate only on the subject which you submit to them; an irresistible power will keep them within the circle which you have drawn. It is this same power which, after the decree of the Legislative Assembly calling for the convocation of a National Convention, caused them to follow scrupulously all the rules indicated by the decree: the means of election and the number of deputies. It is this same power which will cause them to follow the rules you offer them for the form of their deliberation when they consider accepting or refusing the new Constitution. It is the power of reason; the intimate knowlege of the necessity of behaving with uniformity throughout the Republic; the knowledge of the impossibility of indulging in discussions which, as they would vary infinitely in 6,000 primary assemblies, would precipitate the Republic into chaos. This knowledge was victorious at the time of which I have spoken, at the convocation of the National Convention; you flattered yourselves that it would be victorious when the new Constitution was presented. What motive can you have to believe that it will be the less victorious in deciding the fate of Louis?

Discord, intrigue, civil war — images of the greatest disasters have been placed before us. Discord! you thought perhaps that agitators exercised the same control in the departments which a shameful weakness permitted them to usurp in Paris; that is a very great error. It is true that these perverse men are to be found all over the Republic; faithful to their mission, they have used all means to excite disorder, but everywhere they have been repulsed with the same disdain. The people have done no more than tolerate these men of impure blood; they have granted the law the most remarkable respect. In the departments, the general will is obeyed; it is understood that public and private liberty are founded on that obedience. Each primary assembly will send the result of its polling to its district. Each district will send the tally of the ballots of its primary assemblies to the department, each department will send the tally of its districts to the National Convention which will announce the result of the general tally. And I swear by the love of Frenchmen for their country, by their devotion to the cause of liberty, by their unshakable fidelity to the law, not a single voice will be raised in objection.

But intrigue! Intrigue will save the king. You would be made to believe that the majority of the nation is composed of intriguers, aristocrats, *feuillants*, moderates, in short, of those counter-revolutionary *honnêtes gens* of whom Lafayette spoke at this bar. And to give credence to such a black slander against the majority of the people who, in other circumstances are so basely flattered, mankind has been impudently defamed. The cry goes up: 'Virtue has always been in the minority on this earth.' Citizens, Catiline was a minority in the Roman Senate, and if that conspiring minority had prevailed, it would have meant the end of Rome, of the Senate, of liberty. Citizens! In the Constituent Assembly, at least until the revision, Cazalès and Maury were also a minority, and if that minority, half from the nobility, half from the priesthood, had succeeded by its holy and noble insurrections in stifling the zeal of the majority, that would have been the end of the Revolution, and you would still today grovel at the feet of Louis, who retains of his former grandeur only remorse at having abused it.[1] Citizens! Kings are in the minority on earth, and to enslave nations, they also say that virtue is in the minority. They say as well that the majority of the people is composed of intriguers upon whom silence must be imposed by terror, if the empires of the world are to be preserved from a general upheaval.

The majority of the nation composed of intriguers, aristocrats, *feuillants*, and so forth! Thus, according to those who voice an opinion which reflects so honorably on their country, I see that there is no one in the

---

[1]Cazalès and Maury, the first an aristocrat and soldier, the second a priest, were leading supporters of the king in the Constituent Assembly.

entire land who is truly pure, truly virtuous, truly devoted to the people and to liberty, but themselves and perhaps a hundred of their friends whom they will have the generosity to associate with their glory. Thus, so that they might found a government worthy of the principles they profess, I think it will be quite fitting to banish from French soil all those families whose *feuillantisme* is so perfidious, whose corruption so deep; to change France into a vast desert and, for its rapid regeneration and greater glory, to abandon it to their sublime conceptions.

Discord! Intrigue! Civil war! Yet you voted that the new Constitution, as well as the decree which abolished the monarchy, should be presented for the approval of the people. You did not fear intrigues or civil war; why so much assurance in one case, so much dread in the other? If you seriously fear that presenting the judgment of Louis for the ratification of the people might produce civil war, why do you not fear this terrible result from the decree which establishes a republican government? Or, if it is true that you do not fear that the presentation of that decree might create discord, why do you pretend to believe that it would be impossible, without giving rise to discord, to ask the people to sanction the judgment upon Louis? Be consistent in your fears, or renounce all hope of persuading us of your sincerity.

You have sensed how easy it would be to dissipate all these phantoms created to frighten us, and to weaken in advance the replies which were foreseen, the vilest, the meanest of devices has been resorted to: slander. Those who have adopted the opinion of Salle are spoken of as men who conspire against liberty, as friends of monarchy. We are not distinguished from a Lameth, a Lafayette, and all the other courtiers whom we helped to overthrow.

We are accused! Certainly I am not surprised. There are men whose every breath is an imposture, as it is the nature of the serpent to exist only by the distillation of venom.

We are accused! Ah! had we but the insolent pride or the hypocritical ambition of our accusers! If, like them, we took pleasure in boasting of the little good we have done, we would tell with what courage we constantly fought against the tyranny of kings and against the still more dangerous tyranny of the brigands who, in the month of September, sought to found their power on the debris of the monarchy.[1] We would tell of how we concurred, at least by our votes, with the decree which ended the aristo-

---

[1] Throughout the early months of the Convention, the Girondins sought to identify their opponents as the men responsible for the September massacres.

cratic distinctions between active and inactive citizens and called all members of society to the equal exercise of sovereignty. We would tell, above all, that on the tenth of August we did not leave the chair except to come to the rostrum to propose the decree of suspension for Louis, while all those valiant sons of Brutus, so ready to slaughter disarmed tyrants, buried their terror in an underground chamber and there awaited the issue of the battle which liberty waged against despotism.[1]

We are accused, we are denounced, as was done on the second of September before the assassins' steel. But we know that Tiberius Gracchus died by the hand of a misled people, whom he had always defended. His fate holds no terror for us; all our blood is at the disposal of the people; and in shedding it for them, we will have but one regret — not to have more to offer.

We are accused, if not of wishing to provoke civil war in the departments, at least of provoking disturbances in Paris, by upholding an opinion which displeases the true friends of liberty!

But why would an opinion provoke disturbances? Because these true friends of liberty threaten with death those citizens who are so unhappy as not to share their opinions. Is this proof of the freedom of the National Convention? There will be disturbances in Paris, and you announce them! I admire the sagacity of such a prophesy. Does it in fact seem very difficult, Citizens, to predict the burning of a house while one carries the torch which is to light the fire?

Yes, they want civil war, these men who make the assassination of friends of tyranny a precept and who, at the same time, designate as friends of tyranny those whom their hate wishes to sacrifice. They want civil war, these men who call for arms against the representatives of the nation and for insurrection against its laws. They want civil war, the men who demand the dissolution of the government, the abolition of the Convention. They demand the abolition of the Convention, the dissolution of the government, these men who put forth as a principle, not that anyone would seek to disavow it, that in a great Assembly a minority can sometimes know the truth while the majority is fallen into error; but also that it is the duty of the minority to make itself judge of the errors of the majority and to make its judgments legitimate by insurrections. Catiline should reign in the Senate; the private will should be substituted for the

---

[1] On 10 August, the Jacobin leaders, knowing of the planned rising and uncertain of its outcome, stayed away from the Legislative Assembly. The sons of the Tribune Brutus were implicated in a plot to restore Lucius Tarquinius to his Roman throne, and executed at the command of their father.

general will; that is, the will of a few insolent oppressors should be substituted for that of the people and tyranny for liberty. They want civil war, these men who teach maxims destructive of the entire social order in this assembly, in popular gatherings, in public squares; they want civil war, these men who accuse reason of perfidious *feuillantisme*, justice of dishonorable cowardice, and humanity, holy humanity, of conspiracy. Those who call traitor any citizen who has not reached the heights of brigandage and assassination; those, finally, who pervert all notions of morality and by speeches full of artifice and hypocritical flattery constantly push the people to the most deplorable excess.

Civil war for having proposed that homage be rendered to the sovereignty of the people! In your opinion then, is sovereignty of peoples a calamity for mankind? I understand you; you wish to reign.

On the day of the Champ-de-Mars your ambition was more modest.[1] Then you composed and sought signatures for a petition whose object was to have the people consulted about the fate of Louis, then returning from Varennes. Your heart was not tormented by fear of discord; it cost you no pain to recognize the sovereignty of the people. Could it be that then they agreed with your plans, which now they might cross? Is there in fact any sovereignty for you but that of your passions? Madmen! Did you flatter yourselves that France broke the scepter of kings that it might again bend its neck, degraded beneath the yoke?[2]

They have spoken of courage, of greatness of soul; it would be, they said, a sign of weakness not to have the judgment executed before consulting the will of the people. I recognize no greatness in a legislator but that of being true to his principles. I know that in a revolution one is often reduced to veiling the statue of law, but it seems to me that this maxim is being strangely abused.

When one seeks to make a revolution against tyranny, it is necessary to veil the statue of the law which consecrates or protects tyranny. But when you veil the statue of the law which consecrates the sovereignty of the people — you start a revolution which will turn to the tyrant's profit. On the tenth of August, it required courage to attack Louis in all his power. Does it require as much to send Louis, vanquished and disarmed, to the scaffold? A Cimbrian soldier entered Marius' prison to cut his throat. Frightened at the sight of his victim, he fled without

---

[1] On 17 July 1791, a popular demonstration on the Champ de Mars was fired on by the National Guard; a number of people were killed.

[2] The secretary records 'a movement of silent admiration' in the hall.

daring to slay him[1]. If this soldier had been a member of the Senate, do you suppose that he would have hesitated to vote for the death of the tyrant? What courage is there in performing an act of which a coward would be capable?

To hurry us, we are told that if your judgment is sent for the ratification of the people, you will no longer treat Louis like any other man; you thereby violate the principles of equality. But was he treated like any other man when the decree was passed by which you were charged with his judgment? Were these principles respected when he was taken from the tribunals which judge citizens and when attempts were made to induce you to judge him yourselves without observing any form? We all know full well that Louis is not an ordinary prisoner. There are persistant cries that his existence will be the seed of continual ferment. Why should we not ask if his death would not be the cause of still greater disorders?

I respect the pride of my country too much to propose that the Convention should let itself be influenced on so solemn an occasion by considerations of what foreign powers might or might not do. However, as a result of hearing that we must act in this judgment as a political force, I thought it would not be contrary to your dignity, nor to reason, to speak of politics for a moment.[2]

It is probable that one of the motives which keeps England from breaking with its policy of neutrality, and which causes Spain to promise neutrality, is the fear that by joining the league formed against us, they may hasten the death of Louis. Whether he live or die, it is possible that these powers will declare themselves our enemies, but to condemn him will make such a declaration more probable; and it is certain that if such a declaration takes place, his death will be the pretext for it.

I believe that you will conquer these new enemies. I take as guarantee the courage of our soldiers and the justice of our cause. However, let us resist the raptures of our early successes; it would be a considerable addition to your expenses, new recruits to be got for the army, a navy to create, new risks for your commerce which has already suffered so much from the disaster which has struck the colonies. It would mean new dangers for your soldiers who would face the rigors of the elements, the intemperance of the seasons, fatigues, illness, and death, while you here dispose tranquilly of their fate.

---

[1] The story is told in Plutarch's life of Caius Marius.

[2] The international complications and dangers to be expected from the execution of the king were the major theme of Brissot's speech the following day.

And, peace having become more difficult, war, long continued, would bring your finances to a state of exhaustion of which it is not possible to think without a shudder. If it forces you to issue new promissory notes, which will increase enormously the cost of the most necessary goods, if it augments public misery by new blows to commerce, if it causes waves of blood to flow over the continent and on the seas, what great service will your political calculations have rendered to humanity? What gratitude will the nation owe you for having committed in its name, and in despite of its sovereignty, an act of vengeance become the cause, or merely the pretext, of so calamitous a series of events? Will you dare boast to France of your victories? Nor do I mention defeats and reverses; far from me all thoughts of evil. But by the natural course of even the most prosperous events, the nation would be led into efforts which would consume it. Its population will be decreased by the prodigious number of men devoured by war; there will not be a single family without a father or a son to bemoan; agriculture will lack workers; workshops will be abandoned; your spent treasury will require new taxes; the social fabric, wearied by assaults launched from without by powerful enemies and by the convulsive shocks set in motion by factions from within, will fall into mortal langor. You may well fear that in the midst of these triumphs, France will ressemble those famous monuments of ancient Egypt which have conquered time; the stranger who passes by is astonished by their grandeur; and if he wishes to go further, what does he find? Dust and ashes, and the silence of the tomb.

Citizens, he among you who would yield to personal fears would be a coward, unworthy of a seat in the French Senate; but fears for the fate of the nation, though they sometimes imply narrow conceptions, errors of spirit, at least do honor to the heart. I have exposed to you a part of my own fears; I have still more of which I shall tell you as well.

When Cromwell, who has already been mentioned before this assembly, sought to prepare the dissolution of the Parliament by means of which he overthrew the crown and brought Charles I to the scaffold, he made insidious propositions to them, which he knew well should revolt the nation; but he was careful to have them supported by paid applause and great clamor. Parliament yielded. Soon, the ferment was general and Cromwell effortlessly broke the instrument of which he had made use to arrive at the supreme power.

Have you not heard, within these walls and elsewhere, men cry out furiously: 'If bread is dear, the cause is to be found in the Temple; if coin is rare, if the army is ill provisioned, the cause is in the Temple; if we have daily to suffer the spectacle of indigence, the cause is in the Temple'?

Those who speak thus are aware that the price of bread, the lack of money in circulation, the poor administration of the army, indigence, the sight of which afflicts us, have other causes than those of the Temple. What then are their plans? Who will guarantee that these same men who continuously exert themselves to vilify the Convention, and who perhaps would have succeeded if the majesty of the people which resides in the Convention could be subject to their perfidies; these same men who proclaim everywhere that a new revolution is needed, who have such or such a section declared to be in a state of permanent insurrection; who say to the commune, that when the Convention succeeded Louis, it was but an exchange of tyrants, that what is wanted is another tenth of August; that these same men who speak of nothing but plots, death, traitors, proscriptions, who declare in their sectional assemblies and in their writings that a *defender* of the Republic must be named, that there is only one *leader* who can save it[1] – who, I ask, will guarantee that these same men will not cry out with the greatest violence after the death of Louis, 'if bread is dear, the cause is to be found in the Convention; if the wheels of government move hardly at all, the cause is to be found in the Convention charged with directing it; if the calamities of war are increased by the declarations of England and Spain, the cause is to be found in the Convention which provoked these declarations by its hasty condemnation of Louis'?

Who will guarantee that these seditious cries of anarchy and turbulence will not bring forth the aristocracy avid for vengeance, misery avid for change, and perhaps even pity, excited by old prejudices for the fate of Louis? Who will guarantee that in this new tempest, which will bring the murderers of the second of September again from their dens, you will not be presented with a liberator all covered with blood, this *defender*, this chief, who it is claimed is become so necessary. A leader! Ah! if they were ever so bold, they would appear only to be struck down instantly by a thousand blows; yet to what horrors will Paris not be delivered? Paris, your posterity will admire your heroic courage against kings, but they will never conceive of your ignominious servitude before a handful of brigands, jetsam of the human race, who moved in your breast and tore you apart by their tumultuous ambitions and their fury. Who could inhabit a city where desolation and death reign? And you, industrious citizens, whose labor produces all wealth and whose means of labor would be destroyed, you who made such great sacrifices for the revolution, and whose last means of

---

[1] Marat had called again and again for a dictatorship (on the Roman model) in the year before the Republic was proclaimed: in September 1792, he told the Convention that he had changed his mind.

subsistence would be taken, you whose virtues, ardent patriotism, and good faith made you easy to mislead, what will become of you? What resource will you have? What hands will wipe your tears and bear aid to your despairing families?

Will you go to find those false friends, those perfidious flatterers who threw you into the abyss? Ah! sooner flee before them, fear their response. Let me tell you what it will be. You will ask them for bread, and they will say, 'Go to the quarries to dispute with the earth for the possession of some bloody shreds of the victims we slaughtered. Or do you want blood? here, take some. Blood and cadavers, we have no other nourishment to offer.' You shudder, citizens; oh, my country! In my turn, I ask that the record include the effort I am making to save you from so deplorable a crisis.[1]

But no, those days of mourning will never shine on us; the assassins are base; our little Mariuses are base, nourished by the mud of the swamp where that tyrant, possessed at least of some great qualities, was one day reduced to hiding. They know that if they dared attempt to execute one of their plots against the safety of the Convention, Paris itself would rise from its stupor; that from all parts of the Republic citizens would rush together to crush them beneath the weight of their vengeance, to make them expiate, in the most just of punishments, the crimes by which they all too often stained the most memorable of revolutions. They know this; and their baseness will save the Republic from their rage.

At least I am sure that liberty is not within their powers; that, stained with blood but victorious, liberty would find its realm and its defenders in the departments; but the destruction of Paris and the division of the Republic into federal governments which would be the result, all these disorders are as possible and perhaps more probable than that civil war with which we are threatened. Are all these things not of enough weight to be put into the balance in which you weigh the life of Louis?

A previous speaker seemed to be affected by the fear lest this Assembly desire to consult the will of the people; I am much more tormented by a presentiment that it will not. However little one knows the human heart, one knows how powerfully it can be affected by cries of proscription and the fear of seeming to be incapable of action. Furthermore, I know that the view which I oppose is that of many patriots whose courage, wisdom, and honesty I respect greatly.

In any case, I declare that whatever decree the Convention renders, I will regard as a traitor to his country any man who does not submit to it.

[1] This sentence parallels Robespierre's request; above p. 194.

Opinion is free until such time as the will of the majority is manifested; it is free afterward, but then at least obedience is a duty.

If indeed the idea that the people should be consulted carries the day and seditious men rising against the triumph of national sovereignty arm themselves for rebellion, there is your post, there is the camp where you will await your enemies without blanching. What matters death to him who has done his duty? He dies with glory. What matters life to him who has betrayed it? Shame and remorse will shadow him forever.

In summary: Any act emanating from the representatives of the people is an attempt against their sovereignty if it is not submitted for formal or tacit ratification. The people alone, who promised inviolability to Louis, can declare that they wish to make use of the right to punish, which formerly they had renounced. Powerful considerations should hold you to these principles; if you are faithful to them, you run no risk of reproach. If the people desire the death of Louis, they will command it; if, on the contrary, you take their power from them, you will incur at least the reproach of having strayed from your duty; and what a terrifying responsibility such a deviation will bring upon your heads! . . . I have no more to say.

11. PAINE
7 January 1793

On 4 January, Barère spoke against the appeal to the people; it was a very effective speech and its practical arguments were decisive, apparently, for many undecided deputies. Paine's final effort, a few days later, ignores the appeal (which he, like Condorcet, opposed) and returns to the question of death or exile, the hardest question, as it turned out, for the deputies to decide. The proposal that Louis be banished to America was never formally debated. But this naïve plea for the rehabilitation of kings through plain living makes a nice footnote to the politics of the Gironde.

My hatred and abhorrence of monarchy are sufficiently known: they originate in principles of reason and conviction, nor, except with life, can they ever be extirpated; but my compassion for the unfortunate, whether friend or enemy, is equally lively and sincere.

I voted that Louis should be tried, because it was necessary to afford proofs to the world of the perfidy, corruption, and abomination of the monarchical system. The infinity of evidence that has been produced exposes them in the most glaring and hideous colours; thence it results that monarchy, whatever form it may assume arbitrary or otherwise, becomes necessarily a centre round which are united every species of corruption, and the kingly trade is no less destructive of all morality in the human breast, than the trade of an executioner is destructive of its sensibility. I remember, during my residence in another country, that I was exceedingly struck with a sentence of M. Autheine, at the Jacobins, which corresponds exactly with my own idea – 'Make me a king to-day', said he, 'and I shall be a robber to-morrow.'

Nevertheless, I am inclined to believe that if Louis Capet had been born in obscure condition, had he lived within the circle of an amiable and respectable neighborhood, at liberty to practice the duties of domestic life, had he been thus situated, I cannot believe that he would have shewn himself destitute of social virtues: we are, in a moment of fermentation like this, naturally little indulgent to his vices, or rather to those of his government; we regard them with additional horror and indignation; not that they are more heinous than those of his predecessors, but because our eyes are now open, and the veil of delusion at length withdrawn; yet the lamentable, degraded state to which he is actually reduced is surely far less imputable to him than to the Constituent Assembly which, of its own authority, without consent or advice of the people, restored him to the throne.

I was in Paris at the time of the flight, or abdication of Louis XVI, and when he was taken and brought back. The proposal of restoring him to supreme power struck me with amazement; and although at that time I was not a French citizen, yet as a citizen of the world I employed all the efforts that depended on me to prevent it.

A small society, composed only of five persons, two of whom are now members of the Convention,[1] took at that time the name of the Republican Club. This society opposed the restoration of Louis, not so much on account of his personal offenses, as in order to overthrow the monarchy and to erect on its ruins the republican system and an equal representation.

With this design, I traced out in the English language certain propositions, which were translated with some trifling alterations, and signed by Achille Duchâtelet, now Lieutenant-General in the army of the French republic and at that time one of the five members which

[1]Paine himself and Condorcet.

composed our little party: the law requiring the signature of a citizen at the bottom of each printed paper.

The paper was indignantly torn by Malouet;[1] and brought forth in this very room as an article of accusation against the person who had signed it, the author and their adherents; but such is the revolution of events that this paper is now received and brought forth for a very opposite purpose—to remind the nation of the errors of that unfortunate day, that fatal error of not having then banished Louis XVI from its bosom and to plead this day in favour of his exile, preferable to his death.

The paper in question, was conceived in the following terms:

'BRETHREN AND FELLOW CITIZENS:

'The serene tranquillity, the mutual confidence which prevailed amongst us, during the time of the late King's escape, the indifference with which we beheld him return, are unequivocal proofs that the absence of a King is more desirable than his presence, and that he is not only a political superfluity, but a grievous burden, pressing hard on the whole nation.

'Let us not be imposed on by sophisms; all that concerns this is reduced to four points.

'He has abdicated the throne in having fled from his post. Abdication and desertion are not characterized by the length of absence; but by the single act of flight. In the present instance, the act is everything, and the time nothing.

'The nation can never give back its confidence to a man who, false to his trust, perjured to his oath, conspires a clandestine flight, obtains a fraudulent passport, conceals a King of France under the disguise of a valet, directs his course towards a frontier covered with traitors and deserters, and evidently meditates a return into our country with a force capable of imposing his own despotic laws.

'Should his flight be considered as his own act, or the act of those who fled with him? Was it a spontaneous resolution of his own, or was it inspired by others? The alternative is immaterial; whether fool or hypocrite, idiot or traitor, he has proved himself equally unworthy of the important functions that had been delegated to him.

'In every sense in which the question can be considered, the reciprocal obligation which subsisted between us is dissolved. He holds no longer any authority. We owe him no longer obedience. We see in him no more than an indifferent person; we can regard him only as Louis Capet.

---

[1] Pierre-Victor Malouet was a partisan of the British constitution and a spokesman for the right in the Constituent Assembly.

'The history of France presents little else than a long series of public calamity, which takes its source from the vices of Kings; we have been the wretched victims that have never ceased to suffer either for them or by them. The catalogue of their oppressions was complete, but to complete the sum of their crimes, treason was yet wanting. Now the only vacancy is filled up, the dreadful list is full; the system is exhausted; there are no remaining errors for them to commit; their reign is consequently at an end.

'What kind of office must that be in a government which requires for its execution neither experience nor ability, that may be abandoned to the desperate chance of birth, that may be filled by an idiot, a madman, a tyrant, with equal effect as by the good, the virtuous, and the wise? An office of this nature is a mere nonentity; it is a place of show, not of use. Let France then, arrived at the age of reason, no longer be deluded by the sound of words, and let her deliberately examine, if a King, however insignificant and contemptible in himself, may not at the same time be extremely dangerous.

'The thirty millions which it costs to support a King in the éclat of stupid brutal luxury presents us with an easy method of reducing taxes, which reduction would at once relieve the people and stop the progress of political corruption. The grandeur of nations consists, not, as Kings pretend, in the splendour of thrones, but in a conspicuous sense of their own dignity and in a just disdain of those barbarous follies and crimes which, under the sanction of Royalty, have hitherto desolated Europe.

'As to the personal safety of Louis Capet, it is so much the more confirmed, as France will not stoop to degrade herself by a spirit of revenge against a wretch who has dishonoured himself. In defending a just and glorious cause, it is not possible to degrade it, and the universal tranquillity which prevails is an undeniable proof that a free people know how to respect themselves.'

Having thus explained the principles and the exertions of the republicans at that fatal period, when Louis was reinstated in full possession of the executive power which by his flight had been suspended, I return to the subject, and to the deplorable situation in which the man is now actually involved.

What was neglected at the time of which I have been speaking has been since brought about by the force of necessity. The wilful, treacherous defects in the former constitution have been brought to light; the continual alarm of treason and conspiracy aroused the nation and produced eventually a second revolution. The people have beat down royalty, never,

never to rise again; they have brought Louis Capet to the bar and demonstrated in the face of the whole world, the intrigues, the cabals, the falsehood, corruption, and rooted depravity, the inevitable effects of monarchical government. There remains then only one question to be considered, what is to be done with this man?

For myself I seriously confess, that when I reflect on the unaccountable folly that restored the executive power to his hands, all covered as he was with perjuries and treason, I am far more ready to condemn the Constituent Assembly than the unfortunate prisoner Louis Capet.

But abstracted from every other consideration, there is one circumstance in his life which ought to cover or at least to palliate a great number of his transgressions, and this very circumstance affords to the French nation a blessed occasion of extricating itself from the yoke of kings, without defiling itself in the impurities of their blood.

It is to France alone, I know, that the United States of America owe that support which enabled them to shake off the unjust and tyrannical yoke of Britain. The ardour and zeal which she displayed to provide both men and money were the natural consequence of a thirst for liberty. But as the nation at that time, restrained by the shackles of her own government, could only act by the means of a monarchical organ, this organ — whatever in other respects the object might be — certainly performed a good, a great action.

Let then those United States be the safeguard and asylum of Louis Capet. There, hereafter, far removed from the miseries and crimes of royalty, he may learn, from the constant aspect of public prosperity, that the true system of government consists not in kings, but in fair, equal, and honourable representation.

In relating this circumstance, and in submitting this proposition, I consider myself as a citizen of both countries. I submit it as a citizen of America, who feels the debt of gratitude which he owes to every Frenchman. I submit it also as a man who, although the enemy of kings, cannot forget that they are subject to human frailties. I support my proposition as a citizen of the French republic, because it appears to me the best, the most politic measure that can be adopted.

As far as my experience in public life extends, I have ever observed that the great mass of the people are invariably just, both in their intentions and in their objects; but the true method of accomplishing an effect does not always shew itself in the first instance. For example: the English nation had groaned under the despotism of the Stuarts. Hence Charles I lost his life; yet Charles II was restored to all the plenitude of power, which his father had lost. Forty years had not expired when the same family strove to reëstablish their ancient oppression; so the nation then banished from its territories the whole race. The remedy was effectual. The Stuart family sank into obscurity, confounded itself with the multitude, and is at length extinct.

The French nation has carried her measures of government to a greater length. France is not satisfied with exposing the guilt of the monarch. She has penetrated into the vices and horrors of the monarchy. She has shown them clear as daylight and forever crushed that system, and he, whoever he may be, that should ever dare to reclaim those rights would be regarded not as a pretender, but punished as a traitor.

Two brothers of Louis Capet have banished themselves from the country; but they are obliged to comply with the spirit and etiquette of the courts where they reside. They can advance no pretensions on their own account, so long as Louis Capet shall live.

Monarchy, in France, was a system pregnant with crime and murders, cancelling all natural ties, even those by which brothers are united. We know how often they have assassinated each other to pave a way to power. As those hopes which the emigrants had reposed in Louis XVI are fled, the last that remains rests upon his death, and their situation inclines them to desire this catastrophe, that they may once again rally around a more active chief, and try one further effort under the fortune of the *ci-devant* Monsieur and d'Artois. That such an enterprise would precipitate them into a new abyss of calamity and disgrace, it is not difficult to foresee; yet it might be attended with mutual loss, and it is our duty as legislators not to spill a drop of blood when our purpose may be effectually accomplished without it.

It has already been proposed to abolish the punishment of death, and it is with infinite satisfaction that I recollect the humane and excellent oration pronounced by Robespierre on that subject in the Constituent Assembly. This cause must find its advocates in every corner where enlightened politicians and lovers of humanity exist, and it ought above all to find them in this assembly.

Monarchical governments have trained the human race and inured it to the sanguinary arts and refinements of punishment; and it is exactly the same punishment which has so long shocked the sight and tormented the patience of the people, that now, in their turn, they practice in revenge upon their oppressors. But it becomes us to be strictly on our guard against the abomination and perversity of monarchical examples: as France has been the first of European nations to abolish royalty, let her also be the first to abolish the punishment of death, and to find out a milder and more effectual substitute.

In the particular case now under consideration, I submit the following propositions: 1st, That the National Convention shall pronounce sentence of banishment on Louis and his family. 2nd, That Louis Capet shall be detained in prison till the end of the war, and at that epoch the sentence of banishment be executed.

APPENDIX

Excerpts from the Constitution of 1791

Part III, chapter I, *Of the Legislative National Assembly*, Section V:

VII — The representatives of the nation are inviolable. They cannot be examined, criminated, or judged, at any time, with respect to what they may have said, written, or performed, in the exercise of their functions of representatives.

VIII — They may, for a criminal act, be seized as guilty of a flagrant crime, or in virtue of an order of arrest, but notice shall be given of it, without delay, to the legislative body, and the prosecution cannot be continued, till after the legislative body shall have decided that there is ground of accusation.

Part III, chapter II, *Of the Royalty, The Regency, and the Ministers*, Section I :

I — The royalty is indivisible, and delegated hereditarily to the race on the throne from male to male, by order of primogeniture, to the perpetual exclusion of women and their descendants.

Nothing is prejudged on the effect of renunciations in the race on the throne.

II — The person of the king is inviolable and sacred; his only title is 'King of the French'.

III — There is no authority in France superior to that of the law. The king reigns only by it; and it is only in the name of the law that he can require obedience.

IV — The king, on his accession to the throne, or at the period of his majority, shall take to the nation, in the presence of the legislative body, the oath — 'To be faithful to the nation and the law; to employ all the power delegated to him, to maintain the constitution decreed by the constituting national assembly, in the years 1789, 1790, and 1791, and to cause the laws to be executed ...'

v – If, a month after the invitation of the legislative body, the king has not taken the oath; or if, after taking it, he retracts, he shall be held to have abdicated the royalty.

vi – If the king put himself at the head of an army, and direct the forces of it against the nation, or if he do not oppose, by a formal act, any such enterprize undertaken in his name, he shall be held to have abdicated.

vii – If the king, having gone out of the kingdom, do not return to it, after an invitation by the legislative body, within the space which shall be fixed by the proclamation, and which cannot be less than two months, he shall be held to have abdicated the royalty.

This space of time shall be counted from the day in which the proclamation shall have been published, in the place of the sittings of the legislative body. The ministers shall be charged, under their responsibility, to do all the acts of the executive power, the exercise of which shall be suspended in the hands of the absent king.

viii – After abdication, express or legal, the king shall be in the class of citizens, and may be accused and tried like them, for acts posterior to his abdication.

INDEX OF NAMES

Index

Romulus, 5

Rousseau, Jean-Jacques, 62, 72ff., 82, 95, 121, 179n.

Saint-Just, Louis-Antoine-Léon, *conventionnel*, vi, 7, 61ff., 70ff., 93, 130, 139, 158; quoted, 5, 9, 63ff., 71; speeches of, 120–7, 166–7

Salle, Jean-Baptiste, *conventionnel*, 178, 184n., 190n., 198, 201

Schramm, Percy, 12n.

Selden, John, 16

Seligman, Edmond, 55n.

Sèze, Raymond de, vi, 56

Shakespeare, William, quoted, 3, 9, 18, 43

Shklar, Judith, 79n.

Sidney, Algernon, 3, 193

Socrates, 193

Strafford, Thomas Wentworth, earl of, 32, 44f., 62

Sydenham, M. J., 78

Tarquinius, Lucius, king of Rome, 118n., 125, 133, 202n.

Tocqueville, Alexis de, 8

Trevelyan, G. M., 46

Trotsky, Leon, 31f., 80

Turgot, Anne-Robert-Jacques, 139

Ullmann, Walter, 10, 13

Vergniaud, Pierre-Victurnien, *conventionnel*, 56ff., 63, 178; speech of, 194–208

Voltaire, François-Marie Arouet de, 20n., 81

Walsingham, Francis, 51

William I (the Conqueror), of England, 101

William III, of England, 19